D0164464

The Snake and The Fox

The Snake and the Fox offers us a new and exciting way to look at and understand logic. Mary Haight uses graphics to tell the story of how logic works, and why it works the way it does.

Things you will find explained and discussed in *The Snake and the Fox*:

Basic logic concepts such as:

> sound and valid reasoning
> logical form
> formal and informal fallacies
> necessary and contingent statements
> inductive versus deductive reasoning

The logic of statements, using truth-tables
The logic of sets, using Venn diagrams
The logic of statements, using proofs and rules of inference

Mary Haight covers material used in any orthodox introduction to logic course – but she does this in a truly innovative way. She uses arguments in ordinary language, for students to analyse. She also includes some discussion on the philosophical theory underlying the logic: not just how to do it, but why it takes the form it does. *The Snake and the Fox* is user-friendly, interactive, uses questions with answers, and has graphics which will easily guide any student coming to logic for the first time.

Mary Haight teaches at the Department of Philosophy, University of Glasgow. She is also the author of *A Study of Self-Deception*.

The Snake and the Fox

An Introduction to Logic

Mary Haight

London and New York

First published 1999
by Routledge
11 New Fetter Lane, London EC4P 4EE

Simultaneously published in the USA and Canada
by Routledge
29 West 35th Street, New York, NY 10001

Routledge is an imprint of the Taylor & Francis Group

© 1999 Mary Haight

Typeset in Frutiger and Goudy by Routledge
Printed and bound in Great Britain by TJ International Ltd, Padstow, Cornwall

British Library Cataloguing in Publication Data
A catalogue record for this book is available from the British Library

Library of Congress Cataloguing in Publication Data
A catalogue record for this book has been requested

ISBN 0–415–16693–4 (hbk)
ISBN 0–415–16694–2 (pbk)

For my brothers John and Tim Haight
who are interested in such things.

Contents

Preface

This book is for students with no special background in logic or philosophy. Its four parts are divided into short chapters that use a question and answer method. There are twelve questions per chapter, with answers at the back of the book. These answers often supplement the main text, so students should always look them up as they go: they should try to answer the question, then check the answer even if they are sure they know it. The pictures are functional as well: they serve as illustrations, as mnemonics, and to keep the beginner's eye from sliding helplessly down the page. Arts students in particular are used to reading large chunks of text, an entire paragraph at a glance: they find it hard at first to slow down enough to take in an argument-form.

Part I discusses basic concepts such as validity, clarity and logical form, and common forms of argument such as analogy and induction, at greater length than most elementary texts. Part II introduces the logic of statements (also known as 'sentential' or 'propositional' logic), with truth-tables to define the main truth-functional constants, and to assess arguments for validity. Part III uses Venn diagrams in a similar way for the elementary logic of sets. In Part IV I go back to the logic of statements, this time using rules of inference to construct proofs. I do all this without truth-functional symbols: for the reasons why, see my Epilogue. Parts I–III (thirty-six chapters altogether) provide material for a forty-hour introductory course, of the kind taught in the Scottish Higher program, or to first-year university students who may or may not want to go on with logic afterwards. I suggest that each chapter should be the topic for a one-hour class or workshop, *after* students have read it, tried to answer its twelve questions, and digested the answers at the back. Part IV (sixteen chapters) may either be used with the first three in (for example) a sixty-hour course, or (with revision of Parts I–III) form the basis of a second-level forty-hour course like the Scottish Advanced Higher. In an Honours philosophy course, Part IV should introduce one of the many standard texts on quantified logic: I name a few in my bibliography. In a course aimed mainly at assessing how we reason in everyday life, I suggest instead that students use any spare time they have on the kind of book I list under 'Background/Informal Logic', such as R.H. Thouless and C.R. Thouless's classic *Straight and Crooked Thinking*.

When I first planned this book I meant to publish it with an interactive disk, giving extra material for practice. But now that we have the Web, it seems simpler to put it on a web page in a downloadable form. You will find it at http/www.routledge.com.

I would like to thank the many General Philosophy students at Glasgow University who first tried out my question-and-answer method, and the graduate class – some intending teachers, some teachers already – in Dr Catherine McCall's Philosophical Inquiry program at Glasgow, with whom I worked through a first draft of Part I. I would also like to thank Nicholas Dempsey, who programmed the interactive web-page material; Ephraim Borowski, who while Head of the Glasgow University Philosophy Department allowed me to delegate or postpone most of my teaching and administration for one term, when I had no chance of study leave ('a textbook is not research'); Michael Lessnoff for his sympathy and support at every stage of writing; and all the friends and colleagues who so patiently stopped what they were doing to look at the latest portrait of a Biconditional or a Dilemma.

Mary Haight
Department of Philosophy
The University
Glasgow G12 8QQ

Prologue

The Snake and the Fox were rivals to lead a gang of thieves. The Snake proposed a test: 'By night and by day a hundred priests with knives guard the One-Eyed God of Zorro, in a room within a room within a room. Let whoever steals the God's Ruby Eye become our leader.'

The Fox agreed, but added: 'Since my distinguished rival has suggested this test, let him be the first to try it.' Secretly he reasoned:

'The Snake is proud: he will accept. He will then almost surely die in the attempt. Then I shall have no rival, and can easily persuade the band that further tests are a waste of time.

Or he may live, but fail. The result will be the same: for having lost face, he will leave at once for distant parts.

Or perhaps – conceivably – he may succeed. But once he has stolen the Eye, the possibility of MY doing so cannot arise. And the vengeance of the priests of Zorro is horrible and swift. He will not rule for long; and I am his only possible successor.'

How good is the Fox's reasoning?

Part I

Truth and validity

Logicians use the term 'SOUND ARGUMENT' for good reasoning. A sound argument needs two separate things:

> TRUE PREMISES (*input*) – the reasons you give for what you're trying to prove

and

> AN ARGUMENT WHOSE FORM IS VALID (*method of reasoning*).

If you have these, your reasoning will lead safely to a TRUE CONCLUSION (*output*). But if either is lacking, your conclusion is at risk.

Premises are statements, true or false. An argument is a process of reasoning, valid or invalid. A *valid* argument's form is like a reliable sausage machine: if you put good meat in, you get a good sausage out; if you feed truth in, you get truth out.

Consider this argument:

> *My Granny's rich!* Everybody who has a Rolls Royce is rich, and she has one, so she's rich!

Whoever uses it and whenever it is used, THE ARGUMENT IS PERFECTLY VALID. Its validity is due entirely to its form. But this valid form will do little good to the child who makes this boast or to her Granny, if it is false that everybody who has a Rolls is rich, and/or false that her Granny has a Rolls. On the other hand if both premises are true, the form of reasoning guarantees that her Granny *is* rich: it is inevitable.

1 (i) What are the premises of the Granny argument?
   (ii) What is its conclusion?

   (*There are answers at the back of the book.*)

2 Invent a case where the conclusion about the speaker's Granny is false. (Can you do it without denying one or both premises?)

Now consider an invalid argument (pronounced 'inVAlid'):

> *Uncle Marley's a beggar!*
> Beggars wear rags. Uncle
> Marley wears rags. Uncle
> Marley's a beggar!

No matter whether Uncle Marley wears rags, or whether beggars (ever or always) do, THIS REASONING IS NOT VALID. Again that is due to its form: any argument with this form *could* have a false conclusion even when its premises are true. (It would be different if the speaker said 'ONLY beggars wear rags.')

3 (i) What are the premises of the Uncle argument?
   (ii) What is its conclusion?

4 Invent an Uncle Marley about whom this conclusion is false, although both premises are true.

Form is not enough, however. IF YOUR PREMISES ARE NOT ALL TRUE, EVEN A VALID ARGUMENT MAY LEAD YOU ASTRAY, because the conclusion could now be either true or false.

It *could* be false: but even this is unreliable. Here we have a striking difference between argument forms and sausage machines: put bad meat into a sausage machine and you always get a bad sausage.

In the next argument both premises are bad – that is, false – but by chance the conclusion is true.

Insects have eight legs [FALSE]
Spiders are insects [FALSE]

THEREFORE
spiders have eight legs. [TRUE]

5 What do you think – is the Spider argument invalid or valid? (*Hint*: forget the content. Validity depends on an argument's FORM.)

Now some general questions:

6   Can a valid argument have one or more false premises?
7   Can a valid argument have a false conclusion?
8   Can it have a true conclusion, if its premises are false?
9   Can it have a false conclusion, if its premises are true?
10 From all this, work out a simple definition of *valid argument*.
11 Define an *invalid argument* on similar lines.
12 Given all this, what is your first impression of the Fox's argument in the Prologue? Is it valid or invalid?

Clarity (1)

The Granny, Uncle and Spider arguments are unusually simple: two premises (input) and a conclusion (output). But even these need tidying if we want to make their forms absolutely clear. For example:

> *My Granny's rich!* Everybody who has a Rolls Royce is rich, and she has one, so she's rich!

puts the argument's conclusion first. Then we have the two premises; then the conclusion again. This is very common in ordinary conversation. So is putting the conclusion first and *not* repeating it:

> *My Granny's rich!* Everybody who has a Rolls Royce is rich, and she has one!

Anyone who can follow the argument knows that what comes *after* the conclusion (conversationally) is in fact what the speaker accepts *to start with* and gives as reasons for drawing the conclusion.

It makes no difference in which order we take the two premises; logically speaking, both go into the machine together. But the conclusion follows *from* them. Logically, both conversational versions are identical in form to:

Everyone who has a Rolls Royce is rich
My Granny has a Rolls Royce

_____

My Granny is rich.

(The line means 'THEREFORE'.)

Here the written order of statements follows the logical order.

1   Must we also rewrite the Uncle argument (as I put it in Chapter 1) if we want to show its statements in their logical order? If so, do it.
2   What about the Spider argument?

Insects have eight legs   [FALSE]
Spiders are insects   [FALSE]

THEREFORE
spiders have eight legs.   [TRUE]

Whether or not it gets the logical order right, the Spider argument needs tidying in another way. Are the following statements true? YES or NO?

Roses are red.   Spiders have eight legs.

A trick question. Roses may be yellow too: do we mean all roses or only some? 'Roses are red' is true when we mean 'Some roses' and false when we mean 'all'. And do we mean all spiders or only some? If we mean 'all' and we are talking about individual spiders, 'Spiders have eight legs' is almost certainly false: there must be freaks and accident victims.

But the conclusion of our Spider argument is about species, not individuals – or that is how I meant it. It states that not only some, but *all* spiders belong to an eight-legged species; and once this is clear, we know where we are. The statement is true.

The Spider argument's two premises are false. As it happens they are false whether we take them to mean 'some' or 'all': no insects have eight legs (except a few freaks perhaps, who don't count if we are discussing species) and no spiders are insects. But this might not have been so. To avoid mistakes, we should *always* make our meaning clear.

3   Does the Spider argument's first premise claim that all insects have eight legs, or that only some have? Or can't we tell?

4   What about the Spider argument's second premise?

     (These are not questions about whether anything is true or false. They simply ask what the premises mean.)

The Uncle argument:

Uncle Marley's a beggar!
Beggars wear rags. Uncle Marley wears rags. He's a beggar!

needs tidying too.

5   What exactly does 'Beggars wear rags' mean in the Uncle argu-ment? All beggars? Some? Can we tell?

You might think it a waste of time to tidy an invalid argument. But the rule in logic is 'always make the meaning clear': often this is how we find out that the argument is invalid. (See the answer to question 5.)

Now suppose that the Granny arguer said simply:

'My Granny's rich, because *everybody* is who has a Rolls Royce!'.

Is this valid?

Another trick question. Strictly, no: the speaker doesn't tell us what connection she is claiming between everybody who owns a Rolls Royce, and her Granny. But if we *know* that her Granny has a Rolls, and she knows that we know, we may not need telling. In some contexts, then, this too has the logical form

Everyone who has a Rolls Royce is rich
My Granny has a Rolls Royce

My Granny is rich.

Some logicians call a premise 'suppressed' when it is used but not stated. I prefer *implicit*, but shall use both terms so that you get used to them. Conclusions can be implicit too; in fact one spoken (or explicit) statement may sometimes stand in for the whole argument:

'Grannies never have any money.'
'Pooh to you. MY GRANNY OWNS A ROLLS!'

When you decide that something is implicit in an argument, you are trying to read the speaker's mind. *Include only what you can be sure the arguer really concludes or assumes* or you may be either too charitable or unfair, as Bella is here:

> AMY: Harry was lying. He kept saying, '*Well, the fact is…*'
> BELLA: That's ridiculous! Whenever people say '*Well the fact is…*', it means they're lying?
> AMY: I never said that! I'm talking about *Harry* – my brother, whom I've known all my life!

We have a name for Bella's crime: PUTTING WORDS INTO SOMEONE'S MOUTH.

6   Amy's conclusion is '*Harry was lying*'. What premise does she state?
7   What further premise does Bella think is implicit?
8   What is Amy's real implicit premise?
9   Rewrite what Bella thought the argument was, making its logical form clear. (Use a line for '*therefore*'.) Is it valid?
10 Rewrite Amy's real argument in the same way. Is it valid?

Finally, consider the Fox. His argument (in the Prologue) is long – a series of arguments really – but the first step is simple: two premises and a conclusion. He states only two of these:

> **The Snake is proud. He will accept.**

The third is implicit.

11 Which of the three statements in this first short argument –
    two premises, one conclusion – does the Fox leave out?
12 Rewrite the argument – the Fox's first step – with a line for
    '*therefore*', in a way that makes its logical form absolutely clear.

Clarity (2)

The Fox, you will remember, argued as follows:

> 'The Snake is proud: he will accept. He will then almost surely die in the attempt. Then I shall have no rival, and can easily persuade the band that further tests are a waste of time.
>
> Or he may live, but fail. The result will be the same: for having lost face, he will leave at once for distant parts.
>
> Or perhaps – conceivably – he may succeed. But once he has stolen the Eye, the possibility of MY doing so cannot arise. And the vengeance of the priests of Zorro is horrible and swift. He will not rule for long; and I am his only successor.'

The Fox's argument – like most reasoning in ordinary language – needs untangling before its logical form is clear.

First: although we can call the whole passage the Fox's *argument*, it is really a chain of arguments. The Fox works out one conclusion, takes it as a premise towards the next, and so on until his final one. We shall need to take it by stages. I started on his first step at the end of Chapter 2:

> The Snake is proud. He will accept.

Second: many implicit statements – absolutely essential ones, if the reasoning is to be valid – are not simply implicit: their part in the argument is invisible, until you develop an eye for logical form. You have an example in that first step. 'The Snake is proud' is the Fox's reason WHY the Snake will accept. But if his argument were simply

> The Snake is proud
> _____
> He will accept

it would be invalid. Nothing here explicitly connects the Snake's pride with his accepting, and without that connection there is no reason why the premise might not be true and the conclusion false. For example, the Snake's pride might instead make him refuse anything the Fox suggested.

But the Fox is not stupid. He would not give 'The Snake is proud' as a reason for 'He will accept' if he did not believe there was a connection. In the answers to Chapter 2 I suggested two possibilities: 'Anyone proud would accept' and (B) below: 'If the Snake is proud he will accept'. Either would make the argument valid; I prefer the second because it runs less risk of putting unwarranted words into the Fox's mouth. His ideas about *all* proud creatures are less obvious than his opinion of the Snake. The Fox may not be explicitly aware of this part of his reasoning, however. (Were *you* aware of it, before I dug it out?)

So this argument:

> If the Snake is proud, he will accept
> The Snake is proud
> _____
> The Snake will accept

is the first step in the Fox's reasoning. You will find the same thing at later stages: the SURFACE FORM differs from its underlying LOGICAL FORM. That is typical of language. Foreign-language speakers will see a familiar problem here: in French, for example, I don't say that *I am hungry* or *I am bored* by something; instead, I *have hunger* and *bore myself of* something. The translator learns not to be distracted by surface form, but to dig up what is meant. If you look at statements (A)–(M) below with this in mind, you should recognise the Fox's reasoning, translated so as to show its logical form.

To judge how good the reasoning is, we must decide which statements are premises (*input*) and which are conclusions (*output* – although a conclusion may then be used as input towards a further conclusion). If the Fox is to prove his final point he needs two things: his premises must be true, and each argument in turn must have a valid form: that is, one which guarantees a true conclusion *if* the premises are true.

1–9 Decide, for each statement, whether the Fox *assumes it without argument* (i.e. it is a premise) or *works it out* (it is a conclusion). (A)–(C) are here to start you off: you know them already.

(A) 'The Snake is proud.'
   Assumed without argument.
(B) 'If the Snake is proud, he will accept.'
   Assumed without argument.
(C) 'The Snake will accept.'
   Worked out from (A) and (B). It is then used as a premise towards a new conclusion.

(D) 'If the Snake accepts, then either he will die in the attempt, or he will live but fail, or he will succeed.'

(E) 'Either the Snake will die in the attempt, or he will live but fail, or he will succeed.'

(F) 'If the Snake dies in the attempt, the Fox will have no rival, and can persuade the band that further tests are a waste of time.'

(G) 'If the Snake lives but fails, he will lose face and leave for distant parts.'

(H) 'If the Snake loses face and leaves for distant parts, the Fox will have no rival and can persuade the band that further tests are a waste of time.'

(I) 'If the Fox has no rival and can persuade the band that further tests are a waste of time, he will soon become Captain without having to steal the Eye.'

(J) 'If the Snake succeeds, it will become impossible for the Fox to steal the Eye, and the vengence of the Priests of Zorro will destroy the Snake.'

(K) 'If it becomes impossible for the Fox to steal the Eye and the vengence of the Priests of Zorro destroys the Snake, the

Fox will soon become Captain without having to steal the Eye.'

(L) 'If the Snake dies in the attempt, or lives but fails, or succeeds, the Fox will soon become Captain without having to steal the Eye.'

(M) 'Whatever happens, the Fox will soon become Captain without having to steal the Eye.'

Suppose that everything the Fox assumes without argument is true.

10 Must (M): 'Whatever happens, the Fox will soon become Captain without having to steal the Eye', therefore be true?
11 So – is the Fox's reasoning valid?
12 (*Revision*) What is the difference between a valid argument and a sound one?

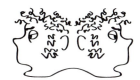

Premises

Most of this book is about the form of arguments. The art of choosing premises is beyond its scope. We can discover rules that will tell us when an argument is valid, because validity is independent of what it is about; but premises *are* what reasoning is about. Since the subjects of argument vary endlessly, so do they.

There are, however, a few dangers common enough to be worth a warning.

Reasoning often has no clear form on the surface because it is not in words at all, or only partly in words, or in words that do not look like argument. We may be unconscious of essential parts of it, often of premises that we use and never question. *But whenever someone draws a conclusion from data, we can express this as an argument, with the data as premises.* If the conclusion does not follow logically from them, the reasoning is unsound in one way – invalidity – but if the premises are false it is unsound in another way. One obvious rule for assessing arguments then is:

Know Your Premises.

Sometimes when you bring these to light, you will find that they are ridiculous; often they will at least be questionable. For example:

A Senior Devil Advises a Junior One

In civilised life domestic hatred usually expresses itself by saying things which would appear quite harmless on paper (the WORDS are not offensive) but in such a voice, or at such a moment, that they are not far short of a blow in the face. To keep this game up you and Glubose [the victims' guardian devils] must see to it that each of these two fools has a sort of double standard. Your patient must demand that all his own utterances are to be taken at their face value and judged simply on the actual words, while at the same time judging all his mother's utterances with the fullest and most over-sensitive interpretation of the tone and context and the suspected intention. She must be encouraged to do the same....Hence from every quarrel they can go away convinced, or very nearly convinced, that they are quite innocent.

(C.S.Lewis, *The Screwtape Letters*)

The double standard works because it is unnoticed. Each 'patient' starts with an idea of what is happening, plus some general ideas about offensiveness, and moves from these to the conclusion '*She/he* is being offensive and *I* am quite innocent'. But if we spell out the patient's hidden reasoning, it seems to be:

I   A speaker is offensive only if his or her words are offensive
    My words are not offensive
    _____

    I am not being offensive

II A speaker is offensive if his or her manner is offensive
    (even when the words are innocent)
    His or her manner is offensive
    _____

    He or she is being offensive.

Once you make the first premises of arguments I and II explicit, it is obvious that both cannot be true. This is the problem, not invalidity. In fact both arguments are valid. They have the forms:

I   All A are B   *Replace A, B and x by:*
       x is not B   x: the speaker (mother or son,
       ————   depending on which is arguing)
       x is not A.   A: offensive speakers
                           B: users of offensive words.

(In other arguments with the same form, different things would replace A, B and x. Think of the letters as holes to be filled differently at different times.)

II   All C are A   A: offensive speakers
       y is C   C: speakers with an offensive manner.
       ————
       y is A.

1   One of two things could fill the x-hole in Argument I, depending on who is speaking. What about y in argument II?

Changing premises halfway through an argument is common enough to have a nickname: SHIFTING YOUR GROUND. And when a new premise is inconsistent with earlier one/s – so that they cannot all be true together – it is called MOVING THE GOAL-POSTS. (In some ground-shifting this does not happen: the arguer just starts using new premises without bothering to contradict the old ones.)

But perhaps each devil's patient, if asked, would accept – in theory – that *any* speaker is offensive whose manner is offensive, even when the words are innocent. But he or she cannot recognize a sneering voice (or whatever) in practice, unless it belongs to someone else. Then the unexamined reasoning is:

All speakers are offensive whose manner is offensive, even
when their words are innocent
My words and manner are both inoffensive
His (or her) manner is offensive

He (or she) is being offensive and I am quite innocent.

Again this is prefectly valid. It has the form:

All A are B or C   (A, B, C, x and y as above)
x is neither B nor C
y is C
All C are A

---

y is A and x is not A.

Any argument of this form will give a true conclusion if the
premises are true. If you don't see this at once, try doing it in two
steps: start by getting a conclusion from the first two premises.

2   What conclusion can we get from the first two premises?

All A are B or C
x is neither B nor C.

The next two premises yield the same conclusion as II above, and
the final conclusion combines the two.
     And again, it is a bad premise that makes the trouble. Once the
assumption *x is neither B nor C* – 'My words and manner are both
inoffensive' – is brought to light, so is its extreme fishiness. And
once *that* is evident, the mother and son have no excuse not to
listen to themselves speaking, as well as each other.

Goalpost-moving

Goalpost-moving has an interesting feature. It is a perfect case of
USELESS VALIDITY, if the point of reasoning is to prove something true.

'It wasn't me, I was in the next county. And if I was here, I never went to the pub. And if I went there, I never saw the man. And if I did see him, we never spoke. And if we spoke, it was perfectly amiable. And if it was not, he hit me first.'

The problem lies in the premises. Spelled out, they are incompatible:

'I was in the next county.
[Well, in fact I was not. I was here.]
If I was here, I never went to the pub.
[Well, in fact I was here and I did.]' – etc.

3   (*Revision*) What is the term for the statements in brackets?

An argument of this form will never allow true premises and a false conclusion.

4   Why not?

So – perhaps surprisingly – it is valid.

5   (*Revision*) Exactly why *is* this a valid form?
6   Why is it also useless?
7   'It wasn't me' is not a premise in the Pub argument. What is it?

Circular arguments

Circular arguments are generally another form of USELESS VALIDITY. (For one example where it is not useless, see Chapter 14.) Here the arguer cheats by taking the conclusion as a premise, then claims to have proved it. Consider this dialogue (a real one – variations turn up in the courts):

'Women who get raped ask for it.'
'What do you mean?'
'Well if they didn't they wouldn't get raped, would they?'

This has the logical form

If not Q then not P   and it is VALID – but only because
_____   a premise and conclusion of this
If P then Q   form state exactly the same thing in
                            different ways.

8 What things replace P and Q in this argument?
9 When we replace them in this way, is the argument sound?

Of course, *if* the premise is true, so is the conclusion. But if the conclusion needs to be proved, so – for identical reasons – does the premise.

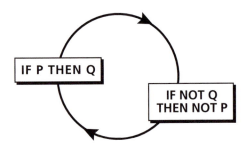

The circle would be formally complete if we asked the arguer where the idea that if women did not 'ask for it' they would not get raped is supposed to come from, and got the answer 'Well – stands to reason, doesn't it? If they get raped, it's because they ask for it'. (Yes, people do argue like this. Try listening in a pub.)

We could define this kind of circular argument by saying that its conclusion is the same as its premise (so we cannot know that the premise is true unless we already know the conclusion is). But the term is also used more generally for any argument where the conclusion appears *among* its premises. So a better definition would be: *a circular argument is one where we cannot know that one or more of the premises is true, unless we already know that the conclusion is.* A traditional name for this is 'begging the question', a translation from the Latin *petitio principii*. This is not very illuminating in English (I would rather call it 'stealing the conclusion'). People who do not know its history often think the term means 'prompting the question' (followed by a question). Do not misuse it in this way – but if you want to be clear about this particular logical sin, it is safer to say 'arguing in a circle', so that people who do misuse 'begging the question' will not misunderstand you.

BOGUS EXPLANATIONS sometimes depend on circularity.

'Please, sir, why does opium put people to sleep?'

'BECAUSE IT HAS SOPORIFIC POWER.'

'Please, what does that mean?'

'IT MEANS THAT OPIUM PUTS PEOPLE TO SLEEP!'

In fact this:

> Opium has soporific power
> ———————————————
> Opium puts people to sleep

is exactly equivalent to this:

> Opium puts people to sleep
> ———————————————
> Opium puts people to sleep.

In real life circular argument often involves a *persuasive definition*. The opium argument is blatantly circular, but at least it is (uselessly) sound: 'soporific' really does mean 'puts people to sleep'.

But a clever arguer can sometimes feed the audience a definition they would not necessarily agree to, given a chance to think; and so (apparently) force them to admit a conclusion they might otherwise reject. For example if you can get your audience to agree that *real* liberty is economic – freedom from want – you can lead them (circularly) to conclude that a state where no one is constrained by poverty must be a free state:

> REAL liberty (in a state) is economic
>
> ───────────────────────────────
>
> A state where people are free from want is free

however bad the state's record on civil rights. If you can get them to accept that real liberty means the absence of any kind of legal restraint:

> REAL liberty (in a state) is the freedom from legal restraint
>
> ───────────────────────────────
>
> A state where people are free from legal restraints is free

you can force them to conclude that a free state is one of anarchy, where the strong are free to prey on the weak…and so on.

The moral is: if you find yourself (apparently) forced to agree to something that you think either fishy or false, because it follows from premises you have accepted – *backtrack*. A defining premise may have been forced on you, as a card-cheater forces a card. If the forcer then accuses you of being inconsistent because you are now denying what you agreed to, hit back by accusing him or her of setting up the argument unfairly. The word 'real' is often a clue: '*real* liberty is…' tends to mean that what follows is not what we usually suppose.

On the other hand you may find that, after thinking, you agree with the suggested definition. If so, it is still better to agree after thinking about it, rather than having it forced on you unawares.

10–11 Spot two persuasive definitions in this example. One is obvious; the other a bit more subtle.
(If this is an abbreviated argument, what is its conclusion?)

> 'Abortion is the murder of an unborn child, and murder is always wrong.'

12 What about this one?
(*Hint*: remember what I said above about 'real'.)

'In the other sense – call it paternalistic – an institution is democratic to the extent that it serves the true needs and interests of its rank and file members, perhaps as determined by somebody else.'

(Antony Flew: *Thinking about Thinking*)

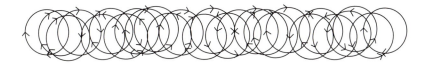

Some traditional fallacies

A fallacy is a mistake in reasoning. The old logic and rhetoric books discuss a series of mistakes that we might generally call *Missing the Point*. Here are three examples, with their Latin names:

(A) APPEAL TO PITY (*Ad misericordiam*)

A weeping student claims that his mark should be not 30 per cent but 50 per cent, because he will lose his funding if he fails the course.

The point of a mark is to state – truly -- how good or bad work is in relation to the standards of the course and to the work of other students. The student's funding is not relevant to this, and a mark loses its point if we pretend that it is. (This does not mean that I might not on a rare occasion use a *false* mark: I did once, when it was not a question of funds but of the student's being sent back to his native country and shot if he lost his student status. But his true mark was less than the 50 per cent I gave him.)

1   Find another example of missing the point by an appeal to pity.

(B)   APPEAL TO FORCE   (*Ad Baculum* – literally 'to the stick')

A terrorist suggests I had better agree his cause is just, because he will blow me up if I don't.

This might make me *pretend* to agree, of course. But again, that is not the point. ('Force' here need not always mean physical force, by the way: any threat would do.)

(C) APPEAL TO AUTHORITY (*Ad auctoritatem*)

'God/Freud/Marx/Stephen Hawking says so. Therefore it's true.'

(Statements are true or false because of what they say, not who says them. So it is knowing your subject that makes you an authority, not being an authority that makes you know your subject.)

2   Find examples of mising the point by appeals (i) to force; (ii) to authority.

(D)   APPEAL TO MARTYRDOM: dying to 'prove' that your cause is right.

3   Why does it fail to prove this?

If you think about it, it does not even prove that you *believe* your cause is right. But for obvious reasons, it is persuasive. (Actions may speak louder than words, but it's not always clear what they say.)

Other members of this family are not hard to spot once you see the pattern: the APPEAL TO THE SNEERING LABEL for example ('bleeding heart', 'egghead', 'do-gooder' – very dangerous to journalists); the APPEAL TO INTELLECTUAL FASHION (very dangerous to the intelligentsia) and so on.

4   Find an example or two where something is unfairly discredited by a sneering label.

Such fallacies are often called *informal*, because we cannot explain them in terms of one specific argument-form that is invalid. Of course we can always find forms that seem to fit the arguments and do show the fallacy. For example:

> x is an authority and x says that P
>
> ―――――――――――――
>
> P   (*Ad auctoritatem*)

is clearly invalid.

5   Explain why.

So is:

> If not P, it will be terrible for me
>
> ―――――――――――――
>
> P.   (*Ad misericordiam*)

6   What is the role of P in these examples (and x in the first one)?

But we might also analyse Missing the Point as a *valid* argument with a false or fishy implicit premise, for example:

> If you don't want me to lose my funding, you should pass me, whatever my work is like
> Surely you don't want me to lose my funding!
>
> ―――――――――――――――――――――――――
>
> You should pass me, whatever my work is like.

7   Which is the fishy premise here?

This also makes the appeal to pity more explicit.

8   How?
Or again:

> If the Professor says so, it's true
> The Professor says so
>
> ―――――――――――――
>
> It's true.

9 What is the form of these arguments?

As I have spelled them out, the fallacies are easy to see. But such thinking is rarely spelled out. This is how informal fallacies get by: neither the listener nor the speaker knows where in the speaker's muddled mind the trouble lies. One way to find out if a bad (unspoken) premise is involved is to put the words explicitly into the arguer's mouth: for example if someone simply quotes Freud to back up a point, ask (politely) 'Does this mean you believe that if Freud said it, it must be true?'. If s/he says 'Yes', ask why. Sometimes the answer may lead you to decide that the implicit premise is neither fishy nor false, after all; but any such premise needs defending.

This passage from *The Daughter of Time*, by Josephine Tey, coins a useful name for one sort of *argumentum ad auctoritatum*. The characters are fictional but the historical issues discussed are real. The speakers are Brent Carradine, an American historian, and Alan Grant, a Scottish detective-inspector. The letter-writer is Grant's cousin Laura. The remarks in bold type are ones I think especially interesting.

❝❝ Tonypandy ❞❞

'Forty million schoolbooks can't be wrong' Grant said after a little.

'Can't they?'

'Well, can they?!'

'I used to think that, but I'm not so sure nowadays…a little affair called the Boston Massacre. Ever heard of it?'

'Of course.'

'Well, I discovered quite by accident, when I was looking up something at college, that the Boston Massacre consisted of a mob throwing stones at a sentry…I was brought up on the Boston Massacre, Mr. Grant. My twenty-eight-inch chest used to swell at the very memory of it. My good red spinach-laden blood used to seethe at the thought of helpless civilians mowed down by the fire of British troops…You can't imagine what a shock it was.'

Grant was staring at the ceiling… 'Tonypandy' he said… 'After all, I've seen the thing at work in my own day.'

'And what in heck is Tonypandy?' Brent asked.

'…If you go to South Wales you will hear that, in 1910, the Government used troops to shoot down Welsh miners who were striking for their rights. You'll probably hear that Winston Churchill, who was Home Secretary at the time, was responsible. South Wales, you will be told, will never forget Tonypandy!'

'And it wasn't a bit like that?'

'The actual facts are these…The rougher section of the Rhondda Valley crowd had got quite out of hand. Shops were being looted and property destroyed. The Chief Constable of Glamorgan sent a request to the Home Secretary for troops…If a Chief Constable thinks a situation serious enough to ask for the help of the military a Home Secretary has very little choice in the matter. But Churchill was so horrified at the possibility of the troops coming face to face with a crowd of rioters and having to fire on them, that he stopped the movement of the troops and sent instead a body of plain, solid Metropolitan police, armed with nothing but their rolled-up mackintoshes. The troops were kept in reserve, and all contact with the rioters was made by unarmed London police. The only bloodshed in the whole affair was a bloody nose or two. The Home Secretary was severely criticized in the House of Commons incidentally for his 'unprecedented intervention' [in withholding troops]. That was Tonypandy. That is the shooting-down by troops that Wales will never forget.'

'Yes,' Carradine said, considering. 'It's almost a parallel to the Boston affair. Someone blowing up a simple affair to huge proportions for a political end.'

'The point is not that it is a parallel. The point is that *every single man* who was there knows that the story is nonsense, and yet it has never been contradicted. It will never be overtaken now. It's a completely untrue story grown to legend while the men who knew it to be untrue looked on and said nothing.'

'Yes. That's very interesting; very. History as it is made.'

'Yes. History.'

'Give me research…The real history is written in forms not meant as history. In Wardrobe Accounts, in Privy Purse expenses, in personal letters, in estate books. If someone, say, insists that Lady Whoosit never had a child, and you find in the account book the entry: "*For the son born to my lady on Michaelmas eve: five yards of blue ribbon, fourpence halfpenny*", it's a reasonably fair deduction that my lady had a son on Michaelmas eve.'

…'Dear Alan [wrote Laura],

Nothing (repeat: nothing) would surprise me about history. Scotland has large monuments to two women martyrs drowned for their faith, in spite of the fact that they weren't drowned at all and neither was a martyr anyway. They were convicted of treason – fifth column work for the projected invasion from Holland, I think. Anyhow on a purely civil charge. They were reprieved *on their own petition* by the Privy Council, and the reprieve is in the Privy Council Register to this day…[Nevertheless] the tale of their sad end, complete with heart-rending dialogue, is to be found in every Scottish bookcase. Entirely different dialogue in each collection. And the gravestone of one of the women, in Wigtown churchyard, reads:

> "Murdered for owning Christ supreme
> Head of his Church, and no more crime
> But her not owning Prelacy
> And not abjuring Presbytry
> Within the sea tied to a stake
> She suffered for Christ Jesus sake."

…And tourists come and shake their heads…All this in spite of the fact that the original collector of the material, canvassing the Wigtown district only forty years after the supposed martyrdom…complains that *many deny that this happened*; and couldn't find any eye-witnesses at all.

P.S. It's an odd thing, but when you tell someone the true facts [behind] a mythical tale, they are indignant not with the teller but with you. They don't *want* to have their ideas upset…If they were merely indifferent it would be natural and understandable. But it is much stronger than that…Very odd, isn't it.'

MORE Tonypandy, Grant thought.

He began to wonder just how much of the school-book which up to now had represented British history for him was Tonypandy.

(Josephine Tey, *The Daughter of Time*)

10–12 Find and discuss some clear and some possible examples of 'Tonypandy'.

More about premises

The premises of an argument (and its conclusion) are statements. So far I have used the word 'statement' as though its meaning were clear.

1   Off the top of your head – try a definition.

Things you might have got wrong:

First, you might have confused a statement with a sentence. A sentence is a string of words: those words and no others. The words

'MY FEET HURT'

(in that order) form an English sentence. Change 'hurt' to 'are sore' and because these are different words, you have a different sentence.

But you could use either sentence to make the same statement. Moreover if *I* wanted to make that statement, which is about *you*, I could use neither. I would need a sentence containing words like '*her* feet' or '*his* feet' or your name. Otherwise I would be making a different statement, about another pair of feet: my own.

2   Suppose I want to make the same statement (about your feet) *to* you. What sentence might I use?

Again, the same person (you perhaps) would use the sentence 'My feet hurt' at different times to make different statements: one today at 10 a.m. (say) about your feet at the moment, the other about your feet at midnight last Tuesday.

A further reason why statements are not sentences is that we can make statements without using sentences, or using words at all. A sentence is only the *typical* way. I might ask '*Do your feet hurt?*' and you, too much in pain to speak, nod. You have made a statement.

3   What have you stated?
4   Does this mean that a nod always states this, or always makes a statement? Why, or why not?
5   Find a few more examples of statements that are made without words.

You can also *speak* a sentence without stating anything, as when you ask 'What is '*My feet hurt*' in French?'

J'ai mal aux pieds   *(La plume de ma tante)*

In short, a sentence – as such – has no truth-value: that is to say, it is neither true nor false.

Second, you might have confused a statement with the SENSE of a sentence. 'My feet hurt' and '*J'ai mal aux pieds*' share a sense. To know this, and to know what sense it is, you need not know who is speaking or when. You need only to understand the English and French words and grammar, and to know that these are used normally. This is quite independent of truth or falsity: like the sentence itself, the sense of a sentence has no truth-value.

6   Which of these share a sense?

(i)   My Granny is rich
(ii)   My mother's mother is rich
(iii) My father's mother is rich
(iv) 7×2=14
(v)   Two times seven is fourteen
(vi) Twice the number of days in a week is fourteen.

My own definition of a statement derives from Plato:

> A statement identifies a subject (or subjects) and says something about it (or them).

A statement therefore occurs only when a sentence (or a nod or whatever) is *used for a particular purpose on a particular occasion:*

different feet,  different statements.

That is why *statements alone* – not sentences or their senses – *are true or false* (have truth-values). Truth is truth about something: it needs a subject. Neither a sentence nor its sense, independent of context, is exact enough to supply one.

This is sometimes disputed. Of course no sentence using a word like 'my' is true or false except when it makes a statement, because 'my' refers to the speaker of the moment.

7   What is the sense of the word 'my'?

The moment also determines when 'now' refers to, and where 'here' is, and the tenses of verbs: past, present or future. Terms like these (they are called 'indexicals') clearly link truth-value to the context of a statement.

However, certain logicians argue that we could in theory always replace indexicals by context-neutral terms – 'I' by the speaker's name, for example, or the present tense by a date – and finally have an *eternal sentence*: one that is always true or always false, without reference to how or when or by whom it is used.

J'ai mal aux pieds

↓

The feet of Marie Dubois hurt / will hurt at 9 a.m., 12/9/97.

But it is an illusion that names are context-neutral. If a sentence were really eternal, the words alone would give us all that we need to tell if it is true, so long as we know the language. But a name does not identify something unless we know its history. Which individual/s (if any) have been given the name 'Marie Dubois'? And if there are more than one, which one do we mean? Dates raise a similar problem. We can seem to locate one date in time by relating it to another; but that in turn must be located…and so on. We can never pin down a date by relating it to *now*, because 'now' depends on a context.

8   Has 'now' a sense? If so, what is it?

The most plausible candidate for an eternal sentence perhaps is one like '2+2=4'. Surely this always, timelessly, says something both intelligible and true about numbers? *But those very shapes might be what a life-form in the Beta Pictoris system writes – and those very sounds the noises it makes – to assert not 'TWO PLUS TWO ARE FOUR' but 'MY FEET HURT'.*

Nearer home, we might use '2+2=4' untypically, as the title of a book for example. If a librarian gives you a form and under TITLE you write '2+2=4', you are not making a statement about numbers. You are stating that this is the name of the book. The way truth depends on context becomes even clearer when you remember that a book might also be called *2+2=5*. Would writing that on the form make you a liar?

Third, if you have already met the term, you might have said that a statement is a proposition. Many philosophers use the word 'proposition' more or less as I use 'statement', so you might not be wrong in that case – just uninformative, since you then need to define 'proposition'. On the other hand some logicians use 'proposition' differently, to mean what is *shared* by statements and other forms of language: a question for example ('Are you rich?'), a command ('Get rich!'), a wish ('If only you were rich') – and a statement ('You are rich').

9   What do all these have in common?
10 What question corresponds to the statement '2+2=4'?

Questions, commands and wishes do not have truth-values. The *answer* to a question may be true or false, but a question is different from its answer. Again a wish may *come* true, or a command be obeyed; but the state of affairs that this brings about is different from the wish or the command, and different again from the (true) statement that says this state of affairs is the case.

11 A sentence – as such – does not make a statement. Can a sentence – as such – give a command or ask a question or make a wish?

So this sense of 'proposition' does not fit what we are studying. Truth-values are what logic is all about: more precisely, the relation between the truth-values of an argument's premise/s and its conclusion.

12 Explain why this is so.

In common usage, too, 'proposition' does not normally mean something true or false, but something to be accepted or rejected (like 'proposal'). This could be misleading.

'Statement', however, does not mislead in this way. Both in logic and in common usage, the word typically means something true or false: think of a policeman taking the statement of a witness. All this explains why I call the first system that I discuss STATEMENT LOGIC, rather than 'sentential' or 'propositional' logic, as it is often named.

Having identified (I hope) what kind of things premises (and conclusions) are, I shall now get back to what makes a good or bad premise.

Logical truth

In Chapters 4 and 5 I discussed badly chosen premises: false or fishy premises that (often) we don't know we're using, premises that can't all be true together, premises that assume our conclusion. To describe these last two kinds – the *argument whose premises are incompatible*, and the *circular argument* – I coined the term 'USELESS VALIDITY': certain arguments are formally valid, but informally fallacious.

1   (*Revision*) Explain why.

What, then, is a well-chosen premise? Quite simply, it is one that we have good reason to believe is true. What counts as a good reason is an issue for epistemology (the philosophical study of knowledge and belief) not logic, except in one respect: *some statements are true (and others are false) for logical reasons.*
      Consider the statement that 2+2=4.

2   Which of these guarantees its truth?

    (i) The fact that every time people have added 2 and 2 they have got 4
    (ii) The meanings of '2', '+', '=' and '4'.

I am assuming of course that we use the terms in their normal sense and context, that of counting and arithmetic.

3 It has been pointed out that whereas one male rabbit plus one male rabbit makes two rabbits, one female rabbit plus one male rabbit may make twelve rabbits. Why does this not contradict the statement that (necessarily) 1+1=2?

Statements like these are called *logical truths*; and any statement whose truth is incompatible with that of a logical truth is logically false: *2+2=5*, for example.

4 What would the denial of a logically false statement be, and why?
5 Which of these statements is true or false because of the meaning of words? (Remember that the words are used in their normal sense.)

(i) If cats are bigger than mice, mice are smaller than cats
(ii) Cats are bigger than mice
(iii) A cat is an animal
(iv) A mouse is a mouse
(v) Some mice are cats
(vi) Some cats are smaller than other cats
(vii) If mice are bigger than cats, cats are smaller than mice
(viii) Some cats are twenty feet high.

When meaning guarantees the truth of a statement, it is through logical form. The forms of such statements contain repetitions. In arithmetic for example there are rules (or rules can be derived) that allow you to substitute '2+2' for '4' and vice versa; or allow you to substitute '1+1+1+1' for both. The truth of '2+2=4' comes from this. It has the underlying form A=A, and the meaning of '=' requires that any statement of that form be true: in any possible world, a thing is equal to itself.

6   Look again at the statements in question 5. Which is true because of repetition?

Sometimes a statement is true because of its meaning, but its surface form contains no repetition. In such cases its underlying form will be different. For example, 'soporific' means the same as 'sends people to sleep'; so 'all soporific drugs send people to sleep' states the same as 'all soporific drugs are soporific' or 'all drugs that send people to sleep, send people to sleep'. Its underlying form is *All As are As*. Some statements in Question 5 are true because of their meaning and therefore because of their logical form; but their surface form does not show this.

7   Find an underlying form for each, which shows that it is necessarily true. Explain how it has this form.

Not all repetition guarantees truth, of course. It may also guarantee that a statement is false, or leave the matter open.

8   Does any statement in Question 5 have an underlying form in which repetition (a) makes it false? (b) leaves the matter open?

9   Say whether these forms guarantee that statements which have them are true, or false, or leave the matter open:

(i) All As are As   (iii) All As are Bs
(ii) No As are As   (iv) All As are Bs or not all As
                                 are Bs.

Logical truths are said to be *necessary*. Philosophers disagree about whether there are necessary truths that do *not* depend on meaning, but this need not worry us: the ones based on meaning are what matter in a logic course. Necessary truths are also said to be *true in all possible worlds*: given what we mean by '2', for example, a world where 2=2 does not equal 4 is impossible. Let me stress again that the *figure* '2' or the *word* for that number may differ: as I have already pointed out, the same figure or letters or sounds could be used to say 'my feet hurt'. But even in a world where feet are called '*two*' and the number two is called '*shrump*', two plus two would still equal four. They would just say it differently.

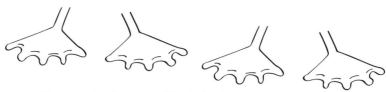

Shrump nko shrump tokku boing!

When a statement is true because of its meaning, we call it *analytic*. 'Analyse' literally means 'take to bits': take such a statement's logical form to bits and you will find repetition, of a kind that guarantees truth.

A word of caution however: the examples I have given are rather simple. It is not always easy to pronounce a statement analytic (or not). In a natural language, words are not strictly defined: aspects that one native speaker may think necessary to what a word means may not seem so to another, and no Language Dictator exists to settle the issue. 'All cats are animals', yes; but what about 'All cats have lungs'?

Some philosophers – W.V.O. Quine for one – attack the whole idea of analyticity. The pros and cons mostly lie beyond an introduction to logic, but these points seem worth making in analyticity's defence:

(i) The fact that there are many undecidable cases does not show that there are no clear ones.

(ii) We do not seem to need exact definitions or synonyms for analyticity. Perhaps we cannot say exactly what an insect is or which kind of insect a moth is – we may even disagree – but if we agree that whatever else it is, a moth is some kind of insect, we agree that the underlying form of 'A moth is an insect' is *an AB is a B*. Whatever A may be, B's repetition makes the form analytic.

(iii) Context is important. There may be uses of 'moth' or 'triangle' or 'cannibal' in which a moth is not an insect, a triangle has no angles, a cannibal lives on milk – but if we know what the words *normally* mean we can still agree that in *normal* contexts the meanings of 'moth', 'triangle' and so on rule this out.

(iv) A statement may also be true analytically not in a normal context but in a special one, when people who use it agree to accept certain definitions. Here Language Dictators may exist. A word like 'infant' for example has a special meaning in English law: 'below the age of majority', I believe. (If you are a lawyer and I'm wrong, please let me know.) Since the age of majority in Great Britain is now eighteen, it will be true by definition *in contexts where this legal term is used* that a twelve-year-old (say) is an infant. We may not always know what counts as aged twelve (what if the child were born on the International Dateline? or on the moon?) – but that is not the point.

Of course this is not to say that 'An English twelve-year-old is an infant' is true in all possible worlds. It is not true in this one where 'infant' is used in its ordinary sense, to mean a baby. If we want a statement that is true in all possible worlds, we shall need to include more, perhaps 'where an unrepealed law declares that the age of majority is eighteen, a twelve-year-old is, in English legal usage, an infant'. And 'English legal usage' will mean the English legal usage of the world where the statement is made (our world); and we must be using language normally when we say all this; just as '2' and '+' and '=' and '4' must be used normally for '2+2=4' to make a statement that is true in all possible worlds.

Analytic statements (obviously) make safe premises. For example any statement – call it S – is either true or false: this covers all possibilities. So a premise with the form *either S or not S* is analytic, because of the meanings of 'either...or' and 'not', and the way that S is repeated. And it is a kind of premise we often use:

> Either he'll agree with me, or he won't.
> (If he does, then...But on the other hand if he doesn't...)

> Every natural number is either odd or even.
> (If it's odd, then...And if it's even, then...).

10 'Every natural number is either odd or even' is not overtly analytic. Explain why not, and what makes it necessarily true.
11 Suppose the man we claim will either agree or not says neither 'Yes' nor 'No', but dithers. Does this mean that our 'necessary' premise was not true after all?

And on the THIRD hand...

There is a fallacy related to the use of 'either...or' in a premise. It is the *Appeal to Non-Exhaustive Alternatives*. This is when the underlying form of your premise is not really *either S or not S*, although it seems to be. For example, *either he'll say YES or he'll say NO* might seem to cover all possibilities. However, it does not: see question 11.

12 Does this mean that it is not a good premise?

When an assumption of this kind lies behind a question, the questioner is said to commit the fallacy of 'Many Questions'. The most famous example is probably

'Have you given up beating your wife yet? YES OR NO?'

– as if the answers 'Yes' and 'No' covered all possibilities. In fact, they only do so if the questions 'Have you a wife?' and 'Have you ever beaten her?' have already been answered 'Yes'. Loaded questions of this kind are common: look out for people who say 'Give me a straight answer – yes or no?'. A quick comeback is 'I can't give a straight answer to a crooked question'. Then explain why it is crooked.

The example above is so well known that if someone asks a question of this kind they're often accused of asking a *have-you-given-up-beating-your-wife?* question. The traditional name, 'Many Questions', is less famous.

Still more about premises

For sound argument, a premise must be true. This chapter says more about what makes a statement true or false, and how we can tell that it is.

1   (*Revision*) When is a statement analytic?

When a statement is not analytic we call it *synthetic*. Literally, 'synthesis' means 'putting together', the opposite of 'analysis'. If we know that a synthetic statement is true, it is not by taking its logical form to bits and finding the right kind of repetition, it is by observing that the ideas it puts together match the way things turn up together in the world. The question about which philosophers disagree – '*Are there any necessary truths which do not depend on the meaning of terms?*' – is the same as '*Are there any synthetic necessary truths?*'. This, as I have said, is a question of epistemology rather than logic.

2   (*Revision*) What is epistemology?

Statements whose truth or falsity is not necessary express *contingent* truths (or untruths). These depend on the way of the world. ('Contingent on' means 'dependent on'.) The statements are also called *contingent statements*. In a different world they might be false.

   Even if synthetic necessary truths are possible, *most* synthetic statements are clearly contingent. Consider '*Sheep exist*', for example.

False!

3   What does the statement 'Sheep exist' say that we may find together, in the world?

I must stress again that deciding whether a statement is necessary is not always simple, even if we limit the question to whether it is or is not analytic. For example, take 'Unicorns do not exist'. This is true, but why? Is it necessary or contingent?

If 'unicorn' just means 'horse-like beast with a single horn', it looks contingent.

4   Explain why.

But if you look in the *Concise Oxford Dictionary* you will find that the first definition – the relevant one – is '*Fabulous* creature with horse-like body and single straight horn'. If this means that *by definition* unicorns are just creatures of fable, the truth now seems to be necessary, because it is analytic.

Ha.

But dictionary 'definitions' are often not definitions in the logical sense. Besides saying what a word means they may, for example, give its origin. 'Fabulous' does just that. Within the fables where the word appears, of course unicorns are real. What would the single horn be attached to, if no animal was there?

English speakers who know what 'unicorn' means would probably agree about the rest: 'Creature with horse-like body and single straight horn'. But is it enough? Stories about unicorns say a lot more than that. And they are our only source for the word's meaning: we cannot reject what they say by referring to real life, (as we might with 'sheep') to show that a story has got it wrong.

5   When and why *would* we agree that a story about unicorns is wrong?

Sometimes we might disagree. We are talking about a species. Anything a story says about this or that individual unicorn will not count, then, unless it is supposed to be typical of unicorns in general. And things are true about the species in certain stories (being able to talk, for example) which we might agree do not have to be true for a creature to be a unicorn. So stories where they lack this feature have not got 'unicorn' wrong. But we may also find that the stories differ in ways which some of us think affect the meaning of 'unicorn', but others do not. Even the basic description, 'creature with horse-like body and single straight horn', may be variously interpreted. How horse-like must the body be, for example?

If this is not a unicorn, 'creature with horse-like body and single straight horn' may give necessary conditions for being a unicorn, but not a sufficient one. This creature (call it a 'mercorn') has a horse-like body and a single straight horn too, and it is not enough.

'Necessary condition' and 'sufficient condition' are two more technical terms. I shall say more about them later, in connection with particular systems of logic. But they are useful concepts in their own right: get them straight if you can. For example:

6   (i) Is being an animal necessary for being a sheep? Is it sufficient?
    (ii) Is being a ram necessary for being a sheep? Is it sufficient?

7   Find three conditions which are necessary for being a sheep, but not sufficient to distinguish a sheep from a goat.

We might never manage to agree on a set of necessary conditions for being a unicorn which add up to a sufficient one – one that allows us to say 'Anything that has all these MUST be a unicorn!' But suppose we did:

8   What would we then need to know, to decide if 'Unicorns exist' is true in some possible world?

It is important that this sufficient condition should be made up of necessary ones. We want to pick out the whole species. If you answered question 6 right, you will know that a sufficient condition may sometimes be too narrow to do this: all rams are sheep, but a sheep need not be a ram. If you met a beast with all the conditions it takes to be a *male* unicorn you could truly say 'Anything that has these features must be a unicorn!', but it is not true that any unicorn must have all these features. Unicorn-stories do not rule out females.

Indeed they do not!

Now suppose that we cannot agree on a definition of the species, though we agree about certain necessary conditions such as being horse-like, with a single horn. Since these are necessary, any species with the right to be called 'unicorn' must have them; but other creatures might have them and still not be unicorns. We might not have thought about 'mercorns', for example, but if we met one, we might agree that it was not a unicorn. But we also agree (surely) that to be just like the creatures in any of the best-known unicorn stories is sufficient. If an animal is just like that, it must be a unicorn, even though not all unicorns need be just like that.

9   In that case, is 'Unicorns exist' contingent?

Of course, to be contingent a statement must avoid not just impossibility, but necessary truth. For example, 'Either there are unicorns or there are not' must fit all possible worlds; so it is not contingent.

10 What about 'Something exists which either is a unicorn or not'? Is this logically true?

Contingent truth is also called *empirical* or *factual* truth, as opposed to logical truth. David Hume makes this distinction in a memorable way (though I think not quite as clearly as he could) in his *Enquiry*, about certain works of which he disapproved. The division into two became known as 'Hume's Fork'.

> '...Let us ask *Does it contain any abstract reasoning concerning quantity or number?* No. *Does it contain any experimental reasoning, concerning matters of fact and existence?* No. Commit it then to the flames; for it can contain nothing but sophistry and illusion.'

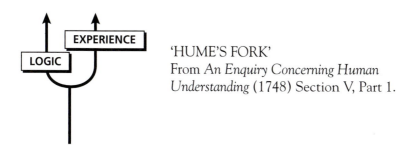

'HUME'S FORK'
From *An Enquiry Concerning Human Understanding* (1748) Section V, Part 1.

I think Hume is not entirely clear about abstract reasoning. It need not concern only quantity or number, unless we call the repetition that makes statements analytic a matter of number. An analytic statement may be about anything. What is important is its logical form, which is why I have labelled the left prong 'LOGIC'.

For the premises of a sound argument, either prong will do. We do not need premises that are true in all possible worlds, unless our conclusion is *about* all possible worlds. All we need is to know they are true in this one. If our experience of this world is not an idle dream, we know for example that sheep exist in it and unicorns do not. (How far, and when, we can trust experience is another question of epistemology rather than logic, though I will say a bit more on this in Chapter 14.) There do seem, however, to be just these two prongs, for learning that something is true: experience and reason.

11 If it's not clear whether 'All cats have lungs' is synthetic or analytic, should we therefore 'commit it to the flames'?

One kind of contingent statement is especially interesting, if we're wondering how it will do as a premise. Although contingent, it becomes true through the act of making it, or of making it in a particular way. The most famous argument to use such a premise is René Descartes's 'Cogito, ergo sum' ('I think, therefore I exist'). He reasoned that *while he was thinking 'I think'*, the statement 'I think' could not be false. And yet it is clearly not a statement which is true in all possible worlds – when the thinking is over, for example.

We call such statements *self-fulfilling*. The negation of a self-fulfilling statement is *self-stultifying*.

12 When is the statement 'I am not shouting' self-stultifying?

Argument-forms (1)

The time has come to discuss in more detail what makes the study of logic and argument possible: the fact that MANY ARGUMENTS HAVE THE SAME LOGICAL FORM. For example, consider:

(1) Everyone who has a Rolls Royce is rich
My Granny has a Rolls Royce
_____

My Granny is rich

(2) All clowns are sad
Bocadillo is a clown
_____

Bocadillo is sad.

(3) Anything you buy from Happy Ed is a bad bargain
I bought my van from Happy Ed
_____

It was a bad bargain.

If you are not language-blind (as some people are colour-blind) you will probably see that all these arguments have the same pattern: and it is one that makes all arguments which share it valid.

All A are B
x is A
_____
x is B

1   A in the Granny argument is 'Rolls Royce owner(s)'. What is A in the Happy Ed argument?

2   B in the Happy Ed argument is 'bad bargain(s)'. What is B in the Granny argument?

3   Which is 'Bocadillo' in the Clown argument: A, B or x?

The arguments' surface form varies without affecting this, because logical form depends not on the words but on what they mean. The only *All A are B* premise that uses the word 'all' is in the Clown argument, but the others come to the same thing. The Happy Ed conclusion uses 'was', not 'is', but it relates x to B in the same way as the others do. The article 'a' is used for singular vans, clowns or whatever, but this is an accident of English idiom and our analysis can leave it out: in the Happy Ed argument, we can replace B by 'bad bargains' or 'a bad bargain' as appropriate. In the same argument 'my van' and 'it' refer to the same thing, so we can interchange them – and so on.

The logical form above is valid. The next three arguments share the same *invalid* form.

(1) No wolves are vegetarians
Annabel is not a vegetarian

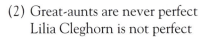

Annabel is a wolf

(2) Great-aunts are never perfect
Lilia Cleghorn is not perfect

Lilia Cleghorn is a great-aunt

(3) Real men don't keep rabbits
Colonel Carruthers doesn't keep rabbits

Colonel Carruthers is a real man.

4   What is the form shared by these arguments? Use A, B and x, so that in the Wolf argument 'wolves' (or 'a wolf' where appropriate) replaces A, 'vegetarian/s' replaces B, and 'Annabel' replaces x.

5   Which is 'rabbit-keeper/s' in the Carruthers argument: A, B or x?

6   Which is 'Lilia Cleghorn' in the Great-Aunt argument: A, B or x?

7   (*Revision*) How does an example (that is, a particular argument) show that its form is invalid? Answer with reference to the Wolf, Great-Aunt and Rabbit arguments: when would they show this, and when not?

Now one more set, whose shared form can be given more simply: instead of names or descriptions, we use letters to represent WHOLE STATEMENTS.

(1) If that malicious little creep sets foot in the house, I leave
He sets foot in the house
_____

I leave.

(2) If it can go wrong, it will
It can go wrong
_____

It will.

(3) If the Snake is proud, he will accept
     The Snake is proud
     _____

     He will accept.

The form these arguments share is

If P then Q
P
_____

Q

(When whole statements replace letters in a form, it is traditional to use P, Q, R etc. instead of A, B or x, y. I'll say more about this later.)

8   In the Creep argument P is 'That malicious little creep sets foot in the house'. What is Q?
9   What are P and Q in the Machine argument?
10 What are they in the Snake argument?
11 Give the form of the following argument. Use P and Q, and make Q 'You are not a sheep'. What is P?

If you are an elephant, you are not a sheep
You are not a sheep
_____

You are not an elephant.

12 Suppose that 'you' here means YOU personally, dear Reader. How does this Sheep argument about *you* show that all arguments of a certain form are invalid?

Chapter 10

Argument-forms (2)

In the answers to Chapter 7 I showed how the Sheep argument

If you are an elephant, you are not a sheep
You are not a sheep
_____

You are an elephant

can be analysed in terms of its logical form. The form I gave you was

If P then Q	P:	You are an elephant
Q	Q:	You ARE NOT a sheep.
———		
P.		

But it has the more detailed form:

If P then Q	P:	You are an elephant
NOT Q	Q:	You ARE a sheep.
———		
P.		

Which analysis we choose depends on what aspects of the argument we need to pick out.

Every argument with the second form also has the first, but not vice versa.

1 Why?
2 Which of these has the first form?

   (1) If you're bigger than a goat, you're bigger than a flea
       You're bigger than a goat
       _____

       You're bigger than a flea.

   (2) If you're bigger than a goat, you're bigger than a flea
       You're bigger than a flea
       _____

       You're bigger than a goat

   (3)   If she loves me, she doesn't love him
                             She doesn't love him
                             _____

                             SHE LOVES ME!!

3 Which of them has the second form?

   The Sheep argument has other forms too. The simplest is

   P   P: If you are an elephant, you are not a sheep
   Q   Q: You are not a sheep

   ___

   R   R: You are an elephant

which it shares with every argument in the world that has just two
premises – the Granny, Spider, Happy Ed arguments and so on –
but not for example a four-premise argument like this one:

   If Fang is a dog, he is a mammal
                        If he is a mammal, he is a vertebrate
                        If he is a vertebrate, he is an animal
                        Fang is a dog
                        _____

                        Fang is an animal.

4   What is the Fang argument's simplest logical form?

And the Sheep argument has this form:

> **If you are A, you are not a sheep**
> **You are not a sheep**
> _____
> **You are A**

which it shares with

> **If you are an insect, you are not a sheep**
> **You are not a sheep**
> _____
> **You are an insect**

A: insects/an insect.

and with

> **If you are a frog, you are not a sheep**
> **You are not a sheep**
> _____
> **You are a frog.**

A: frogs/a frog.

5   What is A in the original Sheep argument?

But unless you mean to spend your time arguing (invalidly, too!) about various non-sheep, the form

> **If you are A, you are not a sheep**
> **You are not a sheep**
> _____
> **You are A**

is not a useful one to study. Nor is:

If you are an elephant you are not B
You are not B

You are an elephant

which our original Sheep argument shares (for example) with

If you are an elephant, you are not a white ant
You are not a white ant

You are an elephant

but not with the Frog or Insect arguments.

6   Why not? (Give one reason.)
7   Explain what makes the White Ant, Frog and Insect examples
     ARGUMENTS rather than argument forms, and what makes
     something an ARGUMENT FORM rather than an argument.

Since validity depends on logical form,
it lies below the quirky surface of language, which can make an
invalid argument look valid and vice versa. Here are two philosophical examples. Note that in each case, more than one logical
form might be assigned, depending how we interpret what the
arguer leaves unsaid. In the first (Miss Nightingale's) neither of the
two most likely analyses can save the argument: if her premises are
acceptable, her argument-form is not, and vice versa. In the second
(Descartes's) I think Rosenberg's interpretation may be unfair –
though he is right to argue that if this *was* Descartes' reasoning, his
argument is invalid. So I give you as well a more charitable interpretation of my own.

   So long as we remember this possibility of rival interpretations,
nothing helps more than digging for the argument-form when we
need to assess an argument.

Miss Nightingale's Argument

In her old age, the great Florence Nightingale acquired a new interest.

> With statesmen and governers at her beck and call…with foreign governments agog for her counsel, building hospitals, training nurses – she still felt that she had not enough to do…What was there left? Of course!…Having set right the health of the British Army, she would now do the same good service for the religious convictions of mankind…Her *Suggestions for Thought to the Searchers after Truth among the Artisans of England* (1860), unravels, in the course of three portly volumes, the difficulties – hitherto, curiously enough, unsolved – connected with such matters as Belief in God, the Plan of Creation, the Origin of Evil, the Future Life, Necessity and Free Will, Law, and the Nature of Morality…Only a very few copies of the book were printed for private circulation. One copy was sent to Mr. [John Stuart] Mill, who acknowledged it in an extremely polite letter. He felt himself obliged, however, to confess that he had not been altogether convinced by Miss Nightingale's proof of the existence of God. Miss Nightingale was surprised and mortified; she had thought better of Mr. Mill; for surely her proof of the existence of God could hardly be improved upon. 'A law', she had pointed out, 'implies a lawgiver.' Now the Universe is full of laws – the law of gravitation…and many others; hence it follows that the Universe has a lawgiver – and what would Mr. Mill be satisfied with, if he was not satisfied with that?
>
> (Lytton Strachey, *Eminent Victorians*)

We might object (obviously) that Miss Nightingale does not seem to have proved the existence of just *one* God. As Lytton Strachey goes on to point out, laws are often

> …as a matter of fact, not dispensed by lawgivers, but passed by act of Parliament. Miss Nightingale, however, with all her experience of public life, never stopped to consider the question whether God might not be a Limited Monarchy.

But has she perhaps proved the existence of *at least one* God, where philosophers (like Mr Mill) confess to failure? If not, where does her argument go wrong? Two analyses seem possible: one locates the mistake in an invalid form, the other in a dubious premise.

I.   On the surface, her argument seems to have the valid form

All A are B	A: system(s) with laws
x is A	B: system(s) with lawgiver(s)
x is B	x: Nature

and the premises appear to be true. But as Mr Mill might have pointed out, the real logical form is different. If the premises seem true, it is because Miss Nightingale uses one sense of the word 'law' in her first premise and a quite different one in the second, without seeing that the meaning has changed. The laws whose existence demands lawgivers – judicial or PRESCRIPTIVE laws – *prescribe* how people should behave. People do not always comply with them, but this does not destroy their status as laws. Scientific laws like the Law of Gravitation are DESCRIPTIVE. They do not tell things how they should behave: they merely *describe* them; and if things do not behave that way in fact, they are not laws at all.

So below the surface the argument really has the form:

All A are B	A: system(s) with prescriptive laws
x is C	B: system(s) with lawgiver(s)
	C: system(s) with descriptive laws
x is B	x: Nature.

The word for this double-meaning fallacy is EQUIVOCATION. It often makes a bad argument seem good.

8   Find an argument with a different A, B, C and x which shows that the form above is invalid.

II.   But perhaps if we accused Miss Nightingale of equivocation, she might say

'But do not Descriptive Laws Also Require a Lawgiver? For how could Nature exhibit Regularity, unless She were so Designed?'

If so, the underlying form of her argument is really

All A and all C are B A: system(s) with prescriptive laws
x is C B: system(s) with lawgiver(s)
_____ C: system(s) with descriptive laws
x is B x: Nature

and it is VALID, though it is now unclear why she should mention the A-set at all. It does not invalidate the argument, but it confuses the issue.

Proof requires more than a valid argument, however. We need true premises as well. And now we must question Miss Nightingale's first premise. It seems evident enough that all systems with *prescriptive* laws need lawgivers to issue the prescriptions (*All A are B*). It is evident too that there is order (regularity) in Nature, so that we can formulate descriptive laws (*x is C*). But it is by no means evident that order cannot arise except by design, so that wherever we find descriptive laws, there must be a Lawgiver or Designer (*All C are B*). Indeed, that is precisely what atheists dispute.

Two arguments from René Descartes's *Meditations*

(From Jay F. Rosenberg, *The Practice of Philosophy*, ch. 2.)

'Here are two short passages from Descartes' first *Meditation*:

I. *Everything which I have thus far accepted as entirely true and assured has been acquired from the senses or by means of the senses. But I have learned by experience that these sometimes mislead me, and it is prudent never to trust wholly things which have once deceived us.*

II. *But perhaps God did not wish me to be deceived in that fashion, since he is said to be supremely good. But if it was repugnant to his goodness to have made me so that I was always mistaken, it would seem also to be inconsistent for him to permit me to be sometimes mistaken, and nevertheless I cannot doubt that he does permit it.*

Each of these…contains or suggests a little argument…in the first instance, he suggests that it could be the case that his senses always deceive him; in the second, that it could be the case that God always permits him to be mistaken. So we may, without too much violence, extract two cleaned-up arguments from these passages, each argument having one premiss [*another way of spelling 'premise'*] and a conclusion:

A1.   My senses sometimes deceive me

       It could be the case that my senses always deceive me

A2.   God sometimes permits me to be mistaken

       It could be the case that God always permits me to be mistaken.

A little scrutiny suggests that we are dealing with two examples of a single pattern of reasoning…

A*   **X is sometimes F**

       It could be the case that X is always F.

If we replace the letter X by 'my senses' and the letter F by 'deceptive', we get argument A1. If we replace X by 'God' and F by 'willing for me to be mistaken' we get argument A2…What we need to do next (to show this form of argument is invalid) is to produce yet another argument of the same form, having an indisputably true premiss and an indisputably false conclusion…

Here is one which occurred to me: replace X by 'paintings' and F by 'forgeries'. What we get then is the following argument:

A3. Paintings are sometimes forgeries

It could be the case that paintings are always forgeries.

The premiss of A3 is clearly, as a matter of fact, true, but the conclusion of A3 is false. For a forged painting is a *copy* of some original painting [or of its style], and it could not be the case that *all* paintings were copies…There would be nothing for the supposed copies to be copies *of*. So the *argument pattern* A* is an invalid pattern and, in consequence, both of the original arguments A1 and A2 are invalid arguments.

9   If (as Rosenberg says) they are invalid, must the conclusions of A1 and A2 be false?

10 Which of the following arguments has the form A*?

A4. It has been Observed upon Divers Occasions that the Elephant, when he is first Confronted with a Mouse, will fall into a veritable Paroxysm of Fright. We may therefore conclude that the Fear of Mice is Universal to the Species; for it is manifestly neither the product of Experience, nor of Reason.

['We may therefore conclude' means 'therefore', and 'It may be' is the same as 'It could be the case that'.]

A5. It has been Observed upon Divers Occasions that the Elephant, when he is first Confronted with a Mouse, will fall into a veritable Paroxysm of Fright. We may therefore conclude that the Fear of Mice is Universal to the Species.

A6. It has been Observed upon Divers Occasions that the Elephant, when he is first Confronted with a Mouse, will fall into a veritable Paroxysm of Fright. It may then be that the Fear of Mice is Universal to the Species.

But does Rosenberg's 'tidying-up' really reflect Descartes' thinking? Given Descartes' own words, A1 and A2 are certainly fair analyses; and yes, as they stand they are invalid. But if we could ask Descartes, he might answer:

'Certainly original paintings must exist to make forgeries possible. But sense experiences and human errors are not like them in this respect.'

If so, we have an extra implicit premise and a different argument-form:

A**   x is sometimes F
       x's being F does NOT depend on x's sometimes being non-F
       _____

       It could be the case that x is always F.

11 Does A** give a false conclusion from true premises if we make
    x 'paintings' and F 'forgeries'?

12 Is A** valid?

(Of course even if it *is* valid, it won't prove Descartes' conclusions
unless his premises are true.)

Monsieur Descartes and Miss Nightingale are dead: we cannot
question them about their unwritten thoughts; and (dead or alive)
many arguers whom we must assess are as far out of reach. What
should we do in these cases? Is there a general rule? I can suggest
one. If you are not sure how to interpret someone's words, first
point out that this itself is a problem. Then look at the argument
from three angles: its surface form, the worst reasonable interpreta-
tion/s of this, and the best.

Start with its surface form, because anyone who puts an argument badly deserves to be attacked for that in the first place.
Misunderstanding is a menace and so are those who abet it.

But if an argument is important, you cannot refuse to consider it
just because it is badly expressed. So after that you should consider
whether any fair interpretation of its surface form suggests a *bad*
underlying argument: if so, criticise that. It may well be what the
arguer meant.

On the other hand if you are interested not in a cheap (and
maybe unjust) victory but in the truth about what is being argued,
you cannot stop here. Consider finally whether a stronger interpretation is possible. If so, this is your real target – because if the
arguer's point can be proved, this is the way it might be done.

Argument-forms (3)

Every argument has several forms. The simplest merely shows that it is an argument, by identifying a premise or premises, a *therefore*, and a conclusion. Take for example the (tidied-up) Granny argument. Its simplest form is (F1).

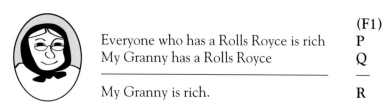

	(F1)
Everyone who has a Rolls Royce is rich	P
My Granny has a Rolls Royce	Q
My Granny is rich.	R

1   The Granny argument is valid, but form (F1) is not. Explain why not.
2   If validity is purely a matter of form, how can the Granny argument have an invalid form?

Here are some more forms:

(F2) **All A are rich**   (F3) **All A are B**
    x is A   **My Granny is A**
    _____   _____
    x is rich   **My Granny is B**

(F4) **All A are B**   (F5) **Everybody who owns a Rolls is B**
    x is A   **x owns a Rolls**
    _____   _____
    x is B   **x is B**

(F6) **If P then Q**
     P
    ―――――――
    Q

(F7) **If x is A then x is B**
     x is A
    ―――――――――
    x is B.

3   Which of these, if any, fit the Granny argument?
4   Which if any are valid?
5   Will any of them fit an invalid argument? Why, or why not?

When you can choose different forms of an argument to study, the best is usually one that is detailed enough to show validity if the argument is valid, but no more. More detail means less scope: the form will fit fewer arguments.

6   Which form of the Granny argument (starting with F1) best meets these requirements?

The Fox again

We have seen that the first step of the Fox's argument

> **The Snake is proud. He will accept.**

is valid, if we supply a premise the Fox almost certainly believes: 'If the Snake is proud, he will accept'. The argument that results is

(Step 1)

If the Snake is proud, he will accept
The Snake is proud

He will accept.

7   Which of Forms (F1) through (F7) does it have?
8   Which of these show/s that it is valid?

In his next step, the Fox takes the conclusion of his first argument as an unspoken premise:

[The Snake will accept.]

He will then almost surely die in the attempt…or he may live, but fail…

or perhaps – conceivably – he may succeed.

We can ignore his use of 'almost surely' and 'conceivably' and his use of 'may' as opposed to 'will': these do not affect his line of reasoning. 'Then' – like 'therefore' – identifies a conclusion. So the Fox's second argument seems to be :

(Step 2)

The Snake will accept

Either the Snake will die in the attempt, or he will live but fail, or he will succeed.

This is formally invalid, since there is nothing to connect *the Snake's accepting* with those three possibilities and no others. If it really were the Fox's whole argument, its premise could be true and the conclusion false. Suppose for example that the Snake accepts, but then hears that the priests have ground down the ruby to make a potion? He will neither have died nor succeeded; but we cannot say that he has failed, if he had no chance to try.

But the Fox is not stupid. If he argues on these lines, he must believe that the connection exists, even though he does not bother to state it. In other words, what he knows of the Snake, the monks, etc. have led him to believe that *if the Snake accepts, then either he will die in the attempt, or he will live but fail, or he will succeed*: no other eventuality need be considered. Add this implicit premise, and we find the dear old argument-form

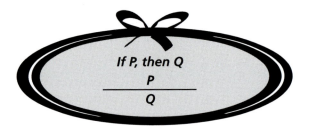

9   What are P and Q?

Q is a long and complex statement. But since that whole statement appears in both premise and conclusion, the single letter Q can represent it.

10 If it has this form, is the Fox's second step valid?
11 Has it a simpler, invalid form? If so, what is it?

Of course if we need to, we can also analyse the Fox's conclusion in greater detail. It is made up of three simpler statements, joined by 'or'. So this same argument also has the less simple form:

If P then (Q or R or S)
P

_____

Q or R or S.

12 What are P, Q, R and S in this new analysis? And is this form
    valid?

We shall need the more detailed form later, because the Fox goes
on to consider each component of his conclusion on its own:

**THE SNAKE WILL ALMOST SURELY DIE IN THE
ATTEMPT.** If so, I shall have no rival, and can easily
persuade the band that further tests are a waste of time.

    OR HE WILL LIVE, BUT FAIL. The result will be the
same: for having lost face, he will leave at once for distant parts.

    OR PERHAPS – CONCEIVABLY – HE WILL SUCCEED.
But once he has stolen the Eye, the possibility of *my* doing so
cannot arise. And the vengeance of the priests of Zorro is
horrible and swift. He will not rule for long; and I am his only
possible successor.

To be continued.

Variables

Variables are the letters like P, Q, A, B or x in argument-forms. They replace what *varies* in different arguments that have the same form. Think of variables as holes to be filled by language.

Furthermore, variables are holes with different shapes, according to what type of language fills them. In my examples so far, there have been just three types: I have used a different kind of letter for each. All three appear in the three possible analyses of the Fox's argument

> If the Snake is proud, he will accept
> The Snake is proud
> _____
> He will accept.

(See Chapter 11, question 7.)

These are

(F1) **P**
        Q
        ___
        R

(F6) **If P then Q**
        P
        _____
        Q

(F7) **If x is A, then x is B**
        x is A
        _____

        x is B.

1   What replaces the variables in each form?

Now look at your answer to question 1, and decide what shape of hole each letter represents. In other words:

2   What kind of expression does a variable represent if it is *a capital letter in the sequence P, Q etc.?*
3   What kind of expression does a variable represent if it is *a small letter in the sequence x, y etc.?*
4   What kind of expression does a variable replace if it is *a capital letter in the sequence A, B etc.?*

Logical constants

A variable in an argument-form is a hole to be filled by a bit of language. Its shape depends on what kind of bit this is. And *that* is determined by the hole's surroundings: those parts of the argument-form that do not change.

One thing that does not change is the difference between input and output (premises and conclusion). Every argument-form contains a 'therefore' and the conclusion must follow after it, or it is not a conclusion. (Remember that I am referring to an argument's underlying form. In casual speech, as we have seen, all kinds of word-order are possible.) Premises must come before 'therefore', or they are not premises.

Apart from this, it does not matter in what order premises appear. So these two:

Anything you buy from Happy Ed is a bad bargain
I bought my van from Happy Ed

It was a bad bargain

I bought my van from Happy Ed
Anything you buy from Happy Ed is a bad bargain

It was a bad bargain

are the same argument, but this:

I bought my van from Happy Ed
It was a bad bargain

Anything you buy from Happy Ed is a bad bargain

is different.

5   Is the third one valid?
6   Could the first be valid if the second was invalid, or vice versa?
    How, or why not?

In an argument's simplest form, there are *only* variables in a certain order, with a 'therefore' before the final one. Form (F1) is like this:

P
Q
──
R.

Each variable should be filled by a whole premise, or by the whole conclusion. Conclusions and premises are always statements, so in these simplest forms all variables are in the sequence P, Q, R... (rather than A, B, C... or x, y, z...), because P, Q and R are statement-holes.

But as soon as we have more detailed forms than (F1), a new kind of non-variable factor appears. For example, the first Happy

Ed argument, like the others, has the form (F1), but it also has the form

All A are B
x is A

---

x is B.

And the argument

 I bought my van from Happy Ed
It was a bad bargain

Anything you buy from Happy Ed is a bad bargain

has form (F1), but it also has the form

x is A
x is B

All A are B.

In both these arguments A, B and x are variables to be replaced; and both arguments replace them in the same way.

7   What are A, B and x ?

But the expressions '*All...are...*' and ' *...is...*' are *not* variables to be replaced: they are the same in every argument that shares this form. Because they are permanent, we call them *logical constants*.

The type of constant used in an argument-form decides what type of variable we need. For example only A, B variables – filled by *general descriptions* like 'things bought from Happy Ed' – go with the constant '*All...are...*'. If we use P, Q variables instead – the kind we replace with whole statements – we get ungrammatical nonsense, like

ALL I bought my van from Happy Ed
ARE it was a bad bargain.

(Form, or rather malform: **All P are Q**.)

We also get nonsense if we fill in '*All:... are...*' with proper names, or with the kind of definite description (like 'my van') that identifies an individual:

ALL my van ARE Happy Ed.

(Malform: **All x are y**.)

Again the logical constant '*...is...*' says that a certain individual (e.g. Happy Ed, or my van) is of a certain kind: 'x is A', 'y is B' and so forth. So here too the wrong kind of variable asks for a nonsense-filling, as in

(i) Bad bargain(s) IS Happy Ed.
   (Malform: **A is Y** or **All A is Y.**)

and

(ii) I bought my van from Happy Ed IS it was a bad bargain.
   (Malform: **P is Q**.)

Here are four expressions:

(i)
'Uncle Marley is a beggar'

(ii)
'Beggars'

(iii)
'Uncle Marley'

(iv)
'People who wear rags'.

8 Say whether each refers to an individual, is a general description, or is a statement.
9 Which of these formulae are malforms, and why?

(i)

If x then y

(ii)

If Q then P

(iii)

If B then A

(iv)

If x then B.

Sometimes an accident of language may make a wrong variable-filling look like sense, or sense look like a wrong variable-filling. But this is only on the surface.

10 'All the world's a stage' looks superficially as if its logical form were **All x is A**: a malform. But since it makes sense, this can't be the case. What is its *real* logical form?

What sort of expression are logical constants, then? Any kind, in theory, so long as they connect the variables in an argument-form. In Chapter 5 we had some that were limited to arguments about sheep or elephants: '*if you are…you are not a sheep*' and '*if you are an elephant you are not…*'. They are rather eccentric constants no doubt; but in the eccentric argument-forms where they figure, that is their role.

11 What type of variable (P, A or x) should replace the gaps in '*if you are…you are not a sheep*' and '*if you are an elephant you are not…*', and why?

In his Descartes arguments, Rosenberg identifies two more constants: '*…is sometimes…*' and '*it could be the case that…is always…*'.

12 What types of variable should replace the gaps here, and why?

Logicians tend to concentrate on a few small families of constants, chosen for their scope and simplicity. Each family (with its own variables and rules) is called a *system of logic*. I shall deal mainly with two. One is the system where we find formulae like *all A are B* and *x is A*: the logic of sets. The other is the less detailed logic of statements, where we find formulae like *if P then Q* and *S or T* and *not R*. I shall take this second system first. In time it will bring us back to the Fox.

Analogy (1)

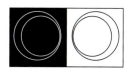

The first part of this book is about logic in general, rather than any one system. I shall end it by discussing a way of arguing that is both indispensable to life and, in its commonest forms, fallacious. This is *argument by analogy*. Earlier I invented the category of USELESS VALIDITY: arguments with contradictory premises for example. Their form will not allow true premises and a false conclusion, but they can't prove anything. Argument by analogy is often a USEFUL FALLACY. LIke many fallacies, it may take alternate forms: either invalid, or valid with an unacceptable premise.

Argument by analogy is useful in one notorious way: it can persuade. The most unlikely analogies will fool people. It is very attractive to approach a difficult x via an easy y, perhaps a y that is visible and can be pictured when x cannot. This of course is why models and diagrams and maps are persuasive; but an honest model uses analogy soundly. Unsound analogy shares its persuasiveness with the other famous informal fallacies: the old rhetoricians taught not only how to recognise and avoid them, but how to use them and deceive. (Just as *know when you're lying* is a more useful rule than you might imagine for thinking clearly, so is *know when you argue badly*.)

Consider for example this answer to what is often called 'the problem of evil'. (A version of it is given by G.K. Chesterton's 'Father Brown', who I am sure was honestly persuaded by it.)

> 'You ask how an all-powerful and benevolent God could have created an obviously imperfect world? In this life we see only the wrong side of the tapestry. On the other side – God's side – the pattern is perfect and complete!'

This has the form:

> **x is like y**
> **y is A**
> _____
> **x is A.**

The premise 'The world is like a tapestry' is implicit, but obviously there:

> The world is like a tapestry
> Perfect tapestries are A
> _____
> The world is A.

1   What is A?

The form is invalid because 'like' is very elastic: a charter for equivocation.

2   (_Revision_) What is equivocation?

A statement with the form _x is like_ y can almost always be true in senses which do not include the A in question. So the conclusion of an argument with this form can be false when the premises are true. Here is a simple example:

 X IS LIKE Y in overall shape (square) and size; in being black-and-white; in being on the same page of this book; in having a pattern made by a smaller ring within a larger one, slightly off-centre…etc.

A= 'white lines on a black ground'.

We can argue validly by analogy. The valid form is:

> x is like y *with respect to (being or not being)* A
> y is A
>
> ───────────────────────────────
>
> x is A.

Example:

> y = a painter's colour sample, 'Russian Cream'
> x = a wall painted with Russian Cream emulsion
> A = matching my cushions.

Assume that x is like y *in colour*. (It should be – that is what a sample is for.) Then if y matches my cushions, I may safely conclude that x will do so. We reason like this without thinking, when we use a model or a map; and if it lets us down we are indignant: x was not like y in the way that we had a right to expect.

But the Tapestry argument must have the first, invalid form, if we can safely accept its premises. Tapestries are created by weavers, and clearly the world is like a tapestry in some ways. Both contain patterns, for example. However, this does not mean we can assume without argument that they are alike in having a creator, or a creator who is like a weaver of tapestries.

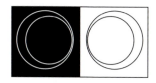

It would be bad enough if we simply did not know whether the analogy between the world and a tapestry is true. But in fact, if the analogy is good, the argument fails as badly as if it were false – but in a different way. If it were sound, the argument would prove the reverse of what the arguer wants. The aim of the Tapestry argument is to show that God could be both all-good and all-powerful in spite of earthquakes, acne, leprosy, tapeworms, infant leukemia and how cats torture mice. But the back of a tapestry is a mess just because tapestry weavers are *not* all-powerful, and because they only care about the front.

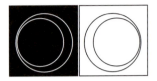

If we take the analogy seriously, the World-Weaver (supposing there is one) turns out to be *less* perfect than a tapestry weaver. The messy side of a tapestry is meant to be hidden and trouble no one. But the imperfect world is the only side we get to see.

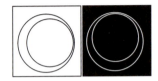

If you think about this argument you will see that there are various ways in which reasoning by analogy can go wrong.

First, we may use a *shaky* analogy: we simply have no reason to suppose that x is like y with respect to A. If we assume it is, our reasoning has a valid form but an unsupported premise. If we do not assume this, but use the more general premise *x is like y*, we may have reliable premises (almost anything is like anything else in some way or other) but the argument is invalid.

Second (and worse), we may use a *bad* analogy. There may be reason to believe that x is *un*like y with respect to A. Here too you could analyse this in two ways, so long as its surface form leaves the matter open: either it is a valid argument with an (even more) fishy premise, or it is an invalid argument.

Third, we may use an *inappropriate* analogy, one which (although we do not realise it) tells against our view rather than for it. In that case if we succeed in proving that x is A, it will not be what we wanted. Here if the analogy is not a good one we are in luck, if only we knew it: we have been saved from an undesirable conclusion.

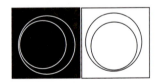

3   Suppose you want to argue that (as many theists claim) a God exists who is both all-powerful and totally good. For your purpose, how (if at all) is the Tapestry analogy wrong?

4   Suppose you want to argue that (as other theists claim) a God exists who is good but not all-powerful, perhaps because of an opposing god who is evil. For your purpose, how (if at all) is the Tapestry analogy wrong?

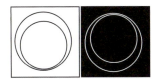

5   Suppose you want to argue that (as still other theists claim) a God exists who is all-powerful but capricious, needing constant propitiation: in short – if they dared to whisper it – not wholly good. For your purpose, how (if at all) is the Tapestry analogy wrong?

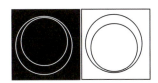

6   Suppose you want to argue (as atheists claim) that there is no God at all. For your purpose, how (if at all) is the Tapestry analogy wrong?

We can criticise Florence Nightingale's argument in Chapter 10 as a failed argument by analogy. Her equivocal use of 'law' leads to a similarly equivocal use of 'like':

> 'A law implies a lawgiver. Now the Universe is full of laws – the law of gravitation and many others; hence it follows that the Universe has a lawgiver – and what would Mr Mill be satisfied with, if he was not satisfied with that?'

7   If we replace x by 'the Universe' in the form on p. 90, what should replace y, and what is A?

8 In what way (according to Miss Nightingale) is x like y?
9 Why in fact is x not like y with respect to (having or lacking) A?

And I think that Rosenberg's criticism of Descartes, quoted in the same chapter, may be unfair due to another bad analogy. Descartes, if you remember, has two arguments:

I.   'Everything which I have thus far accepted as entirely true and assured has been acquired from the senses, or by means of the senses. But I have learned by experience that these sometimes mislead me, and it is prudent never to trust wholly things which have once deceived us.'

and

II. 'But perhaps God did not wish me to be deceived in that fashion, since he is said to be supremely good. But if it was repugnant to his goodness to have made me so that I was always mistaken, it would seem also to be inconsistent for him to permit me to be sometimes mistaken; and nevertheless I cannot doubt that he does permit it.'

Rosenberg says that these are invalid because they are like the clearly invalid

III. Paintings are sometimes forgeries; therefore it could be the case that paintings are always forgeries.

He believes that the way in which I and II are like III guarantees likeness with respect to validity.

10 In what way does he say they are alike?

He therefore thinks that his criticism of Descartes fits the valid form for arguing by analogy.

11 If we replace x in this form by 'arguments I and II', what would replace y and A?

But I think the likeness between I and II on the one hand, and III on the other, does not guarantee likeness with respect to validity.

12 Why not?
    (*Hint*: Remember that valid arguments can have invalid forms as well as valid ones.)

So if Rosenberg's first premise has the form *x is like y* it is true (like his *y is A*) – but his argument is invalid. On the other hand, if his first premise has the form *x is like y with respect to A* his argument is valid, but this premise is false.

Analogy (2)

If someone tries to make a point by analogy illegitimately, you can do various things. Simply denying the analogy is the most straightforward ('We're talking about the universe, not a tapestry!'). Carefully dissecting it (as I did the Tapestry Argument in the last chapter) may be the best, if the situation allows it. If it does not, you might try to turn the analogy to your own ends ('If the tapestry has a messy side, the weaver *can't* be all-powerful!'). If that won't work, find a counter-analogy that supports your own case. But if you want to do this honestly, be careful: analogies invite us to beg the question. The analogy that comes first to mind will almost certainly be inspired by the conclusion we want to reach.

1   (*Revision*) What is 'begging the question'?
2   Suppose I defend a policy that will cause a lot of suffering by saying 'You can't make an omelette without breaking eggs.' Think of some ripostes.

More legitimately, even a doubtful analogy may be useful heuristically – that is, as an aid to enquiry. Faced with the unknown, compare it to anything at all that you do know, and at least this will start you thinking: if you consider it, what else could? It seems no accident that a species living by its wits should be hooked on analogy. The moral is: use it – indeed you have no choice – but use it with care.

This leads to my next example, a kind of argument by analogy so famous that it needs its own section. It comes under the heading 'Useful Fallacy' in that (according to how we analyse it) the logical form is either invalid or circular. On the other hand, although logic shows that it cannot prove its conclusions, I think its *use* can be logically justified. So 'fallacy' may not be the right word after all.

Induction

Imagine that I am on my way to a political meeting where I disapprove of the speaker. I am a rowdy person and inarticulate, so I usually argue (invalidly) by throwing things. I have a dozen raw eggs. If you ask 'Why eggs?' I explain that they make a nice mess but do not break bones. I am rowdy but not cruel. I am always careful to avoid the eyes.

How do I know that my eggs will shatter and not hurt? A lifetime of eggs hitting solid surfaces, both in and out of politics, leads me to expect it. Any animal that lives by its wits relies on experience.

We do not usually spell this out; but if we did, it might take one of two forms. In the case of my eggs, these would be

(version 1) All the eggs I've known that hit solid surfaces (such as politicians) shattered harmlessly
_____

Today's eggs, hitting this politician, will shatter harmlessly.

(version 2) (i) All the eggs I've known that hit solid surfaces (such as politicians) shattered harmlessly
_____

All eggs that hit solid surfaces (such as politicians) shatter harmlessly.

(ii) All eggs that hit solid surfaces (such as politicians) shatter harmlessly
_____

Today's eggs, hitting this politician, will shatter harmlessly.

'Eggs' in this context is short for 'hens' eggs', by the way. An ostrich egg might well break a bone, and fish eggs are too soft to shatter. Of these arguments, only the second step of version 2 is valid.

But in each case we should add an implicit premise. When I rely on experience, I assume that *all future eggs will be like those I have known* (version 1) or that *ALL eggs – past, present and future – are like those I have known* (version 2). This is why induction is an argument by analogy. If so, I must use the valid form of analogy, if I want it to work.

3   (*Revision*) Give the valid and invalid forms of argument by analogy.

I need the valid form because it is not enough to assume that future eggs, or eggs in general, are simply like the eggs I have known in some way or other. (That is safely true, or I would not call them 'eggs'). They must be like the eggs that I have known *in fragility*. This will follow if I assume – as I normally might – that future eggs, or eggs in general, are like past eggs in all respects; but I might also be more cautious. Version 1 then, at its most cautious, seems really to be

> All future eggs will be like the eggs I've known, when it comes to fragility
> All the eggs I've known that hit solid surfaces (such as politicians) shattered harmlessly
> _____
> Today's eggs, hitting this politician, will shatter harmlessly.

I say it *seems* to be, because some people say that induction predicts only probabilities. In that case the implicit premise is not '*All* future eggs…' but '*Most* future eggs…', or some more definite proportion, with a conclusion to match. I shall come back to this idea.

4   What corresponds here to x and y in the valid analogy form?
5   What corresponds to A in the valid analogy form?

Part (ii) of version 2 is as before. But (unless induction is about probabilities) part (i) at its most cautious is really:

> All eggs (past, present and future) are like the eggs I've known, when it comes to fragility
> All the eggs I've known that hit solid surfaces such as politicians shattered harmlessly
>
> ___
>
> All eggs (past, present and future) that hit solid surfaces such as politicians shatter harmlessly.

6   Which part – (i) or (ii) – is an argument by analogy, and what form has the other?
7   What corresponds here to x, y and A in the valid analogy form?

The extra implicit premises:

> *All future eggs will be like the eggs I've known, when it comes to fragility* (version 1) and
> *All eggs (past, present and future) are like the eggs I've known, when it comes to fragility* (version 2)

make my arguments valid. But what right have I to assume these premises?

Version 1

My premise is 'all future eggs will be like the eggs I've known, when it comes to fragility'. But why should I suppose that the future will be like the past, in this way or any other? If I say 'because it always *has* been like the past', this is circular. 'It always has been' only justifies 'it will be' if we have already established that the future will be like the past.

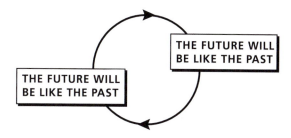

Circular arguments are valid but prove nothing.

8   (*Revision*) Why are they valid, and why do they prove nothing?

If 'The future will be like the past' is in fact true, this argument is not only valid but sound; but it still proves nothing. I need an independent reason to prove my claim that future eggs will be like those I have known.

Version 2

My premise is 'all eggs (past, present and future) are like the eggs I have known, when it comes to fragility'. If I claim this, my only evidence must be my life's experience of how samples relate to wholes. And my life's experience is itself a sample (of samples). Even if I appeal not just to my own experience but to that of everyone who has lived so far, that is only a sample (of samples). To justify my claim that a sample guarantees the whole, it might seem that I have to know already that a sample guarantees the whole.

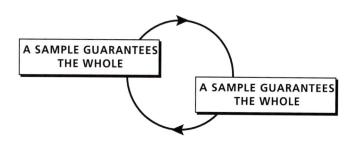

But this is too sweeping. We have all met misleading samples: good mushrooms do not foretell the one that makes you sick, stairs do not warn you of one that is missing. The premise I need is really 'although bad samples are not like the whole, good ones are'. But I cannot reach this either, unless I argue in a circle. For a start, a sample of samples cannot tell us *anything* about the whole class of samples, unless we have already established that we can rely on a (good) sample to be like the whole. But that is just what we wanted to know.

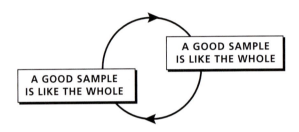

And in this case there is an extra twist. What makes a sample good? I cannot just say it is *the kind of sample that is like the whole*: that is a bogus explanation.

'Please, sir, when is a sample like the whole?'
'WHEN IT'S A GOOD ONE.'

'Please, what kind of sample is a good one?'
'ONE THAT IS LIKE THE WHOLE!'

I may speculate that some special feature will do the trick: being a large sample, say, with no counterexamples. But *even in the case of the samples I have met* – my sample of samples – I cannot be sure that this will work, unless I also know the whole, to check against my sample. Now and then I might know it (see 'enumeration' below); but this is not typical. For one thing, a whole which is already known cannot include future cases. I can find out for example that a poll matched the way people were about to vote in the last election. The final count gives me the whole, so I can check. But I cannot know that such polls will also match how people will vote in elections to come. Most of the wholes that interest me will be like this: unknowable, because they are open-ended. So, even in the case of samples that I have known, all I can usually claim is 'They *seem* to guarantee the whole – but the jury is still out'.

So once again, a sample will not prove the conclusion I want: in this case that ALL eggs (past, present and future) are like those I have known. The arguments that suggest it are circular, so I need independent reasons for my conclusion.

Experience cannot supply such reasons. Experience refers to yesterdays's eggs or today's, never tomorrow's; and yesterday's eggs and today's (even if we knew them all, from the dawn of time) are only a sample of all eggs, past, present *and future*. To quote David Hume:

> There can be no *demonstrative* arguments to prove, *that those instances, of which we have had no experience, resemble those, of which we have had experience.* We can at least conceive a change in the course of nature; which sufficiently proves, that such a change is not absolutely impossible.
> (A *Treatise of Human Nature*, Book I, part III, section vi)

No matter how many premises I list stating that *this* egg shattered harmlessly, and *this* one and *this* and *this*, they could all be true, but 'the next egg to hit a solid surface will shatter harmlessly' could be false – whether due to a change in the course of nature or simply to aspects of nature that I have not yet seen. Or they could be true and 'ALL eggs that hit solid surfaces shatter harmlessly' false, whenever *all eggs* covers more than the eggs that my premises mention.

I can of course argue validly that *all the members of a set are A* from particular instances if I list them all, as in

My mother's mother is dead
My mother's father is dead
My father's mother is dead
My father's father is dead

All my grandparents are dead.

This is *enumeration*, not induction. And I can argue validly that all grandparents are parents, or that the next grandparent I meet will be a parent, without listing any grandparents at all: it follows from my definition of 'grandparent'. This is logical deduction – what Hume calls a 'demonstrative argument'.

But when I argue inductively, any form that my argument can take will allow true premises and a false conclusion, unless it is circular – and then it fails to prove its conclusion. I think that typically induction *is* circular, implicitly: without stopping to reflect, we make the assumptions (about the future, about good samples) that I have suggested.

And this circularity goes deep. As I have mentioned before, samples that seemed adequate may fail us: life contains surprises. But when that happens we do not see it (typically) as discrediting induction. We decide instead that this cannot after all have been a good sample: we were not considering the right facts or enough facts. And so (bogusly) we explain the failure away.

'Please, sir, why did this sample fail?'
'BECAUSE IT WAS A BAD ONE.'

'How do we know that it was a bad one?'
'BECAUSE IT FAILED!'

Since Hume, the 'problem of induction' has worried philosophers for two main reasons. One is that it might undermine science; the other is that it seems to make common sense irrational.

Induction and science

One source of the trouble here comes from a view that now seems wrong to most philosophers and (I think) most scientists: that the method of science is to make empirical observations ('This egg is fragile, and this, and this') and from them to infer general laws ('All eggs are fragile') *which are certain*. They could only be certain if, in such cases, all eggs (past, present and future) are like known eggs with respect to fragility; and if you have followed the chapter so far, you will know we cannot claim this without circularity.

So if this picture of science is true, science is a fraud. Its methods cannot deliver what they promise. But in fact, neither the alleged method nor the promise seem right. Scientists do not get their theories from brick-by-brick induction, or at least not usually – although like other analogies, induction can be useful heuristically.

9 (*Revision*) What does 'heuristic' mean?

And no scientist aware of the subject's history – that graveyard of superseded 'laws' – is likely to think of today's 'laws' as certain. A theory endures as a conjecture that *may* be true so long as it is not shown to be false; and the role of experiment and observation is not to prove it (which cannot be done) but to test it. Testing appeals not to induction but to a necessary truth: that a general statement ('All hen's eggs are fragile') is incompatible with even one clear counterexample ('This one bounces').

10 (*Revision*) When two statements are incompatible, what can we say about their truth-values?

This account of scientific method is called *hypothetico-deductive*, and it is largely due to Karl Popper. Its details, and the comments and objections that it has inspired, are beyond the scope of an introduction to logic. I shall mention just two points that seem important.

First, if the role of scientific (that is, experimental) method is to test laws, a scientific law must be testable. We must be able to predict things from it which experience could falsify. If we cannot, by this account the law is not a scientific one even though it may be true, and even though scientists may find it heuristically valuable.

11 Which of these 'laws' are – in theory – testable and which are not? (If you think that the answer is not clearly 'yes' or 'no', explain why.)

(i) 'Hens' eggs are either fragile or not fragile.'
(ii) 'Hens' eggs contain *gallinan* – an ingredient undetectable by any process.'
(iii) 'Hens' eggs explode when suddenly heated to 200° Centigrade.'
(iv) 'An obsession with hens' eggs is caused by a repressed childhood phantasy.'*
(v) 'Hens' eggs break because they are fragile.'
(vi) 'All hens' eggs eventually rot.'

*In case you're not up in the jargon: 'phantasy' is a phancy way to spell 'fantasy', more or less – something the child imagines. A *repressed* memory has been buried (usually because of guilt or fear) so that the patient now cannot recall it; but it may still be active unconsciously.

Second, testing a law has a circular aspect too, and we are stuck with it. The Fragile Egg Law, for example, has passed many tests. This makes us think we can trust it better than a law that we have tested sketchily or not at all. Popper says that successful testing *corroborates* a law, though it cannot prove it. But a well-corroborated Fragile Egg Law has no more chance than any other to be true about *tomorrow's* eggs, unless 'those instances, of which we have had no experience, resemble those, of which we have had experience'.

One effect of this is that even when we adopt the principle, 'One clear counterexample disproves a law', induction may sneak in as we accept or reject examples. The more used we are to fragile eggs (from past corroboration) the more we will distrust one that is – it seems – not fragile. At worst this can lead to quite blatant question-begging:

'Please, sir, why do you say this egg doesn't count?'
'BECAUSE THERE MUST BE SOMETHING WRONG
WITH IT.'

'Please, how do we know that?'
'BECAUSE WE KNOW EGGS DON'T BOUNCE!'

However, it also leads to a caution that we usually think essential to good scientific method: insisting, for example, that an experiment be repeated before we accept its result. But our caution and later our acceptance make sense only if we expect the future to be like the past. If the course of nature may change between bouncing egg Number 1 and bouncing egg Number 2, Number 2 cannot tell us anything about whether Number 1 was genuine, or vice versa.

The same objections hold when people say that induction predicts not certainties but probabilities (a popular move). We cannot predict *anything* from past experience, unless the future – in the relevant respects – is going to resemble it. Probability is one such respect.

Mathematical probability is independent of time, but it cannot predict. This is because it is not inductive. It is based logically on what the options are: if a coin may fall in just two ways (heads or tails) with nothing to choose between them, heads is said to have a

probability of 1 in 2; if a die has six sides, any one side (the three-spot, say) has a probability of 1 in 6.

12   What is the probability of any one of my ten fingers being a thumb? (I have normal human hands.)

But gamblers can only trust this to tell them what coins or dice will *do* if the real behaviour of coins and dice reflects this pattern. Up to now it seems to have done so: keep on throwing a die, and any one side does seem to come up about once in six. But we can at least conceive (as Hume might say) that, starting tomorrow, the three-spot will never come up again, in spite of its being one of six that could.

Induction and common sense

This circularity applies not only to science but to everyday life. In all our generalisations from experience, we are stuck with it. How far is this a problem?

Some philosophers argue that we should not even *try* to assess inductions by deductive standards:

> Of course, inductive arguments are not deductively valid; if they were, they would be deductive arguments. Inductive reasoning must be assessed, for soundness, by inductive standards...To ask whether it is reasonable to place reliance on inductive procedures is like asking whether it is reasonable to proportion the degree of one's convictions on the strength of the evidence. Doing this is what 'being reasonable' *means* in such a context.
>
> (P.F. Strawson, *Introduction to Logical Theory*)

(By 'inductive standards', Strawson means things like preferring well-corroborated laws.)

I think we can do better than 'This is what "reasonable" *means* in such a context'. If inductive and logical reasoning are so distinct, why do we use the same word for both? We may use different kinds of reason for different requirements; but it does not seem reasonable that one of them (logic) should undermine the other (induction). They should at least be compatible; and it makes better sense if they support each other.

Induction does support logic, in that logic has always *worked* – at least up to now. Gamblers who flout the laws of chance get into trouble. And I need not count rabbits to know that two rabbits plus two rabbits add up to four; but if I do count Flopsy and Mopsy, Cottontail and Peter, the result confirms my arithmetic.

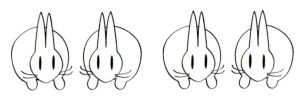

I think that logic also supports the use of induction, even while showing that induction cannot prove its conclusions.

First: remember that circular arguments can be sound. Circularity is valid and a circular argument's premises can be true. In such cases it entails a true conclusion, though it cannot prove one. If induction is (implicitly) circular, logic therefore shows that a belief in its conclusions need not be irrational, as it would be to believe what must be false.

Second: it would be illogical to believe in a system that undermined itself. But on balance induction supports itself: most past samples seem 'good', and we can explain the 'bad' ones away. The premises we (circularly) adopt to do so are unproven, but consistent with the rest.

And finally: logic suggests that even though I cannot prove it, I should assume that *nature – past, present and future – is consistent* and that *my experience reflects this well enough to give me information, if I am careful*. These are my grounds for any assumption about samples being like the whole, or the future like the past. But I must adopt these as working principles only, not claim they are certain.

(The following argument is adapted from one by Karl Popper about science. To do science, we must adopt the working principle that science is possible: that there are laws of nature we might discover.)

Think of it as a bet that I must make, one way or the other. Either I back the possibility that nature is consistent and my experience reflects it adequately – in other words I bet on induction – or I do not. I should back it, for the following reasons:

(a) I want to make reliable predictions and general statements.
(b) If induction is a reliable method, I can: what I have not experienced will be like what I have (if what I have experienced is a good sample). If induction is not reliable, I cannot.

(c) If I bet that induction is not reliable, I lose out either way. If I am right, there is no chance of basing predictions or general statements on experience; if I am wrong, there is a chance, but I do not take it.

(d) If I bet that induction is reliable and I am *wrong*, I lose again. But this bet also gives me a chance to win, which the other does not. For if I am *right*, reliable general statements and predictions are possible, using induction.

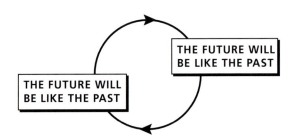

Points (b) and (c) need some expansion. Why assume that if induction is unreliable, I lose my only chance of making true predictions or general statements? Might I not bet against it in favour of a rival method – prophetic vision maybe, or tossing a special coin – that works as well or better?

But if it did, how could I know? If I bet on prophetic vision (say) because visions have worked in the past, I appeal to induction: my 'rival method' is really a parasite. If I say, 'a vision told me that visions work', this is circular. If I appeal to one non-inductive method to justify another ('Tossing my special coin told me that visions work') I now need to justify the one I have appealed to. This will either lead me into another circle – 'tossing my coin told me that visions work and a vision told me that coin-tossing works' – or into an infinite chase: 'a vision told me that coin-tossing works and an astrologer told me that visions work and my Granny told me that astrology works and I found it written in the sand that what Granny says works...' with nothing to explain at any stage why this should be so. I could offer an explanation ('My visions are true because God sends them!') but if I try to justify *that*, I land in another circle ('I saw in a vision that God sends my visions') or else in another endless chase.

Induction is circular too, as we have seen. And the principles it rests on (regularity in nature, the reliability of most experience) explain why it works, if it does; but they are not provable. Unlike all other methods, however, (except logic) *this is the one we naturally use*. How could it be rational for me to twist my mind – even if I could – to any of a million others which at best can be no better? And which (by the way) induction probably contradicts? For I have never been able in the past to rely on visions to get me through the day, or special coins, or astrology...

So I think we can accept the parts of (b) and (c) that seemed doubtful: 'If induction is unreliable, I can't', and 'If I bet that induction is unreliable, I lose out either way.'

To sum up: induction rests on unproven principles. What my argument shows is not that it is secure, but that it is my best bet. If I must bet (and I must) it is rational to choose my best bet, and irrational to choose any other. And the argument that, for reasons (a)–(d) it *is* my best bet is quite easy to prove logically: I shall give it to you as an exercise later in this book, when you are doing statement logic.

 **This is the end of Part I.**

Part II

Statement logic

In Chapters 10–14 I discussed different ways of analysing arguments. Each way had its own logical constants.

1   (*Revision*) Define variables and logical constants.

Some of these were very limited in scope. You could only use them in arguments about sheep perhaps; or insects; or *sometimes being something* and *always being something* (Rosenberg); or being like something else, in one way or other (analogy). If you tried to base a general method for analysing arguments on this sort of constant you would end up with a vast patchwork, each patch fitting just a few cases. But at the end of Chapter 12, I mentioned two logical systems whose scope is very wide, using only a few constants. One is the logic of sets; the other is the logic of statements. Almost every study of logical form starts with one or the other: our use of language more or less dictates it. I shall begin with statement logic.

In the simplest form of any argument, variables are always holes for *statements*: the argument's premises and its conclusion:

$$\frac{P}{Q} \quad \text{or} \quad \frac{\begin{array}{c}P\\Q\end{array}}{R} \quad \text{or} \quad \frac{\begin{array}{c}P\\Q\\R\end{array}}{S} \quad \text{etc.}$$

The only validity that this kind of form can show is the circular sort where the conclusion is also a premise, since we then find the same variable in both places:

$$\frac{P}{P} \quad \text{or} \quad \frac{\begin{array}{c}P\\Q\end{array}}{P} \quad \text{or} \quad \frac{\begin{array}{c}P\\Q\\R\end{array}}{P} \quad \text{etc.}$$

(When a variable turns up more than once in a formula or argument-form, we must replace it by the same thing every time.)

But we have already seen that other, more complex forms exist, which can show other kinds of validity. For the moment I want to consider only those which depend on the logical relations between statements. For example look at the Fox's first two arguments:

(a) If the Snake is proud (then) he will accept
He is proud
_____

He will accept

(ii) If the Snake accepts (then) he will die in the attempt, or he will live but fail, or he will succeed
He will accept
_____

He will die in the attempt, or he will live but fail, or he will succeed.

They share a valid form. It uses just two variables: P and Q. Each stands for a statement.

2   What is that form? What, in each case, are P and Q (are they the same in both arguments)?

Here are two more arguments:

> Either Randolph is asleep, or he's dead
> Randolph is not asleep
> _____
> Randolph is dead

> Either it's measles or these are fleabites
> It's not measles
> _____
> These are fleabites.

They share an invalid shortest form:

$$\frac{P\quad Q}{R.}$$

3   What is P in each argument? And what is R?

But they also share a *valid* form in statement logic. Again it uses only two variables, P and Q. In the Measles argument, Q is 'These are fleabites'.

4   What is P in the Measles argument, and how many times does it appear in the valid argument-form?
5   What are P and Q in the Randolph argument?
6   What is this shared valid form, and what are its logical constant/s?
7   How does this form show validity, when the form

$$\frac{P\quad Q}{R.}$$

does not?

However you put your answer to Question 7, it must have used the idea of a COMPLEX STATEMENT: one that can be broken down into shorter statements, plus logical constants. 'Randolph is asleep or he's dead' splits into 'Randolph is asleep' and 'Randolph is dead', plus 'or'. 'Randolph is not asleep' splits into 'Randolph IS asleep' and 'not'.

We show complexity in an argument-form whenever our variables represent not whole premises or conclusions, but smaller statements within them. A statement like 'Randolph is asleep', which cannot be divided in this way, is called a SIMPLE STATEMENT. In statement logic, there is only one way to represent a simple statement in an argument-form: by a single letter, like P.

8 Consider the statement 'If I had measles I'd have a fever, and I haven't got a fever'. We can analyse this in four different ways. What are they? (Say which statements your variables represent in each.)

The four basic constants

The four basic constants commonly used in statement logic are 'AND', 'IF-THEN', 'OR' and 'NOT'. The best general translation of 'NOT' is 'It is not the case that', to be followed by the statement you want to negate ('It is not the case that I have a fever').

9 Which of statements (A)–(E) below are complex?
10 What statement-logic constants (if any) do they contain?
11 What simple statements occur within the complex ones?
12 Is there a form that they all share?

(A) If that malicious little creep sets foot in the house, I leave.

(B) Not all insects have wings.

(C) Once long ago, in a faraway land, there lived a Princess who was really a fox.

(D) All the world's a stage, and all the men and women merely players.

(E) All witches have cats, and my Granny is a witch.

Clarity again

Punctuation can be vital.

Compare this:

and this:

The difference between a chance of life (if you meet the witch) and unavoidable death is one of logical form. Where English sentences use things like commas to show this, an argument-form has brackets: the first statement's form is *(P or Q) and R*, and the second's is *P or (Q and R)*.

1   What are P, Q and R?

The formula without brackets – *P or Q and R* – is ambiguous between the two, and therefore not properly anything: a malform. The opposite of a malform is a *well-formed formula*, often called a

('Formula' is the usual term for 'statement-form'.)

A wff in statement logic is *any combination of the logical constants in our system, and/or brackets, and/or variables, that yields a clear and grammatical statement when we substitute a statement for each variable.* Wffs in other logical systems are constructed in a corresponding way. So an expression may fail to be a wff for many reasons, not just through a lack of brackets.

2   Which of these is a wff in statement logic, and how does each malform fail to be a wff?

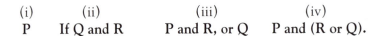

(i)	(ii)	(iii)	(iv)
P	If Q and R	P and R, or Q	P and (R or Q).

A wff is always a wff within a particular logical system. *All A are B* is not a wff in statement logic, although in a different system it could be. Nor is *P because Q*, even though if you substitute statements for P and Q you will get a statement. 'Because' is not a constant in our system.

3 Which of these is a wff in statement logic, and how does each malform fail?

| (i) | (ii) | (iii) |
| A or B | P (and R or Q) | P and (R or Q) |

Here is another pair of statements.

ONE

Your head will be chopped off if you resist or run away

(so you'd better do neither)

TWO

Your head will be chopped off if you resist – or you'll run away!

(so don't resist – RUN!)

The first has the form **if P or Q then R**.

P: You resist
Q: You run away
R: Your head is chopped off.

4 Explain why this is NOT ambiguous, and IS a wff in our system.

The second without brackets would be **If P then R or Q.**

5 Where should we place the brackets in this, and why do we need them?
6 How many wffs do we get by bracketing **P and Q or R and S** in different ways?

Unnecessary brackets

Sometimes you may find it convenient to add brackets where they are not needed. For example

If P or Q then R

(as we have seen) is not ambiguous; but you might see its shape more clearly if you wrote

If (P or Q) then R.

This is all right: it's still a wff, provided that

(i) the brackets you insert are a pair – a left-hand one followed at some later stage by a right-hand one – and
(ii) what they enclose is itself a wff.

7 One of these is a malform in statement logic, and one is a wff. Which is which, and why?
   (i) **((((P and Q) or R)**   (ii) **(((P and Q) or R))**

8 Which brackets in the wff above are allowable but unnecessary?
9 Are these malforms or wffs?

(i)	(ii)	(iii)
If P then Q and R	**P (or Q) and R**	**P and P**

10 Is this a wff in statement logic? If not, explain why not.

       If P then R
       Not R
       ───────
       Not P.

11 If P is 'I'll get up early', Q is 'I'll go for a run' and R is 'I'll be back by seven', what are the logical forms of these?

(i) If I get up early I'll go for a run and be back by seven.
(ii) If I get up early and go for a run, I'll be back by seven.

Brackets after 'NOT'

You might think that the formula *not P or Q* is ambiguous without brackets: should it be

(Not P) or Q   or   **Not (P or Q)?**

But by convention, 'not' in statement logic negates *the shortest statement, or the shortest wff, that follows it.* In the case of *not P or Q*, this wff is P. So if you want to say *(Not P) or Q* you do not need brackets: *Not P or Q* says the same thing. But if what you mean is *Not (P or Q)*, you need them.

12   In these examples, which wff does each 'not' negate?

(i)	(ii)	(iii)
Not not P	**If not (P or R) then Q**	**If not P or R then Q.**

The Fox again

So far we have followed the Fox through two arguments, each with the valid form

If P then Q

P

––––––––––

Q.

1   Does this form contain any logical constant(s), and if so, which?

In his first argument, P is 'The Snake is proud' and Q is 'The Snake will accept'.

In the second, P's surface form is different in the two premises where it appears: in the first – following 'If' – we find 'The Snake ACCEPTS'; in the second we find 'The Snake WILL ACCEPT'. This is unimportant at the level of logical form. From now on, I will use a timeless present when analysing the argument: this makes P 'The Snake accepts' and Q 'Either the Snake dies in the attempt, or he tries but fails, or he succeeds'.

The conclusion of this second argument – 'Either the Snake dies in the attempt, or he tries but fails, or he succeeds' – becomes a premise for a later argument.

On the surface, this premise is split into three, with other bits of text between them:

> THE SNAKE WILL ALMOST SURELY DIE IN THE ATTEMPT. If so, I shall have no rival, and can easily persuade the band that further tests are a waste of time.
>
> OR HE WILL LIVE, BUT FAIL. The result will be the same: for having lost face, he will leave at once for distant parts.
>
> OR PERHAPS – CONCEIVABLY – HE WILL SUCCEED. But once he has stolen the Eye, the possibility of MY doing so cannot arise. And the vengeance of the priests of Zorro is horrible and swift. He will not rule for long; and I am his only possible successor.

Again this is unimportant at the level of logical form (as are 'almost surely' and 'perhaps – conceivably'). The twice-repeated 'or' tells us that we have three parts of the same or-statement here. Its logical form is **P or Q or R**. (In the next chapter I shall introduce a convention that requires brackets here: **P or (Q or R)** for example, or **(P or Q) or R**. But for the moment we can forget it.)

2   What are P, Q and R?

Note that this is exactly the same statement that we represented by the single variable Q at an earlier stage: 'Either the Snake dies in the attempt, or he lives but fails, or he succeeds.' That was in the Fox's second step, where the whole statement can be taken as a unit. This does not happen again until the end, when the Fox uses the whole statement as a premise in order to reach his very last conclusion.

Before that stage, each step deals separately with just *one* of the three possibilities connected by 'or'.

3   What is the Fox's very last conclusion? Does the Fox state it, or is it implicit?
(If in doubt, look again at Chapter 3.)

The Fox clearly wants to show that – whatever happens – this final conclusion must be true. His next step (after the two we have analysed already) works out what will happen if the first of his three possibilities happens.

(Step 3)

> **If the Snake dies in the attempt I shall have no rival, and can easily persuade the band that further tests are a waste of time.**

On the surface this has the form *if P then Q*: not an argument at all, just a statement. But if we follow the Fox's reasoning, it is clear that he uses this statement to stand in for a short argument, of which it is one premise.

4   (*Revision*) Why is a statement not an argument?
5   What replaces Q here? (Don't worry about its length. *Any* whole statement – however long – can replace a single variable in statement logic.)

The argument's second premise, and its conclusion, are implicit. The argument-form is

(Step 3)
If P then Q
If Q then R
─────────
If P then R.

6   We know what Q is. What are P and R? (Are they the same as in the answer to question 2?)
7   Is this form valid?

Next the Fox works out what will happen if the second possibility comes true. Again the argument is only partly spelled out.

(*Step 4*)

> If the Snake lives but fails, the result will be the same: for having lost face, he will leave at once for distant parts.

('The result will be the same' = 'I shall have no rival, and can easily persuade the band that further tests are a waste of time'.)

But if we add a few unspoken but obvious bits, we can represent it as

If P then Q
If Q then R
If R then S
_____

If P then S.

8   What are P, Q, R and S? (Are P, Q and R the same as in earlier answers?)
9   If the Fox's third step was valid, can this new argument be invalid? Why, or why not?

The Fox's fifth step is about what will happen if his third possibility comes true.

(*Step 5*)

> Suppose the Snake succeeds. Once he has stolen the Eye, the possibility of MY doing so cannot arise. And the vengeance of the priests of Zorro is horrible and swift. He will not rule for long, and I am his only possible successor.

Success here means stealing the Eye, and 'suppose that' boils down to 'if'. So we can rewrite the first part:

> If the Snake steals the Eye, the possibility of MY doing so cannot arise.

And as before, what interests the Fox here is his *final* conclusion: he is arguing that in this case too, it must follow.

I abbreviated this part somewhat in Chapter 3, when I separated what the Fox assumes from what he works out. (Look at (J) on page 18.) Now I want to expand it, so as to show his line of thought more clearly. The Fox's final conclusion – as we have seen – is that he will soon become Captain, without having to steal the Eye. So far I have taken that statement as a whole; but we can also analyse it as two statements joined by 'and':

> The Fox does not have to steal the Eye.
> The Fox soon becomes Captain.

He concludes these for different reasons. He thinks that he will soon become Captain because if the Snake steals the Eye, the priests of Zorro will soon destroy the Snake; he thinks that he will not have to steal the Eye because once the Eye is stolen, it cannot be stolen again. His argument therefore splits into parallel strands: Step 6a and Step 6b.

(Step 6a)   *Form:*
If the Snake steals the Eye, nobody else can   **If P then Q**
If nobody else can, the Fox doesn't have to   **If Q then R**

If the Snake steals the Eye, the Fox doesn't have to. **If P then R.**

10   What are P, Q and R? Is this argument valid?

(Step 6b)   *Form:*
If the Snake steals the Eye, the priests of Zorro
soon destroy him   **If P then Q**
If the priests of Zorro soon destroy him, the Fox is
soon the only candidate   **If Q then R**
If the Fox is the only candidate, the Fox soon
becomes Captain   **If R then S**

If the Snake steals the Eye, the Fox soon becomes   **If P then S.**
Captain.

11   What are P, Q, R and S? Is this argument valid?

Now our clever Fox surely takes for granted the following valid argument, which pulls the two strands together:

(Step 6c)
If the Snake steals the Eye, the Fox doesn't have to
If the Snake steals the Eye, the Fox soon becomes Captain

If the Snake steals the Eye, the Fox doesn't have to AND soon becomes Captain.

That is, 'If the Snake steals the Eye, the Fox will soon become Captain without having to steal the Eye'.

12   What is the logical form of this argument, and is it valid?

To be continued.

The logical constants (1)

'AND'

In statement logic this always joins WHOLE STATEMENTS. In English it can join other things as well.

1 (*Revision*)   When do words (or a gesture, or whatever) express a statement?
2 Does 'and' link statements in (i) and (ii) below, if we analyse them to show their logical form? Rewrite them in a way that illustrates your answer. (Remember to look for *what is being stated*, not just the surface form.)

> (i) Hansel and Gretel are children.
> (ii) Hansel and Gretel are brother and sister.

3   What about 'and' in 'Paul and Evangeline are married'?

Furthermore if I join two statements by 'and' in statement logic, this means one simple thing: *if the whole statement is true, both component statements are true*. Ordinary English can be more complicated: for example it can make a difference which of the two components comes first. Compare 'He hit me and I hit him' with 'I hit him and he hit me'.

When 'and' is a logical constant these are equivalent, and neither says who started it.

Other English expressions also tell us that both the statements they join are true; and again they may suggest more. But if any extra shades of meaning do not affect the fact that *the statements they join are true*, we can use our logical constant 'and' here as well, when we are giving logical form.

4   Do statements with these forms claim that P and Q are both true, whatever else they may suggest?

(i) **P, although Q**   (ii) **P but Q**   (iii) **P instead of Q**
(iv) **P as well as Q**   (v) **Not only P but Q**   (vi) **If P then Q.**

(In some of these, if you substitute the whole *sentence* that normally expresses such a statement, it will look strange: for example if P is 'It's cold' and Q is 'It's bright', I would not say 'It's cold as well as it's bright' but 'It's cold as well as bright'. As usual, don't worry about surface form. Concentrate on what is meant.)

Finally, the statement-logic 'and' always links just two statements. This is only a convention, since the meaning of longer statements like 'I fell down and I broke my leg and I howled' is perfectly clear. Any such statement says that ALL the statements joined by 'and' are true. When I did fall down and break my leg and howl, 'I fell down and I broke my leg and I howled' is true; in all other cases (e.g. when I fell down and broke my leg but didn't howl; or fell down and just grazed my knee, and howled) it is false. But the 'only-two' rule makes 'and' easier to use in proofs and truth-tables, as you will see.

So from now on we must tidy up such statements with brackets, for example

I fell down and (I broke my leg and I howled).

The first 'and' here is the main constant or *main connective*.

5 Which two statements does it connect?
6 Which two does the other 'and' connect?

What is true of the statement is also true of the related formula *P and Q and R*. By convention, we define 'and' so that *P and Q and R* is not a wff: it needs brackets.

7 Is *P and (Q and R)* the only way we can bracket it? If not, give another. Say which 'and' is the formula's main connective in each case.

Technical terms

The 'and' relation is called *conjunction*. A statement made of two statements joined by 'and' is *a* conjunction; and the two statements joined by 'and' are this conjunction's conjuncts ('CONjuncts').

8 Which of these represent conjunctions, and what are their conjuncts?

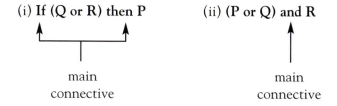

(i) **If (Q or R) then P**

main
connective

(ii) **(P or Q) and R**

main
connective

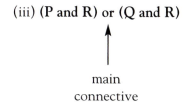

(iii) **(P and R) or (Q and R)**

main
connective

9   Is this statement a conjunction? If so, what are its conjuncts?

The witch has turned Oscar, Ludmilla, Fritz and Clara into ginger-bread.

'NOT'

This is the only constant that relates to one statement at a time, not two. As we have seen, it *negates the statement that immediately follows it.* If this statement is complex, we must be careful.

10 Which of these negates *P or Q*, and what does the other one mean?

   (i) **Not (P or Q)**   (ii) **Not P or Q.**

Even in ordinary language, the correct negation of statements can be tricky. The secret (as always) is to concentrate not on surface form, but on what the statement we want to negate *means*. Its negation will always be false if that statement is true, and true if it is false.

11–12   Negate these statements:

   (a) All wolves are carnivores.

   (b) No one can stay up a tree forever.

   (c) Branches sometimes break.

   (d) Some animals are not friendly.

   (e) They can't climb trees or jump this high.

   (f) Eventually they will get tired or bored.

The logical constants (2)

'OR'

In English this word has two senses: INCLUSIVE ('and/or') and EXCLUSIVE ('either, but not both'). An example of the exclusive sense:

You may already have won a trip to the Bahamas or £10,000 in our Priize Draw!!

and of the inclusive sense:

Applicants for language courses must have some prior knowledge of French or German.

To avoid ambiguity, 'or' has only one sense in statement logic. It is INCLUSIVE: 'and/or'. A statement with the form *P or Q* is therefore true in any of three situations: when P alone is true, or when Q alone is true, or when both are.

1 When is it false?
2 Since 'or' is always inclusive in statement logic, the exclusive sense, as in: 'You may have won *either* a trip to the Bahamas *or* £10,000 (but not both)' must have a different logical form. What is it?

(Make P: 'You may have won a trip to the Bahamas' and Q: 'You may have won £10,000'.)

If in doubt, try question 2 again when you have finished this chapter.

My examples show that the English word 'or' may seem on the surface not to join two statements, although it really does so (as 'and' does in 'Hansel and Gretel are children', though on the surface it seems only to join two names). For example the word 'French' does not make a statement, and neither does 'German'. But the sentence containing them converts easily to 'Applicants for language courses must have some knowledge of French or they must have some knowledge of German': logical form *P or Q*.

3 What statement is P here? What is Q?

On the other hand – as with 'Hansel and Gretel are brother and sister' – we cannot rewrite *every* sentence that contains 'or' in this way. For example 'Every number is even or odd' does not mean 'Every number is even, or every number is odd'. It does *not* have the logical form is *P or Q*.

4 What about '2 is even or odd'?

Finally (as with 'and') we stipulate in statement logic that 'or' must link TWO statements and no more, and that the order of these statements is irrelevant. By convention then, *P or Q or R* needs brackets.

5 Which of the following will do?

(a) **P or (Q or R)**   (b) **Q or (R or P)**
(c) **(P or R) or Q**   (d) **P or (R or Q).**

6 Will any others do? If so, give one.

Technical terms: The 'or' relation is called *disjunction*, and any statement made of two statements joined by 'or' is called a disjunction. The two statements joined by 'or' are called disjuncts ('DISjuncts').

7 Which of these represent disjunctions? What (if any) are the disjuncts in each?

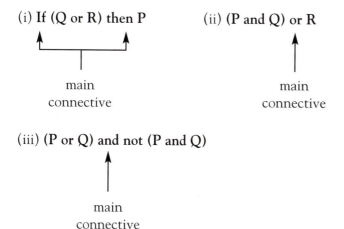

(i) **If (Q or R) then P**

main
connective

(ii) **(P and Q) or R**

main
connective

(iii) **(P or Q) and not (P and Q)**

main
connective

(I shall discuss our fourth logical constant – 'If-then' – in Chapters 22 and 23.)

Truth-functions

A statement with the form *P or Q* may be either true or false, and this depends on its P-statement and Q-statement. More precisely, it depends on just one aspect of them, their *truth-values* – that is, whether they are true or false. If I know these, I can tell you at once whether their disjunction is true or false. I do not even need to know what they state.

Suppose Shrdlu (a green Martian) states '*Quorflogs are spppingle!*' and Qwertyuiop (a yellow Martian) states '*Spligs are dddivyptu!*'. Green Martians invariably lie and yellow Martians always tell the truth.

8 What is the truth-value of '*Quorflogs are spppingle OR spligs are dddivyptu*'?

9 Do we know the truth-value of '*Quorflogs are spppingle AND spligs are dddivyptu*'? If so, what is it?

10 What about '*Quorflogs are NOT spppingle*'?

After answering 9 and 10, you will realise that *P and Q* and *not P* are like *P or Q* in this respect: when a statement has the form *not P*, its truth or falsity depends on that of its P-statement; when its form is either *P or Q* or *P and Q*, its truth or falsity depends on the truth or falsity of its P- and its Q-statements.

We call such formulae *truth-functions*, because the truth-value of any statement with that form is a function of – that is, it is determined by – the truth-values of its component statements. The logical constants in these formulae – 'and', 'or' and 'not' – are *truth-functional operators*.

This is only possible because, as we have seen, 'and', 'or' and 'not' in statement logic are pared down versions of the same words in common usage.

11 (*Revision*) Normally 'I hit him and he hit me' means something different from 'He hit me and I hit him'.
Explain why, in this case, 'and' cannot be a truth-functional operator.

12 (*Revision*) A statement with the form *P and Q* is true in just one case. At all other times it is false. What is that one case, and what are the others?

Truth-tables

In statement logic a conjunction is true in just one case: when both conjuncts are true. At all other times it is false. These truth-values are all we need to know in order to know a conjunction's truth-value. We can therefore define the truth-function *P and Q* by a matrix called a truth-table. I introduced the basic table for 'or' – that is for the form *P or Q* which all 'or'-statements share – in the answers to Chapter 19. Here is the basic table for 'and'.

	P	Q	P and Q
(1)	T	T	T
(2)	T	F	F
(3)	F	T	F
(4)	F	F	F

These four lines cover all the possibilities. When both P and Q are true, as in line (1), *P and Q* is true; so we write T beneath it in the table. In lines (2)–(4), where other combinations of truth-values make *P and Q* false, we write F.

1   Which line or lines tell us that *P and Q* is false when only one conjunct is true?
2   Which line or lines tell us that *P and Q* is false when both conjuncts are false?

Now consider 'or' again. *P or Q* is true in *three* possible cases, and false in just one. Here is its truth-table, with the truth-values of *P or Q* left out.

	P	Q	P or Q
(1)	T	T	
(2)	T	F	
(3)	F	T	
(4)	F	F	

3 (*Revision*) Without looking back to the answers for Chapter 19, fill them in. Remember that 'or' is inclusive ('and/or') as in

Applicants for language courses must have some prior knowledge of French or German.

4 The truth-table defining 'not' should be shorter than the previous two. Why?
5 Draw it.

How to build a truth-table

Once you know the simple tables for logical constants like 'and' and 'not', you can build a table for *any* complex formula in statement logic, since we use only these constants (and variables, and brackets) to put it together. This makes the truth-table a useful tool for studying argument-forms, and therefore validity – as you will see.

There is a fixed pattern for writing truth-tables. If you follow it they are easy to read; if not, they are chaotic. Here is how to build a truth-table step by step. I shall start with the table for *P and Q* – a simple one that you have met already.

First, write the formula at the top, on the right. Give each variable its own column at the left, in alphabetical order.

Variables ——▶ P   Q   P and Q ◀—— *Formula*
_____

Next, in the variable columns, write all the possible truth-values. Start with the variable at the right: in this table it is Q. A statement replacing Q might be either true or false, so put T in the first line and F in the second.

	P	Q	P and Q
(1)		T	
(2)		F	

When your formula has only one variable you need no more lines. The table for *not P* is like that, and so is this one:

Variables ——▶   Q   Q or Q ◀—— *Formula*
_____
                   T
                   F

6   A disjunction is true when either disjunct is true, or both are; otherwise it is false. With this in mind, fill in the Q *or* Q column above.

But with two variables, your table will double. A statement replacing Q might be true or false when the one replacing P is TRUE:

– but also when it is FALSE.

	P	Q
(1)	T	T
(2)	T	F
(3)	F	T
(4)	F	F

With three variables, the length doubles again.

7 Show why this is so, using the variables P, Q and R (in that order).

Finally, fill in the truth-values for the formula itself, based on those of its variables.

	P	Q	P and Q
(1)	T	T	T
(2)	T	F	F
(3)	F	T	F
(4)	F	F	F

You can do this in one step for *P and Q*. But with a more complex formula, this part too must be done by stages. Consider the formula *not (P and Q)*. Like all negations, its truth-value will always depend on that of the formula it negates.

8 (*Revision*) In what way?

Here you set up your table as usual (it will have two variables).

	P	Q	Not (P and Q)
(1)	T	T	
(2)	T	F	
(3)	F	T	
(4)	F	F	

Next, use your variable columns to work out the possible truth-values, line by line, of *P and Q*. (Easy.)

IMPORTANT: to avoid chaos, ALWAYS line up the Ts and Fs very accurately under the logical constant they refer to: in this case 'and'.

	P	Q	Not (P and Q)
(1)	T	T	T
(2)	T	F	F
(3)	F	T	F
(4)	F	F	F

From this, you can work out the values for the *negation of P and Q*, since a statement's negation is always false when that statement is true, and true when it is false.

	P	Q	Not (P and Q)	
(1)	T	T	F	T
(2)	T	F	T	F
(3)	F	T	T	F
(4)	F	F	T	F

And that's it.

**Congratulations!
You now know how
to build a truth-table.**

In truth-tables we need to identify *one* connective as the main one, whose line of Ts and Fs applies to the formula as a whole. In the table above it is 'not'. This explains why 'and' and 'or' must link only two statements, so that *P or Q or R* (for example) needs brackets. However we bracket it, the final column of truth-values will be the same: 'T' for every line except 8, where P, Q and R are all false. But we will not know where to write this in until we have put in brackets, and worked out the bracketed formula first.

Here are a few more questions, for practice.

Consider the statement:

'Quorflogs are NOT spppingle, NOR are spligs dddivyptu'.

Like all complex statements, we can analyse this in several ways, depending on how much detail we want. Four such analyses are conjunctions.

9 What are they? (Give the formula for each, and say what statements replace the variables.)

10–11 Draw the truth-table for any of these formulae whose table you have not drawn before.

12 Finally, try the table for an even more complex formula, the one for *P or Q but not both*: that is

(P or Q) and not (P and Q).

After you have set up your variable-columns, you will need three stages.

Necessity and contingency (2)

In my examples so far, the truth-table's main column has both Ts and Fs. A statement with one of these forms – P *or* Q, P *and* Q etc. – may be either true or false, depending on the truth-values of its P and its Q.

For example 'I have at least a million pounds' has the logical form P *or* Q:

P: I have EXACTLY a million pounds
Q: I have MORE than a million pounds.

(Remember that logical form depends on what a statement *means*, not on surface grammar.)

When 'I' refers to the writer of this book, 'I have at least a million pounds' is false. It fits line (4) of the P *or* Q truth-table.

	P	Q	P or Q
(1)	T	T	T
(2)	T	F	T
(3)	F	T	T
(4)	F	F	F

But in a better world it could have been true: in that case, it would fit one of the other lines.

1   There is one line that it could never fit. Which, and why?

By contrast 'I have at *most* a million pounds' is true in the real world. It too has the form *P or Q*.

2   If P is the same as before, what is Q?

Given what I have said about my finances, we know which line of the *P or Q* truth-table table fits the facts.

3   Which, and why?

But look at the truth-table: *P or Q* can be true in three different ways. 'I have at *most* a million pounds' could fit a different line (in a better world) and still be true. And again there is one line that it could never fit.

4   Explain which other line it could fit, and in which circumstances; and why one line is impossible.

We call statements whose form allows them to be either true or false *contingent*. A formula that fits such a statement has both Ts and Fs as truth-values. By extension, we call these formulae 'contingent' too. You may also remember however that some statements cannot fail to be true: their logical form ensures this.

These are the necessary truths: for example 'Either I have a million pounds or I do not', which has the form *P or not P*.

5   Draw the truth-table for *P or not P*, and see how the values work out.

Again some statements are bound to be false because of their logical form: these are the *necessarily false* statements, or *self-contradictions*. And by extension we also use the terms 'necessarily false' or 'self-contradiction' for the formulae that show this necessity. The simplest form of self-contradiction is *P and not P*.

6   Draw its truth-table, and see how the values work out.

But remember that statements, like arguments, may be analysed in more than one way; and some ways are too simple to show necessity. For example, any statement may replace a single letter in a formula. So the necessarily true 'Either I have a million pounds or I do not' and the self-contradiction 'I both have a million pounds and I do not' share the simple (and contingent) form P.

'Either I have a million pounds or I do not' is a disjunction, so it also has the form *P or Q*. And 'I both have a million pounds and I do not' is a conjunction, so it has the form *P and Q*.

	P	Q	P or Q
(1)	T	T	T
(2)	T	F	T
(3)	F	T	T
(4)	F	F	F

	P	Q	P and Q
(1)	T	T	T
(2)	T	F	F
(3)	F	T	F
(4)	F	F	F

7   What statements replace P and Q in these cases?
8   Do these forms show the two statements to be necessary? How, or why not?

Finally, some general questions.

9   Suppose a statement has *some* necessarily true logical form/s. Is the statement itself therefore necessarily true?

10 Suppose it has *some* contingent logical form/s. Is the statement therefore contingent?

11 If it has *some* necessarily false logical form/s, is a statement necessarily false?

12 Could the same statement have two forms, one a self-contradiction and the other necessarily true?

The logical constants (3)

'IF-THEN'
is tricky for logicians. We can write truth-tables for 'and', 'or' and
'not' because they are truth-functions; but we cannot write a similar
table for 'if-then', as these words are normally used.
Consider:
(i) If you were a fish, you would have fins
(ii) If you were a fish, you would have feathers.

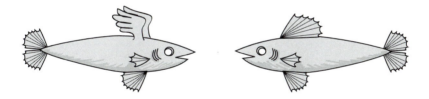

Both (i) and (ii) have the same form: *if P then Q*.

1   What are P and Q in (i)? And in (ii)?

Now P and Q in (i), and P and Q in (ii), have the same truth-
values: both are false. (Or so I suppose. You are not a fish, are you?
And you have neither fins nor feathers?) But normally we would
say that 'IF you were a fish, you would have fins' is true, and 'IF you
were a fish, you would have feathers' false, because of what their
different Q-statements say.

A truth-table for *if P then Q* therefore seems to be impossible. Truth-tables (like the truth-functions they illustrate) take no account of which statements may replace a P or a Q. They show what is true of a *general form* of statement, however the variables are filled.

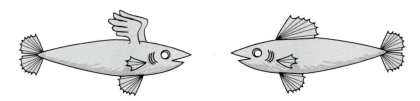

And yet 'if-then' (in some sense of the words) seems so basic to human reasoning that a truth-functional logic without it would not be much use. We cope with this by distinguishing two kinds of 'If-then'. One – called the STRICT sense – is more or less the 'If-then' of ordinary speech. Here, as we have just seen, the truth-value of a statement with the form *if P then Q* depends on the *meaning* of whatever statements replace P and Q, rather than their truth-values.

The other is TRUTH-FUNCTIONAL: it depends on truth-values alone, and takes no account of meaning. It keeps some main features of the strict sense, but in other ways is not very like it – in fact, less like it than the logical constants 'and', 'or' and 'not' are like their common-usage equivalents. We can write a truth-table for this second 'if-then', however: it was devised with that in mind. We get our truth-functional operator by asking:

Is there anything crucial, to do with truth-conditions, that ALL true 'IF P THEN Q' statements share?

There is.

(i) We can find true statements of this form where both P and Q are true, like 'If you are human, you have bones'. You are – I suppose – and you have.

2 Give another example. (Remember to spell out what replaces P and Q.)

 (ii) We can find true statements of this form where both P and Q are false, like 'If you were a fish, you would have fins'. You are not – I suppose – and you have not; but you would have, if you were.

 (iii) We can find others still where P is false and Q is true, like 'If you were a fish, you would have bones'. You are not a fish, I suppose, but you would have bones if you were; and you have bones anyway, being human.

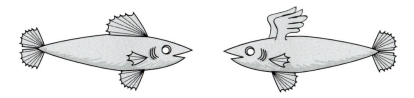

3 Give other examples of types (ii) and (iii), spelling out which statements replace P and Q.

But the meaning of the words 'If-then' will not allow any statement of the form IF P THEN Q to be true, when P is true and Q is false.

Try to think of one: you can't.

This gives the rule for a simplified, truth-functional 'If-then'. Statements of the form *If P then Q* are held to be FALSE in just one condition: when P IS TRUE AND Q IS FALSE. At all other times, we hold them to be TRUE.

4 Following this rule, fill in the truth-table below. (Line up the values under 'then'.)

	P	Q	If P then Q
(1)	T	T	
(2)	T	F	
(3)	F	T	
(4)	F	F	

↑

This 'if-then' is called *material* (as opposed to 'strict'). And just as the truth-functional 'and' does not differentiate between 'He hit me and I hit him' and 'I hit him and he hit me' – though in ordinary language if one is true, it often implies that the other is false – material implication fails to notice certain differences that strict implication would. For example, it does not differentiate between 'If you were a fish, you would have fins' and 'If you were a fish you would have feathers'. It cannot, because the difference between them does not involve truth-values.

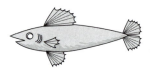

5 According to this rule, what is the truth-value of 'If you were a fish, you would have feathers'?

The same rule gives us a statement of equivalence:

(By definition) **If P then Q = NOT (P and not Q).**

6 Draw the truth-table for *Not (P and not Q)*. How does it compare with the other?

So long as we are careful about its limitations, the truth-functional 'if-then' is very useful. By and large, it provides a good way to assess arguments in real life. For example, the rules of inference that you will meet later in this book (and in other logic courses) work for both senses: strict and material. Modern formal systems depend on it: again, it was devised with this in mind.

Technical terms: 'If-then' statements (whether 'if-then' is strict or material) are called *conditionals* or *conditional statements*, and *if P then Q* means that P's truth is a *sufficient condition* for the truth of Q. The P-statement is called the *antecedent*; the Q-statement is the *consequent*. The 'if-then' relation (whether strict or material) is called *implication* or *entailment*, and we say that P *implies* or *entails* Q.

7 Which of these are conditional statements? Give the antecedent and consequent of those that are, and explain why the others are not.

(i) If pigs can fly then I'm a Dutchman.
(ii) I'll come to the party if Sally can babysit.
(iii)I don't know if Sally can babysit.
(iv)If you're going to the library, will you take this book back?
(v) If you can't be good, be careful.

8 Which of these are conditional forms? Give the antecedent and consequent of those that are, and explain why the others are not.

(i) **If (Q or R) then P**

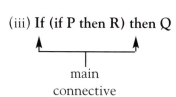

main
connective

(ii) **(If P then Q) and R**

main
connective

(iii) **If (if P then R) then Q**

main
connective

9 Draw the truth-table for (i).
10 Draw the truth-table for (ii). If you need practice, draw the table for (iii) as well.

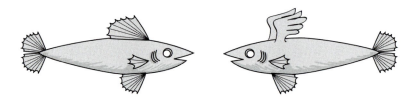

Here are some statements with antecedents and consequents whose truth-values (I think) you will know.

(i) If you were a bird, you wouldn't be reading this.
(ii) If you were a bird, you *would* be reading this.
(iii)If today is Monday, tomorrow is Tuesday.
(iv)If today is Monday, tomorrow is Thursday.

11 In each case, give the truth-value for the whole conditional when 'if-then' is (a) strict and (b) material; and explain in each case what this truth-value depends on.

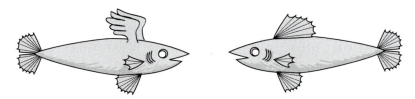

12 Is *if P then Q* necessarily true, necessarily false, or contingent? Use its truth-table to explain why.

'If-then' and validity (1)

So far I have suggested that we can simply *see* when an argument is valid or invalid. Most people who know what validity is have no problem (for example) recognising whether this argument is valid

I.   Either Randolph is asleep or he's dead
     Randolph is not asleep
     _____

     Randolph is dead

or this one:

II. Either Randolph is asleep or he's dead
     Randolph is asleep
     _____

     Randolph is dead.

1   Are they valid?

But we can make mistakes. For example you might still not feel sure at once about

III. If Randolph is dead, he is not asleep

If Randolph is asleep, he is not dead.

2   Is it valid or invalid?
(*Hint*: forget what these particular statements state. Must any argument of this form have a true conclusion, if its premise is true?)

When in doubt, we can sometimes show *invalidity* by finding another argument with the same form whose premises are true, but its conclusion false.

3   Give an example to fit the invalid form

If P then Q
Not P

Not Q.

But this is not always easy. And so far we have had nothing comparable to show validity. It would be useful to have a method that can do both. And now –

GOOD NEWS

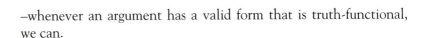

–whenever an argument has a valid form that is truth-functional, we can.

An argument (you will remember) is VALID whenever its form will not allow true premises and a false conclusion. A truth-functional 'if-then' statement – as you now know – is TRUE whenever it does not have a true antecedent and a false consequent. All we need do therefore, to find out if an argument's form is valid, is construct an 'if-then' formula whose antecedent represents *all the premises* (joined by 'and', as necessary) and whose consequent represents *the conclusion*. We can call this the argument's 'validity-formula'. Then we test this formula with a truth-table.

Suppose that in any line, the formula has the value 'F':

Variables	If	[premises]	then	[conclusion]
			F	

This can happen only when the antecedent is true and the conclusion false:

Variables	If	[premises]	then	[conclusion]
		T	F	F

that is, when an argument with this validity-formula has true premises and a false conclusion.

A formula may have the value 'F' in two cases. Either it is contingent (in which case its truth-table will show a mixture of 'T' and 'F'); or it is necessarily false (in which case every line will show 'F').

4 Sum up what we know about an argument's premise/s and conclusion, when its validity-formula is contingent.

5 Suppose the formula is necessarily false. What does this tell us about the argument?

But in some cases the validity-formula is necessarily true. Then you may find any or all of these patterns:

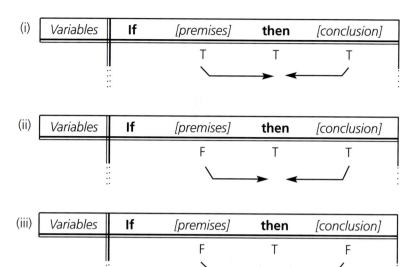

– since any of these values, by definition, make a truth-functional 'if-then-' statement TRUE. But never, in any line, will you find the antecedent true and the consequent false.

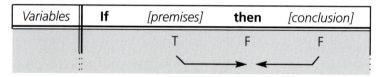

6   What does this tell us about any argument with a necessarily true validity-formula?

Take the first Randolph Argument:

> Either Randolph is asleep or he's dead
> Randolph is not asleep
> ———————————————
> Randolph is dead.

This has the logical form

> **P or Q**
> **Not P**
> ———
> **Q.**

7 What statements replace P and Q?
8 What formula do we get if we join this argument-form's premises by 'and'?

Your answer will be the antecedent of the first Randolph argument's validity-formula. Its consequent is that argument's conclusion: Q.

9 What is the validity-formula?
10 Draw its truth-table, and explain exactly why this table shows that Randolph Argument I is valid.

By contrast, Randolph Argument II has the form

P or Q
P
──────
Q.

11 What is its validity-formula?

12 Draw the truth-table for this formula, and explain how it shows that Randolph Argument II is invalid.

'If-then' and validity

My GOOD NEWS

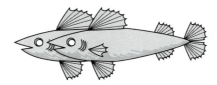

was that when an argument has a form that is truth-functional, we can now test it for validity.

1   (*If you'd like more practice.*) Test the argument-form

If P then not Q

If Q then not P.

Unfortunately there is also some

BAD NEWS.

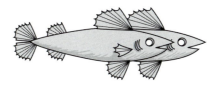

The truth-table test works *in theory* for any argument in statement logic. Unfortunately, in practice it is often unworkable: the table is too big. Remember that the number of lines doubles with each variable; and again if your premises are long, or you have more than just two or three, the antecedent of your validity-formula may be huge, and the formula even more so. Take the rather simple Fang argument:

If Fang is a dog, he is a mammal
If he is a mammal, he is a vertebrate
If he is a vertebrate, he is an animal
Fang is a dog

_____

Fang is an animal.

It has the valid form:

If P then Q   P: Fang is a dog
If Q then R   Q: Fang is a mammal
If R then S   R: Fang is a vertebrate
P   S: Fang is an animal.

_____

S.

2   If you wanted to test it by truth-table, what would the validity-formula be? (You can bracket it in several ways – but be careful!)
3   How many lines would your table need?

Luckily there is a short cut that often helps: you'll find it in Chapter 26. Often we need not write out the whole table. A proof using rules of inference can be even better, once you know how to use it (see Part III of this book).

But as you will see, the rules on which these proofs depend are themselves testable by truth-table (when they are truth-functional). So here too, truth-tables support the rest.

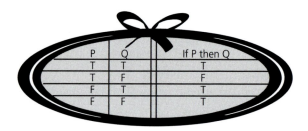

Here are some general questions on what you have done so far:

4   Which of these is right, and why is the other wrong?

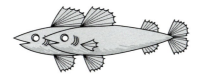

  (i) 'An argument is valid when its validity-formula is valid.'
  (ii) 'An argument is valid when its validity-formula is true.'

5–11 Say which of these is wrong and which is right, and explain
     why.

  (i)   'An if-then statement is false when its antecedent is false.'
  (ii) 'An if-then statement is true when its consequent is true.'
  (iii) 'An if-then statement is false when its consequent is false.'
  (iv) 'When an argument is valid, its validity-formula is neces-
        sarily true.'
  (v)   'When an argument is invalid, its validity-formula is neces-
        sarily false.'
  (vi) 'Every form of a valid argument is valid.'
  (vii) 'Every form of an invalid argument is invalid.'
  (viii) 'No validity-formula of a valid argument can be contin-
        gent.'
  (ix) 'Every validity-formula of an invalid argument is contin-
        gent.'

(I am referring to truth-functional logic throughout.)

And finally

You will remember that Qwertyuiop (a yellow Martian) always tells the truth. Shrdlu (a green Martian) invariably lies.
'*Ggruds are yulop*' is TRUE, '*Syps slep*' is FALSE, and the Martian language is strictly truth-functional.

12 Say which is speaking.

    (i) 'If ggruds are yulop, then syps slep.'
    (ii) 'If ggruds are yulop and are not yulop, then syps slep.'
    (iii)'If syps slep or do not slep, ggruds are yulop.'
    (iv)'If ggruds are yulop, ggruds are yulop.'
    (v) 'If syps slep, then syps do not slep.'

(If in doubt, refer back to the truth-table for *if P then Q*.)

Logical constants (3)

Material implication is useful to test validity. But why treat it as a logical constant in its own right? The equivalent formula *not (P and not Q)* represents validity too. When P is the conjunction of an argument's premises and Q is its conclusion, *not (P and not Q)* says 'It is not the case that this argument's premises are true and its conclusion false'. And we already have its constants, 'and' and 'not'. Do we really need more? Well, try it in a truth-table.

1   Suppose you want to show that this form (that of Randolph Argument I) is valid. What validity-formula should you test by truth-table, using 'Not (…and not…)' instead of 'If-then'?

P or Q

Not Q

———

P.

Unwieldy. The equivalent 'if-then' formula is easier to use.

But we might still ask, 'Why call this new logical constant *if-then?*'. Material implication seems so unlike 'if-then' in common usage, where (typically) we expect *if P then Q* to suggest *why* Q might be true if P is. Fish are finny and never feathered: that is why the counterfactual 'If you were a fish, you would have feathers' is (we say) false. The equally counterfactual 'If you were a fish, you would have fins' we say is true, for the same reason. But in truth-functional logic, *all* counterfactuals are true.

2   Which line/s in the truth-table for *if P then Q* show that 'If you were a fish, you would have feathers' is true?

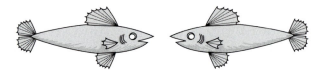

We also have special words in English – 'were' instead of 'are', 'would have' instead of 'have' – to show when a condition is counterfactual. In statement logic these disappear: we treat 'If you were a fish, you would have feathers' as identical to 'If you ARE a fish, you HAVE feathers'. How many such rules can we drop, and still plausibly claim that this statement-logic operator means 'if-then'?

Other unexpected things happen too, when 'if-then' is material. For example

(i) Any *if P then Q* statement whatsoever is true if P is false. Therefore 'If sharks are snails then 2+2=4' is true, just because sharks are not snails; and so is 'If sharks are snails then 2+2=7'.

(ii) Any *if P then Q* statement whatsoever is true if Q is true. Therefore 'If sharks are snails then 2+2=4' is true for this reason too; and so is 'If sharks are NOT snails then 2+2=4'.

3   What, according to the rules of material implication, is the truth-value of 'If sharks are NOT snails then 2+2=7'?

4   What are the truth values, respectively, of 'If sharks are NOT snails then sharks ARE snails' and 'If sharks ARE snails then sharks are NOT snails'? Which line/s in the table for *if P then Q* make it so in each case?

To sum up: a false statement materially implies *anything* (any statement, that is), however unrelated; and *anything* materially implies a true statement.

This is particularly startling when applied to self-contradictions or logical truths. If a statement has the form *P and not P* for example, it materially implies everything, because it is false in all possible worlds. If it has the form *P or not P* it is true in all possible worlds, so everything materially implies it. These things so often worry people that they have come to be called *paradoxes* of material implication: 'paradox' here meaning something that seems to defy common sense.

I think this is unfair.

For a start, not all *if P then Q* statements in ordinary language offer P as either a reason or a cause for Q, so that we expect a connection between them. It can sometimes be important – in scientific research for example – simply to note a *correlation*: that Q is true whenever P is, never mind why. (A one-way correlation: P need not also be true whenever Q is. For that we need to add *If Q then P*.)

Here is an example: the ethologist Oskar Heinroth noted that although ducklings rush away from human beings as soon as they hatch, newly hatched goslings 'stare calmly at human beings and do not resist handling'. In such circumstances, goslings will later treat the human who first handled them as a parent, rejecting their mother (or any adult goose). There is, in fact, a correlation between *an animal's being a newly hatched gosling whose first handler is human*, and *its behaving in the way described*.

Of course where we see a correlation, we may hope to find a reason or cause. Heinroth decided that the first thing the gosling sees is imprinted as the image of its parent. Further experiments by Konrad Lorenz confirmed that there is such a mechanism, and established more details of how it works in different species. (For an account of all this, see R. Harré, *Great Scientific Experiments*, ch. 5.) But we may not find such a connection when we observe *If P then Q*; or if we do, it may not be what we expected. If we think of material implication as an 'if-then' of pure correlation, its logic seems less strange.

Material implication agrees with common usage in other important ways. For example, trusty friends like these are still valid when 'if-then' is truth-functional:

If P then Q P ――――― Q	If P then Q If P then R ――――― If P then (Q and R)	If P then Q If Q then R ――――― If P then R.

And these well-known traitors are still invalid:

If P then Q Q ――――― P	If P then Q Not P ――――― Not Q	If P then Q ――――― If Q then P.

5   Find an example for each traitor which shows its treachery.
6   (*Revision*) Examples provide an alternative to truth-tables in showing that a form is invalid. Do they also provide one for showing that a form is valid? How, or why not?

Given all this, it seems to me that so long as we remember the difference between material implication and other kinds, and watch out for when it matters, there is no reason at all why the truth-functional 'if-then' should worry us, or need any apology.

Back to the Fox

Now that we have a way to show validity, we can use it for the Fox's arguments. Go over the six steps that we have looked at so far (in Chapters 2 and 3, Chapters 11 and 12 and Chapter 17). You will find that they rely entirely on the forms I call 'trusty friends' above. Remember that any argument with the form

If P then Q
If Q then R
If R then S
―――――――
If P then S

can also be analysed in two stages as:

If P then Q	If P then R
If Q then R	If R then S
―――――――	―――――――
If P then R	If P then S.

7   Use a truth-table to show that the 'trusty friend' with *two* variables is valid.

The Fox has now derived four separate statements, each necessary for his final conclusion. They are:

(i)   Either the Snake will die in the attempt, or he will live but fail, or he will succeed.
(ii) If the Snake dies in the attempt, the Fox will soon become captain without having to steal the Eye.
(iii) If the Snake lives but fails, the Fox will soon become captain without having to steal the Eye.
(iv) If the Snake succeeds, the Fox will soon become captain without having to steal the Eye.

He will conclude 'Whatever happens, the Fox will soon become captain without having to steal the Eye'.

If you have an eye for argument, you can probably see the line he will now take. First he must combine the information in (ii), (iii) and (iv) into a single statement, by the following argument:

(Step 7)
If the Snake dies in the attempt, the Fox soon becomes captain without having to steal the Eye

If the Snake lives but fails, the Fox soon becomes captain without having to steal the Eye

If the Snake succeeds, the Fox soon becomes captain without having to steal the Eye

---

If the Snake dies in the attempt, OR lives but fails, OR succeeds, the Fox soon becomes captain without having to steal the Eye.

Then he can use this conclusion as the premise in a final argument, with (i) as his other premise:

(Step 8)
If the Snake dies in the attempt, OR lives but fails, OR succeeds,
    the Fox soon becomes captain without having to steal the Eye
Either the Snake dies in the attempt, or he lives but fails, or he
    succeeds

The Fox soon becomes captain without having to steal the Eye.

8   Give the logical form of the Fox's *seventh* step.

(Remember that 'or' can join only two statements, so you'll
need brackets when you deal with the three-part disjunction in
this argument. There are several ways you could do it.)

9   Give the simplest logical form for the Fox's *eighth* step that
shows it to be valid.
10   What is its more complex form?

You've already shown by truth-table that Step 8 has a valid form.
You can do the same for Step 7. BUT

11   What is the validity-formula for this seventh step?
12   How many lines would its truth-table need?

When you are stuck with tables as huge as this, be grateful that you
will soon learn a short-cut that will help (and if you go on to the
section about rules of inference, you will learn to use a proof
instead).

To be continued.

A shorter way with truth-tables

Many quite simple arguments need an enormous truth-table to test their validity. But a short-cut exists.

For example the argument-form

> **If P then Q**
> **If P then R**
> _____
> **If P then (Q and R)**

is valid.

The Fox uses it to conclude 'If the Snake succeeds, the Fox will soon become Captain without having to steal the Eye'. But its validity-formula is long:

> **IF (if P then Q and if P then R) THEN if P then (Q and R)**

and it has three variables, which means an eight-line table. The short-cut depends on the fact that when an argument is valid in statement logic, its validity-formula is necessarily true.

1   (*Revision*) What is a necessary truth, and how does a truth-table show one?

So instead of working through every line of a long table, we might try to find one line – one is all we need – where the argument's validity-formula is FALSE.

P	Q	R	If [if P then Q and if P then R] then if P then [Q and R]
			F

If we cannot, we know that statements with this form are necessarily true, so our argument is valid.

Since it is a conditional, this formula can be false in just one way: ANTECEDENT TRUE, CONSEQUENT FALSE. Starting with the consequent:

P	Q	R	If [if P then Q and if P then R] then if P then [Q and R]
			F F

for this to be the case   *we need this*

2 What is the consequent? If it is false, what truth-value must P have, and why?
3 What truth-value must the formula Q *and* R have, and how does this affect the truth-values of Q and of R?
4 So in how many different ways can *If P then (Q and R)* be false?

For the validity-formula to be false, its antecedent must also be true.

P	Q	R	If [if P then Q and if P then R] then if P then [Q and R]
			T F F

?

5   Explain why the 'T' must be under 'and' in the table, rather than anywhere else.

6   For this 'T' to be correct, what truth-values must the formulae *if P then Q* and *if P then R* have, and how does this affect the truth-value of P, of Q and of R?

7   Given the values we have already given P, Q and R, is this possible? Have we found what we were looking for: a line where the validity-formula is false?

Now try the same test on another of the Fox's argument-forms:

If P then Q
If Q then R
_____
If P then R.

8   What is its validity-formula?

As before, if we can find a line in this formula's truth-table where it is false, the related argument is invalid; otherwise it is valid.

9   What truth-value must the formula's *consequent* have if the formula itself is false? How does this affect the truth-values of P and R?

10   What truth-value must the formula's *antecedent* have, and how will this affect the truth-values of P, Q and R? Can we find a line where the validity-formula is false?

The only Fox's argument-form that we have not yet tested is

If P then R
If Q then R
_____
If (P or Q) then R.

11   Test this by truth-table, using the short cut. Have we now shown that the Fox's argument is valid?

And now we come to the end of the story…

**THE SNAKE STOLE THE EYE, SHOWED
IT TO THE THIEVES, SNEAKED IT BACK
AGAIN AND SAID TO THE FOX:
'NOW IT'S YOUR TURN!'**

12   What does this show about the Fox's reasoning?

Logical constants (5)

We now have four truth-functional constants: 'and', 'not', 'or' and 'if-then'. One more relation between statements is important when we apply logic to real life: it turns up everywhere, especially in laws and definitions. This is '*if and only if*', abbreviated

It is also known as the *biconditional* ('bi-' for 'double', as in 'bicycle').

The truth-table that defines it is simple, because 'iff' is the relation of equivalence. *P iff Q* is true whenever P and Q have the same truth-value. Otherwise it is false.

	P	Q	P iff Q
(1)	T	T	T
(2)	T	F	F
(3)	F	T	F
(4)	F	F	T

Note that this is *truth-functional* equivalence only: the statements that replace P and Q do not have to be equivalent in meaning, only in truth-value.

1 How exactly does the table show that 'iff' means (truth-functional) equivalence?

2 Draw the truth-table for *Q iff P*. What relation does it have to the table for *P iff Q*?

We could survive without giving this relation a name of its own. As you will see, we do not need it for the rules of inference that I shall later introduce, and we can write it (at some length) using constants we already have. But just as it makes life easier to write (and think in terms of) *if P then Q* rather than *not (P and not Q)*, so it does to use 'iff' instead of something longer. Still, why call this relation of having the same truth values 'if and only if'?

The answer is that the underlying logic of equivalence is *iffy*. It is the conjunction of two other important iffy concepts: *necessary* and *sufficient conditions*. I have already mentioned these from time to time, and shall say more in the next chapter. But I want first to explore the relation between the terms 'if', 'only if' and 'if and only if' ('iff'). Beginners often find this tricky unless taken slowly, so let us do so.

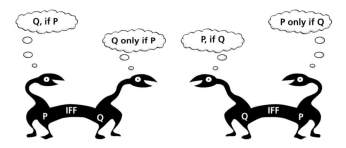

Consider this statement:
  'You can join the Red-Headed League IF you have red hair.'

Since this is the same as 'If you have red hair then you can join the Red-Headed League', its logical form is *if P then Q*.

3   What are P and Q?

Suppose this is all that we know about the rules of the Red-Headed League.

4   Do we know that you can NOT join the League if you do NOT have red hair?
5   Do we know whether Ginger (an undoubtedly red-haired cat) can join?

Now suppose that we do NOT know this IF-rule. Instead we know the rule:

> 'You can join the Red-Headed League ONLY IF you have red hair.'

6   Do we know now that you can NOT join the Red-Headed League if you do NOT have red hair?
7   What is the ONLY-IF rule's logical form? (Make P and Q the same as before, and remember that 'only if' is not a constant in our system: you'll need to translate.)
8   Given this ONLY-IF rule (and nothing more), may we conclude that the IF-rule

> 'You can join the Red-Headed League IF you have red hair'

also holds?
9   Given the ONLY-IF rule (and nothing more), do we know whether Ginger can join?

Finally, suppose that *both* rules hold:

> 'You can join the Red-Headed League IF AND ONLY IF you have red hair.'

Now we know exactly where we stand: both who may join and who may not. Ginger, yes (because of the IF-rule); the red-headed Irish Secretary yes (the IF-rule again); his black-haired Irish sister no (because of the ONLY-IF rule)…et cetera.

Next step: suppose instead that the rule is

'You can join the Red-Headed League if and only if you have red hair AND ARE OF IRISH ORIGIN.'

P: You have red hair, and are of Irish origin.

Q: You can join the Red-Headed League.

10 Which of these are still true?

(i)   You can join the Red-Headed League IF you have red hair

(ii) You can join the Red-Headed League ONLY IF you have red hair

(iii) You can join the Red-Headed League IF AND ONLY IF you have red hair.

Because it makes the qualifying conditions absolutely clear, the biconditional is useful for laws, regulations and definitions. Suppose for example that I want to define the word 'uncle'. If I say only

(i)   You are an uncle IF you are a parent's brother

this is not enough to distinguish 'uncle' from wider terms. You are also (among other things) *male* if you are a parent's brother; and you are *not an only child* and *part of a family* and *not a teapot* and you *exist*. Being a parent's brother suffices (is enough) for all of these; but they are not what I set out to define. Furthermore, although (i) specifies *one* way of being an uncle, if you did not know what 'uncle' means you might think there were others: being a brother's parent for example. This is not the case. And if I say merely

(ii) You are an uncle ONLY IF you are a parent's brother

this is not enough to distinguish 'uncle' from narrower terms.
You can be a *wicked* uncle only if you are a parent's brother; or the *uncle of twins* or *Jimmy's uncle* or *a great-uncle*. *Being a parent's brother* is necessary for all of these, although other things are needed too. And if you did not know what 'uncle' means, you might think other things were needed for *that*. In fact they are not. But

(iii) You are an uncle IF AND ONLY IF you are a parent's brother

pins it down exactly: this is what it is to be an uncle.

Compare my definition of 'valid argument': its underlying form is biconditional.

Q: The argument's form will not allow true premises and a false conclusion.

If Q then P

If P then Q

P: The argument is valid.

Q   IFF   P

11 Find examples (as for the Uncle definition) that show why neither *P if Q* alone, nor *P only if Q* alone, can adequately define 'valid'.

One last point. *P iff Q* is a truth-function. Its truth-table defines material equivalence: a two-way correlation, just as the truth-function *if P then Q* is a one-way correlation. P and Q always have the same truth-values, never mind why. But just as there are two kinds of conditional (strict, and truth-functional), there are two kinds of equivalence. *Strict* equivalence, like strict implication, depends not on the truth-values of P and Q, but on what these statements say. So we have two kinds of definition, fitting the two kinds of equivalence. Here is an example.

Plato suggested that we define 'human being' as 'featherless biped'. (He meant the species, of course. A legless war veteran does not falsify Plato's definition; and the joker who – it is said – shaved a hen and threw it into Plato's Academy missed the point.) Material equivalence fits this. We could write:

x is human IFF x is a featherless biped

because what we have here is mere correlation. 'This is a human' and 'This is a featherless biped' are indeed both true or both false wherever they occur, because we happen to be the only case of either. But we would not call being a featherless biped what it is to be human, nor vice versa. Other human features count more; and other featherless bipeds might exist.

What seems to have interested Plato was that although it does not explain what it is to be human, *as things are* the definition gives you a rule. If you want to find featherless bipeds look for humans, and vice versa. It could be the start of further enquiry.

Aristotle has a more ambitious definition: 'the rational animal'. This does try to say what being human is. The equivalence may not be as secure as he thinks: on the face of it, other rational animals seem possible. (Aristotle himself might say that nature has room for only one.) But *being an animal* and *being rational* do both seem to be true of us not just as it happens, but strictly. Intelligent non-animals – angels, or Triffids, or robots – would not qualify. Neither would animals who were like us in other ways, but non-rational: without speech, for example. Even if we stretched the term 'human' to cover any of these in some special context, we would still think them essentially different from ourselves.

Aristotle's definition therefore involves strict implication. But if it is true, the truth-functional

  x is human IFF x is a rational animal

is true as well. All strict equivalence is also material (though not vice versa).

12 Why?

So we can often treat strict and material equivalence interchangeably. But we should keep the difference between them in mind: it is sometimes important.

Logical constants (6)

In the last chapter I mentioned that equivalence combines two important iffy concepts (which we have met before): sufficient and necessary conditions.

Suppose all we know about the Red-Headed League is that red hair is a NECESSARY condition for joining. No grey ex-redheads, no non-redhaired members' relations need apply.

1   Which if any of these means the same?

(i)   'You can join the Red-Headed League IF you have red hair'
(ii) 'You can join the Red-Headed League ONLY IF you have red hair '
(iii) 'You can NOT join the Red-Headed League if you do NOT have red hair'.

2   If all we know is that red hair is a necessary condition, do we know whether Ginger the cat can join?

Our original IF-rule:

'You can join the Red-Headed League IF you have red hair'

states a *sufficient* condition for being able to join the League.

3   If red hair is a sufficient condition for joining, can Ginger join?

Now suppose that the Irish Rule holds as well:

'To join the League, you must be of Irish origin.'

4   Can red hair still be a sufficient condition for joining? Why, or why not?
5   If the rules are as the secretary tells Ginger (in the answers to Chapter 27) does 'You are of Irish origin' state a sufficient condition for 'You can join the Red-Headed League', or a necessary one, or what?
6   Given what the secretary says, what do we know about O'Reilly, a red Irish fox? Can he join the League?

Now look back at question 1.

7   What is the logical form of the rule that says red hair is a necessary condition for joining the league? (Make P 'You can join the Red-Headed League' and Q 'You have red hair'.)

Suppose we learn that being a red Irish fox is sufficient.

8   Does it follow that being a red Irish fox is necessary for joining the League?

You may by now have spotted some equivalences.

P is a necessary condition for Q

means that Q cannot be true unless P is:

If not P then not Q.

But we can also express this by saying

Not (Q and not P)

which is equivalent (by definition) to

If Q then P.

in other words, P must be true if Q is. And that is also to say

Q only if P.

However you put it, it is important to remember that P's being necessary for Q does not make it sufficient. You cannot join the League unless you have red hair; but you might (like Ginger) have red hair without being able to join.

Here is another set of equivalences.

P is a sufficient condition for Q

means that Q must be true if P is:

If P then Q

which is another way of saying

Not (P and not Q)

and is also the same thing as

P only if Q.

Again it is important to remember that P's being sufficient for Q does not make it necessary. Being a red Irish fox is sufficient to get you into the League; but the Secretary is a member, and he is not a fox.

Sometimes several necessary conditions add up to a sufficient one, though each is insufficient on its own. For the Red-Headed League as I finally described it, being red-haired is necessary but not sufficient: Ginger cannot join. Being of Irish descent is also necessary but not sufficient: Clodagh, the Secretary's black-haired sister, cannot join. But if these are the *only* necessary conditions, then being red-haired AND of Irish descent is a sufficient condition. That is why O'Reilly qualifies.

And since it is also the sum of two necessary conditions, being red-haired AND of Irish descent is itself necessary.

9   If P is 'You can join the Red-Headed League' and Q is 'You have red hair and are of Irish origin', which of these gives the

logical form of

'Red hair plus Irish descent is a necessary and sufficient condition for joining the League'?

(i)   **If P then Q**
(ii)   **If Q then P**
(iii)   **If not Q then not P**
(iv)   **If not P then not Q**
(v)   **If P then Q and if not P then not Q**
(vi)   **If P then Q and if Q then P**
(vii)   **P iff Q.**

10 Write the truth-table of (v). How does it relate to the table for *P iff Q*?

11 Write the truth-table of (vi). How does it relate to the table for (v) and, again, to that of *P iff Q*?

12 Here are some questions for practice.

(i) Is being a grandmother sufficient for being a mother?

(ii) Is being a mother sufficient for being a grandmother?

(iii)Is being a grandmother necessary for being a mother?

(iv)Is being a mother necessary for being a grandmother?

(v) Is being a grandmother necessary and sufficient for being a mother?

(vi)Is being a mother necessary and sufficient for being a grandmother?

(vii) Define 'mother' by giving a necessary and sufficient condition.

(viii) Define 'grandmother' by giving a necessary and sufficient condition.

 **This is the end of Part II.**

Part III

I have now introduced one system (statement logic), and a way of showing whether its forms are valid (the truth-table). I shall come back to it when I introduce proofs: but already you know enough to be going on with: you can recognise and assess it in arguments. So I now want to look at a different system.

The logic of sets

The logic of statements, unlike statement logic, can show us what is wrong with this:

> No wolves are vegetarians
> Annabel is not a vegetarian
> ───────────────────────────
> Annabel is a wolf

and right with this:

> Everyone who has a Rolls-Royce is rich
> My Granny has a Rolls
> ───────────────────────────
> My Granny is rich.

Instead of statements, it deals with sets and individuals. Instead of truth-tables, it uses *Venn diagrams* to show invalidity and validity. You may know something about these already, from elementary mathematics; but though the general principle is the same, logicians use a different form. Be ready to forget some things you think you know. I shall start by showing you how to cope with – and then asking you to try

LEWIS CARROLL'S PUZZLE.

Find a conclusion that can be inferred from these ten statements.

(1) The only animals in this house are cats.
(2) Every animal is suitable for a pet, that loves to gaze at the moon.
(3) When I detest an animal, I avoid it.
(4) No animals are carnivorous, unless they prowl at night.
(5) No cat fails to kill mice.
(6) No animals ever take to me, except what are in this house.
(7) Kangaroos are not suitable for pets.
(8) None but carnivora kill mice.
(9) I detest animals that do not take to me.
(10) Animals that prowl at night always love to gaze at the moon.

If there is such a conclusion, it must follow validly from (1)–(10). But statement logic cannot show this. Validity here depends on relations between sets: the set of cats, the set of carnivora (that is, carnivores), the set of animals that love to gaze at the moon, etc. We use *general terms* like 'cat' to identify sets. Each general term stands for a *concept* that determines which things we include in a set, and which we do not.

To solve Lewis Carroll's puzzle, we must use every statement in his list as a premise; and we must use nothing else, unless it is a conclusion drawn from an earlier stage of the argument. We can use Venns to show validity. This means it has to be done in steps: a sequence of syllogisms (two-premise arguments).

Every premise and/or conclusion in the puzzle has one of two underlying forms:

All A are B   or   **No A is B.**

A and B are variables that we replace with general terms. Carroll's first premise – rewritten to show its basic form – is 'All the animals in this house are cats'; A is 'animals in this house', and B is 'cats'.

1   Rewrite (2)–(10) to fit one or the other of these forms. Say in each case what replaces A, what replaces B, and what logical constant/s the form uses. You will need these general terms:

'animals I avoid'   'animals I detest'
'animals in this house'   'animals suitable for a pet'
'animals that take to me'*   'animals that do NOT take to me'*
'carnivores'   'cats'
'kangaroos'   'moon-gazing animals'
'mousekillers'   'night-prowling animals'.

*You'll see why you need both when you do the puzzle.

After this tidying-up, your next move will be to start with any premise. I suggest (1); find another that usefully combines with it in a syllogism – for example (5); and draw a conclusion. This will be the first premise in your second syllogism. Add a new premise from Carroll's list, draw a second conclusion — and so on. The final step, when you have used all ten premises, will be the answer to the puzzle. They are easy syllogisms: you should have no trouble seeing the valid conclusion each time. But we want to show that it is valid; so before you go on, here is how to do this with a Venn.

A circle represents a set.      CATS

We cannot tell from this whether the set is occupied or empty, that is whether there are cats or not. We show that a set is empty by shading it: think of this as blacking out the set.

This says that there are no unicorns.   UNICORNS

For Lewis Carroll's puzzle we need to show that certain sets are empty. We do not need to say, explicitly, that any set is *not* empty: I shall come to that later. Just remember for the moment that an *un*shaded circle – a blank one – does *not* say that the set is empty, nor that it is occupied. It leaves the matter open.

Overlapping circles show how sets relate to each other. Here, spaces 1, 2, 3 and 4 identify four separate sets, all defined in terms of the set of cats and the set of unicorns:

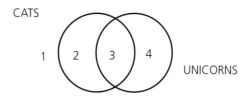

1   Anything that is neither a cat nor a unicorn
2   Cats that are not unicorns
3   Cats that are unicorns (or unicorns that are cats)
4   Unicorns that are not cats.

2   How would we shade the cat-unicorn diagram to say (i) 'No cats are unicorns'? (ii) 'No unicorns are cats'? (iii) 'There are no cats'?

When our diagram has no frame, set 1 includes *everything* that is neither a cat nor a unicorn: cakes of soap, doors, numbers, pigs, languages, roses…But it is sometimes useful to limit our universe of discourse (as it is called) by framing. Cats and unicorns are both kinds of animal: we might agree to leave non-animals out of the discussion by doing this:

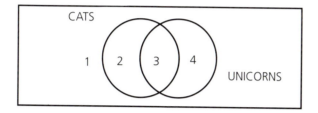

3   2, 3 and 4 are the same as before. What set is 1 in this diagram?
4   How would we shade this diagram to say (i) 'No cats are unicorns'? (ii) 'No animals are unicorns'? (iii) 'There are no cats'?

More about 'All A are B'

All A are B may be taken in two ways. Sometimes it seems to say there are As in the world, and sometimes not. If a man says 'All my daughters are lawyers', for example, we assume that (for this to be true) he must have daughters. If he says 'All unicorns have horns', we do *not* assume that (for this to be true) there must be unicorns.

It is dangerous to confuse the two senses, because an argument may be valid for the first but not the second. So (as with 'OR', etc.) logicians take one sense to be standard, and decree that we must put the other in a different way. For a long time they chose the first sense, following Aristotle: they said that *all A are B* entails that there is at least one A.

But the logic of sets (and modern logic generally) avoids certain problems in the Aristotelian system by choosing the other, the 'All unicorns have horns' sense. That is, we take *all A are B* to mean *no A is NOT B*, which leaves the existence question open.

If we want the Aristotelian sense, we must now say *all A are B AND there is at least one A*. (You will learn later how to say *there is at least one A* in a Venn.) One advantage is that anything *all A are B* entails is (of course) also entailed by *all A are B AND there is at least one A*.

5 (*Revision*) Explain why.
6 How would we shade this diagram to say 'All geniuses are mad'?

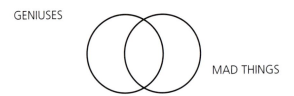

GENIUSES

MAD THINGS

7 Draw a two-circle Venn for premise (1) of Lewis Carroll's puzzle.

By putting THREE circles together, we can identify EIGHT separate sets.

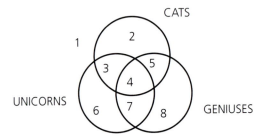

CATS

UNICORNS

GENIUSES

8 What are 1–8?

And with three circles, we can do Lewis Carroll's syllogisms. If we start off with premises (1) and (5), our first step has the form:

All A are B
All B are C

All A are C.

9   What are A, B and C?

B's role is crucial. It is called the *middle term*, and without it our premises would not give a useful conclusion. If (as I have done) you start with premise (1), only (5) or (6) are any use as a second premise, because these are the only two that give us a middle term: in (6) it is 'animals in this house'.

10 Now look carefully at the diagram below.

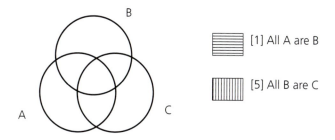

[1] All A are B

[5] All B are C

Substitute the names of the appropriate sets for A, B and C. Then use horizontal shading to state Lewis Carroll's premise (1): if in doubt, look at your answer to quesion 7. Use vertical shading for (5). What does the result tell us about the relation between A and C? Is the conclusion *all A are C valid?*

199

11–12 Go on with the puzzle by taking your conclusion as the first premise in a new syllogism. Find another in Carroll's list, one that will give you a middle term, and draw a conclusion. Keep on like this until you have used premises 1, 2, 4, 5, 8 and 10 (not in that order); and use a Venn diagram to test each step.

That will be your first five syllogisms. We'll do the rest in the next chapter.

Lewis Carroll's puzzle continued

By the time you have used premises 1,2,4,5,8 and 10 you should have worked out (in five syllogisms) that all the animals in this house are suitable for pets. Every syllogism fits a Venn diagram of this form:

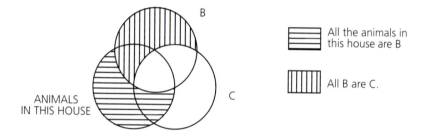

and each conclusion has as its subject *all the animals in this house*.

1   (*Revision*) In this diagram, which letter represents the middle term of each syllogism, and which part of the diagram corresponds to it? What is the middle term's role?
2   For syllogism number 6, find a premise that makes 'animals in this house' the middle term. Write the syllogism and show that it is valid with a Venn.
3   Among the premises you still haven't used, which would do for syllogism 7? Explain why.

Syllogism 7 has a different logical form, whose premises are *All A are B* and *No C is B*.

4 Which letter stands for the middle term here, and what can we conclude about the other terms? (Give the whole argument-form.)

5 What are A, B and C in syllogism 7?

6 Show by Venn diagram that this syllogism is valid.

7 Which premise looks the most promising for syllogism 8, and why?

If you got that question right, you know that the conclusion of syllogism 8 will be

All kangaroos are animals I detest.

But if our premises are the conclusion of syllogism 7 and the answer to question 7, too many sets are involved for a three-circle Venn: we have no middle term.

8 What sets do these statements refer to?

One extra step will put things right. ANIMALS THAT TAKE TO ME and ANIMALS THAT DO NOT TAKE TO ME are *complementary* sets: without overlapping, they complete the set of ANIMALS. Since kangaroos are animals too, we can use a frame to show by Venn that the conclusion of syllogism 7 – 'No kangaroos are animals that take to me' – entails something we can use for syllogism 8.

9 What part of this diagram represents the set of ANIMALS THAT TAKE TO ME?

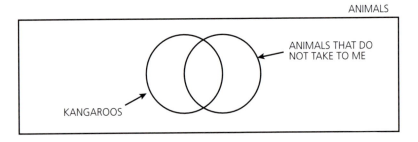

10 With this in mind, shade the diagram above to state the conclusion of syllogism 7: 'No kangaroos are animals that take to me'. What does the result show about the relation between KANGAROOS and ANIMALS THAT DO NOT TAKE TO ME?

11 Write a revised syllogism 8 with this result as a premise, and use a Venn to show that it is valid.

12 Use your conclusion to 8 and the one premise that is left in a final syllogism and Venn, to get THE ANSWER TO LEWIS CARROLL'S PUZZLE.

More about shading

First some general questions:

1 Does an unshaded diagram make a statement? If so, what do these diagrams state?

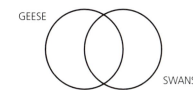

2 Does a shaded diagram make a statement? If so, what do these diagrams state?

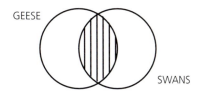

3   What about these?

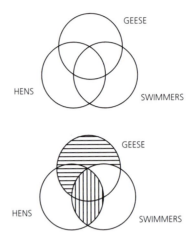

4   Does the frame below mean the diagram states that geese, hens and anything that swims are all birds? If not, what is it doing?

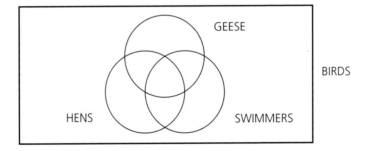

I can use shading to make any statement that says a set represented in my diagram is empty. These can be quite complicated. For example I can say, 'All Swiss people speak either French or German or both':

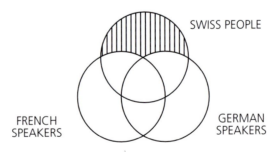

and I can also say, 'all Swiss people speak either French or German, but not both'.

5   How would I say that, using three circles?

6   Now say each of them again, using two circles and a frame instead.

I am limited only by the fact that I cannot have more than three circles (plus or minus a frame) in a single diagram. The three-circle diagram gives eight separate sets, which between them represent all the possible combinations of the major sets A, B and C:

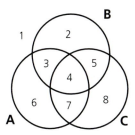

7   What set is 4? What is 4+7? What is 6+7+8?

If you had four major sets (A, B, C and D instead of A, B and C), you would need to split each of these eight into two: 1s that are D and 1s that are not D, 2s that are D and 2s that are not, etc. A four-circles diagram cannot do this. You *can* do it if you use not a fourth circle, but three circles and a sort of doughnut; but the diagram is virtually impossible to read, so we do not use it.

8   To enhance your feeling for Venns, try it. (You will need some ingenuity.)

Here are a few more patterns. These say (i) *EVERYTHING is either A or B*, and (ii) *EVERYTHING is either A or B, but nothing is both.*

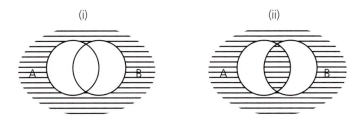

(Since a frameless Venn refers to the whole universe, think of the outer shading as shretching infinitely in all directions.)

These say (i) *Everything is both B and A*, and (ii) *Everything either is both B and A, or is neither.*

These say (i) *Everything is A, B and C*, and (ii) *Everything is A or B or C.*

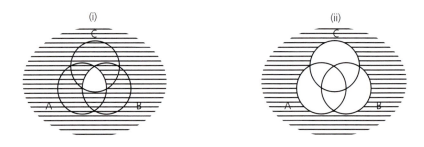

(Unless we specify otherwise, 'or' means 'and/or'.)

9   How would I say *ONLY A are B*?

10   How would I say 'ALL and ONLY those with red hair can join
     the Red-Headed League'?

Suppose that this is the first premise of an argument, whose second
premise is 'All foxes have red hair'.

11   Draw a diagram to show whether foxes can join, if both these
     premises are true.

12   (*Revision*) When I say all this, am I saying that any foxes exist,
     or creatures with red hair (etc.)? If so, what part of my diagram
     states this? If not, what exactly am I saying?

Venns and invalidity

All the arguments in Lewis Carroll's puzzle are valid. When we draw the premises of a valid argument into a Venn, the conclusion *draws itself in*: we look at the diagram, and there it is. Now consider

All frogs are animals

All animals are frogs.

By this time you should not need to note its true premise and false conclusion to recognise that this argument is INVALID: its form should be enough. And with a Venn diagram, you can show this.

1   How many sets are involved here, and what are they? How many circles will the diagram need?
2   What is this argument's form, in the logic of sets?
3   Draw the diagram for this form, and explain how it shows that the form is invalid.

Now consider the form:

No A is B
No C is B

All A are C.

4   Find an example that shows it is invalid.
5   How many sets are involved, and how many circles will its diagram need?

6   Draw the diagram for this form, and explain how it shows that the form is invalid. (Use a different kind of shading for each premise.)

7   What about this one?

All A is B or C
All B is C or A

All C is A or B.

Show by a Venn whether it is invalid or valid.

8   What about this argument?

All prophets are pessimists
Realists are never pessimists

No realists are prophets.

9   And this?
Philosophers are never pessimists
No pessimist is an optimist

All philosophers are optimists.

It is a good thing to use a different kind of shading for each premise. If you do not, the diagram will tell you whether or not your conclusion is valid, but it will not show how you reached it. For example the three argument-forms below would all end up with the same diagram:

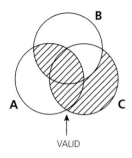

VALID

But different shading for each premise would show how unlike they are, even though they all validly reach the same conclusion:

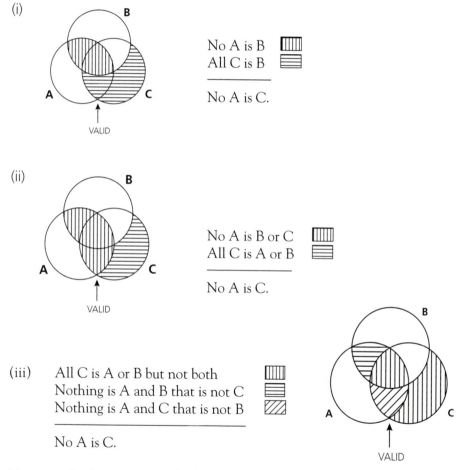

(i)

B

VALID

A   C

No A is B   ⦀
All C is B   ☰

No A is C.

(ii)

B

A   C

VALID

No A is B or C   ⦀
All C is A or B   ☰

No A is C.

(iii)   All C is A or B but not both   ⦀
Nothing is A and B that is not C   ☰
Nothing is A and C that is not B   ▨

No A is C.

B

A   C

VALID

Here is a final exercise in shading, before we go on to the next stage.

Yossarian hopes to be grounded (relieved of combat duty) on the plea that he is crazy.

'Can't you ground someone who's crazy?' Yosarian asked.

'Oh sure. There's a rule saying I have to ground anyone who's crazy. But first he has to ask me to. That's part of the rule.'

'And then you can ground him?'

'No. Then I *can't* ground him.'

'You mean there's a catch?'

'Sure there's a catch', Doc Daneeka replied. 'Catch-22. Anyone who wants to get out of combat duty isn't really crazy.'

(Joseph Heller, *Catch-22*)

10 What is Doc Daneeka's conclusion, and what are his premises? *Hint*: there are three premises, which express

(i) the first part of Doc Daneeka's rule;
(ii) the second part of Doc Daneeka's rule;
(iii)the catch.

Premises and conclusion should each state the relation between two of these three sets: AIRMEN WHO ASK TO BE GROUNDED; CRAZY AIRMEN; AIRMEN THE DOCTOR CAN GROUND.

11 Using these premises, draw a three-circle Venn to show that Doc Daneeka's premises make his conclusion inevitable.

12 If this is so, what is wrong with the argument? (Something must be!)

Venns and existence

At times we want to say explicitly that a set is NOT empty. We do this by drawing a stroke in the circle which represents that set.

 UNICORNS   This says that there is at least one unicorn.

When circles overlap, we have to be careful where to put the stroke. To make exactly the same statement in a *two*-circle diagram, I must do this:

WHITE THINGS 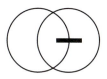 UNICORNS

because I want only to say that unicorns *exist*, without saying anything about their colour.

1   What do I say exists, if I put the stroke like this instead?

WHITE THINGS 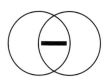 UNICORNS

Technical term: in the logic of sets the word 'some' (unlike the word 'all') implies existence. From now on I shall use *some A is B* to mean the same as *there exists at least one A that is B*, and *something is A* to mean the same as *there exists at least one A*.

The stroke in the first two-circle diagram does NOT say that both white and non-white unicorns exist.

2   How would you say that in a Venn?
3   Does this diagram say that there are no non-white unicorns? How, or why not?

WHITE THINGS 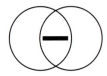 UNICORNS

Sometimes we need a curved stroke. This three-circle diagram is another that says that there is at least one unicorn.

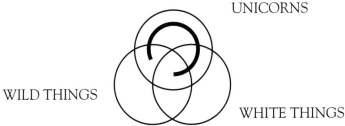

UNICORNS

WILD THINGS

WHITE THINGS

4   Explain why the stroke must be curved.
5   Does it say that any wild things exist? How, or why not?
6   What exactly is the role of the circles for WILD THINGS and WHITE THINGS?

7 What does this diagram say?

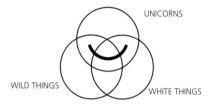

8 Do these two diagrams say the same thing?

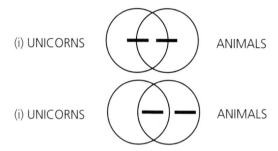

9 What about these?

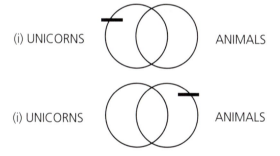

10 Are these two diagrams compatible? Explain why or why not.

11 What about these?

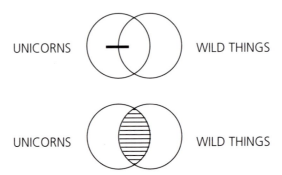

12 Draw a diagram that says 'Sheep exist but unicorns do not'.

(I hoped you'd get around to me eventually.)

Individuals (1)

In the next two chapters I shall use the ideas of an *individual* and a *referring term* to raise some issues in the philosophy of language – enough to give you an idea of what they are. You may find it useful to look again at Chapters 6–10, where I used the idea of a premise in the same way. The links are obvious.

Besides relations between sets, and whether sets are occupied or empty, the logic of sets deals with individuals. We identify an individual by a referring term. This may be a *description*, which (in context) picks out one thing of the kind described: 'my uncle' for example or 'Uncle', when I'm the one who is speaking and we know which of my uncles I mean. It may be a *proper name* like 'Joe'. Or, as in 'Uncle Joe', it may have aspects of both.

A description describes: that is, it says what something is like. Used literally, 'my uncle' means a brother of the speaker's father or mother: it would misdescribe anything else. And so we know what kind of thing the descriptive term 'my uncle' would refer to, even when we do not use it to refer.

The same thing is true of 'my pet unicorn'. This can never refer, literally. There are no pet unicorns.

1 (*Revision*) What is the literal use of language, as opposed to its figurative use?

But again, because the words are descriptive, they have a sense. We know the kind of thing they would refer to, if they did.

2 Without using the words 'my', 'pet' or 'unicorn', say what kind of thing 'my pet unicorn' (used literally) must refer to.

By contrast proper names have meaning if and only if they *do* refer. Their role – in theory – is not to describe a thing at all, but just to pick it out. Philosophers disagree about how this could work, and whether there *are* proper names in a language like English. Read what follows carefully, and see what you think.

In English 'my uncle' literally means the brother of the speaker's father or mother. 'Uncle' with a capital U can mean the same. But the same words might *name* anything at all: a boat, a film, a tune. You might call your boat 'Uncle' on a whim: you hit on the name by closing your eyes and sticking a pin in a book. Still, *because you have made this its name*, we can use the word 'Uncle' to speak of the boat.

Using 'Uncle' as a name is untypical: its first use is to describe. On the other hand we have words like 'Joe' or 'Joseph', whose first use – it seems – is to name. And some expressions contain both, like 'Uncle Joe'.

Words can describe in two ways: literal or metaphorical.

3   (*Revision*) What is a metaphor?

Metaphor is not any term's first use: it appeals to uses that are there already. Take 'Uncle Joe': people sometimes used this of Joseph Stalin. When they did, they were not literally calling him a mother's or father's brother. He may or may not have been – it is irrelevant. But the words do seem to imply an analogy. In some way which the speakers thought relevant, he was somehow like a (typical) parent's brother.

4   How might this apply to Stalin? (You need not agree with the speakers of course.)

Like a literal description, this is different from a name. If a name suggests what its owner is like, even metaphorically, this goes beyond its role as a name. 'Uncle Joe', like 'Uncle', could be the name of a boat. No doubt if the name was not picked at random there will be some link between its owner and its sense (if it has a sense); but many links might do. You might call a boat 'Uncle' not because it is uncle-ish, but because your uncle bought it. Often the link is descriptive, however: the word we use as a name suggests what its owner is like, or (we hope) will be like. We name daughters 'Rose' but never 'Onion'.

5   If 'Rose' says what a girl is like, is this literal or metaphorical?

But once 'Rose' is her name, we can use it to talk of her no matter un-rose-like she may be. Legal names ensure this, but they only make official what we do anyway. We might give Stalin the nickname 'Uncle Joe' because we think he is somehow uncle-ish, but go on using it when we are quite sure he is not. 'Uncle Joe' then functions purely as a name.

We might indeed decide he is not Joe-ish either. A name like 'Joe' can be used to describe. 'He's not a Joe – more of a Joseph' is not about what the man is called, but about what suits him.

This looks like metaphor again. But how can it be, if names do not originally describe? If 'Joe' does not typically say what its owner is like, how can it make sense to say someone is like a (typical) Joe?

6 Without working out why you think so – what might the difference be, descriptively, between a Joseph and a Joe?

Here is something that might help to explain the situation. A metaphor is an implicit analogy; but the analogy need not be based on a term's literal sense (also known as its *cognitive meaning*). Words have *evocative* meaning too, apart from their literal sense. Sometimes the accidental sound is enough. Salmonella is a bacterium that makes people sick, and citronella is an insect repellent; but the sound of both suggests a girl, like the name 'Cinderella' – enough to make them useful joke-names. Sometimes what is evoked is the word's social background: 'Mum', 'Mummy', 'Mommy', 'Mom', 'Mamma', '*Maman*', 'Maw' and 'the Mater' all literally describe someone as a mother, but they suggest different kinds.

7 What kinds? Give some examples.

When two words literally describe the same thing, one of them may be poetic and one prosaic ('morn' and 'morning' for example), one approving and one disapproving ('philanthropist' and 'do-gooder'), one plain and one pompous…and so on.

8 Think of more pairs like this: words whose cognitive meaning is the same, but whose evocative meanings are different.

A proper name, though it has no cognitive sense, can evoke descriptions in this way. Writers like P.G. Wodehouse know it: Bertie Wooster, an upper-class type, could never have been Bert. If we then use the name *as if* 'upper-class type' were its sense ('He's not a Bert, he's a Bertie'), we use it metaphorically.

9   Go back to question 5. See if you can now explain what you instinctively felt, about the difference between a Joseph and a Joe.

Evocative meaning is often found in the non-verbal side of language – tone of voice, accent, facial expression, timing – though these can have cognitive implications too. A speaker's tone, for example, may decide whether the words 'You're going home now' make a statement, ask a question or give a command.

10 Why is the difference between a statement, a question and a command a cognitive one?
    (*Hint*: Put each use of 'You're going home now' another way, where not the tone but the words themselves show the difference. Can we use the same for all three?)

People who write about logic often bypass evocative meaning: it seems even harder to pin down and make rules about than other aspects of a natural language. They may indeed give up on natural languages altogether, and limit themselves to ideal ones where such meanings are (typically) unknown. Or they may work only on areas in natural language where meanings are cognitive and explicit. Traditionally they have looked to theology or the law for examples; more recently they have turned to science. This can be valuable, but it is unrealistic if you want to use logic in ordinary life. Think of Wormwood's 'patient' in Chapter 4.

Even if we stick to the cognitive and explicit there are problems about the idea that a name in no way describes, but can still refer. Suppose that 'Mary Haight' refers to me, without saying anything about what I am like. Must not it then (cognitively) pick out everything about me: the air in my lungs, the hairs on my head and all? I lose a hair, I breathe out, and the thing whose name it was has gone – unless we want my name to pick out everything from my beginning to my end, in sequence. And in that case (i) there are borderline problems: what *is* my beginning, or my end? (ii) There are problems about counterfactuals: how can we now say 'Mary Haight might have worn different clothes today' without contradiction? 'Mary Haight' means someone wearing *these* clothes today. And (iii) this is just not how we use our names.

11 What natural words or gestures really come closest to referring without description?

On the other hand, if we start saying 'That change doesn't count – Mary Haight could be wearing different clothes – but this change does', we seem to be sneaking in descriptions. If putting me through a mincer would produce something that my name no longer fits, 'Mary Haight' seems to entail that its owner is unminced.

12 (*Revision*) Make this point again using 'necessary condition' and/or 'sufficient condition'.

But perhaps something totally simple could be named? We would then avoid problems of change or counterfactuals: these depend on a thing's having more than one aspect, so that it can be partly what you first named and partly not. Some famous attempts at an ideal language suggest this, from Plato in ancient Greece to Bertrand Russell and Ludwig Wittgenstein in this century. The idea is that you might *name* the 'simples', and *describe* other things in terms of them. But Wittgenstein later attacked this idea (Plato's, Russell's, his own), I think irrefutably, on the grounds that nothing can be that simple. (If you are interested, you will find this in his *Philosophical Investigations*.)

The things we name in real life are far from simple (people for example). And what we call names in English often seem to describe: 'Joseph' (normally used) seems to guarantee a male and 'Josephine' a female, just as 'uncle' and 'aunt' do. 'Normally used' is crucial; but so it is for 'uncle' and 'aunt'. We could be cagey and say that 'Joseph' (when normally used) *suggests* rather than *entails* that its owner is male; but I think that English is not so precise.

Individuals (2)

Here are a few questions to test you on the last chapter.

1   Is the word 'I' literally descriptive? If so, what kind of thing does it describe?

Descartes's *cogito* argument makes a claim about the use of 'I' to refer (or the use of its Latin equivalents: like the first-person ending *cogitO*).

'COGITO, ERGO SUM.'
('I think; therefore I exist.')

2   What is this claim?
3   Give an example in which the word 'I' appears, but does not refer.

In the last chapter, I said that English proper names (so-called) often seem to describe. We might insist that a name ('Joseph') never entails a description ('male'), it only suggests it. However, that seems artificial. I also suggested that if a name does not *somehow* describe, it is hard to see how we can use it. If 'Mary Haight' just picks out everything I am, it cannot refer to something even minutely different. This is not how we use 'Mary Haight'. On the other hand, if it selects some aspects of me and not others, it implicitly describes me: I am (for example) unminced.

This is the tip of a philosophical iceberg. We cannot explore it here, and luckily we need not. Whether or not names like 'Joe' or 'Mary Haight' can refer without (even implicitly) describing, they still refer. We can also distinguish them from *explicit* descriptions like 'the writer of this book' or 'my uncle': whatever they are, they work differently. Consider 'my uncle' and 'Joe' again.

Being a girl would normally disqualify you for both. But being my father's or mother's brother would *qualify* you for 'my uncle', while no description qualifies you for 'Joe'. Nothing makes you Joe except being given the name. And this is true of any named individual, normal or not: boys called Joe, girls called Joe, ponies called Goat (I used to know one), boats called Uncle and pubs called The Prince of Wales. There is just one rule for a name's use: that it was given.

This does not mean we have no rules for *giving* names in particular cases: naming people for example. Some are prescribed by ritual or law. We also have conventions.

(An example to show the difference between a rule and a convention:

Rule: When you write the truth-table for *P and Q*, the formula is TRUE when P and Q are.

Convention: When you write the truth-table for *P and Q*, the variables are lined up on the left.

You could use another convention and still have the table for *P and Q*; but the rule is essential.)

In Britain, I believe, the rule for legal names is that a child's parents or guardians must register it, but can register it as anything they like. It is conventional, however, to use the father's surname, not to call a daughter 'Joseph' or 'Onion' – etc. In France, I think (unless this has changed) only certain given names are allowed. 'Joséphine' is legal for your daughter, but I do not know if 'Joseph' is, for a girl; 'Oignon' definitely is not, although it could be a surname.

Legal rules for naming are only one kind, of course. If you ask whether it is a rule of the English language that you do not name a girl 'Joseph', or only a convention, I would repeat that English usage is not precise enough to say. At most we can say that this is what a normal English speaker expects, unless told differently.

But again, for our purpose it does not matter: what matters is that a name refers. It is a proper name if and only if it is given to something, as you might stick on a label. A name – if it *is* a name – therefore implies its owner's existence at the time of naming, though not necessarily its existence now. You cannot stick a label on nothing.

In the Venn diagrams that follow, I shall use a small letter to abbreviate proper names. The diagram below says 'Margaret Thatcher is a politician'.

A term is a proper name only if it refers. So, if the diagram above makes a true statement, this one must do so as well:

4   (*Revision*) What does the stroke in the circle mean?
5   Is the reverse true? Does the second diagram, if accurate, tell us that the first is?

A story-name like 'Cinderella' is not a name really. It does not refer. It is a descriptive term (like 'my pet unicorn'), used in a special way. Fiction is a game of make-believe, where the teller pretends that there is (or was) such a person – dressed in rags, with ugly sisters, a fairy godmother (and so on) and named Cinderella. The story itself tells us what kind of person this word describes, just as unicorn stories provide us with the meaning of 'unicorn'. But 'Cinderella' is not just a description: it is also part of the word's meaning that it is a pretend-name. If we happened to find someone real (fairy godmother and all) who matched the story, the story-name 'Cinderella' would not refer to her. She would have the *real* name 'Cinderella' because she had been given it at a real christening, and she would have it even if the story did not exist. And if both she and the story did exist, the word 'Cinderella' would have two distinct uses (as of course many words do): one as a real name, the other not.

The use of name entails its owner's existence because if it is a name, it refers. A description is a description whether it refers or not; but when I know that it does, I can use a letter in a Venn for it too. The diagram below says that the queen of England loves horses.

HORSE-LOVERS   q: The Queen of England.

The present tense of 'loves' and the year in which I write this (1997) give a context where I know that the words 'the queen of England' pick out a real individual, a.k.a. Elizabeth Windsor.

6   Which of these terms refer (if I use them normally)? Answer YES, NO or UNCERTAIN, and in each case explain why.

(i)   'The present king of France'
(ii)   'The tallest man in the world'
(iii) 'France'
(iv)   'The Diskworld'
(v)   The even number between three and five'
(vi)   'The even number between four and six'

So far I've spoken of referring to an individual; we can also refer to more than one individual at once. 'My parents' refers to my mother and my father. What matters is that (in context) my words are definite: not just anyone's parents, but these. I can use a single letter to pick out a couple if I have reason to (or a trio or a quartet, etc.) so long as it is a specific couple (or trio, etc.).

So these two diagrams state the same fact: that my parents were American.

p: couple consisting of my mother and father
m: my mother   f: my father

But these circles do not pick out the same set. One represents a set of individual people, the other a set of individual couples.

We could use two-circle diagrams to say the same thing, if we had reason to:

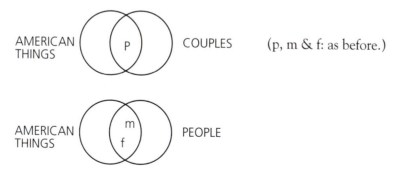

7   (*Revision*) Draw a Venn diagram that says 'Some couples are American'.

A general term like CATS is not definite. It describes whatever cats there are if there are any, but does not specify any individual/s, either singly or in a group. That is why we can take 'All cats purr' to mean the same as 'No cats do not purr'.

8   (*Revision*) Draw the Venn for 'All cats purr'.

'THE cats' is different. Typically we would use it to specify a group, as when 'All the cats have come in for their supper' states the same as 'Paddy, Quincey and Mehitabel have come in for their supper', a state of affairs that we might draw like this:

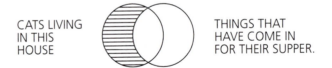

CATS   p   THINGS THAT   p: Paddy
            q   HAVE COME IN   q: Quincey
            m   FOR THEIR SUPPER   m: Mehitabel

9   Draw   (i) a one-circle Venn for this statement, still referring
                 to each cat by name;
            (ii) a two-circle Venn stating the same fact in terms of a
                 trio of cats.

But English is slippery: we might sometimes use 'all the cats' as a general term, short perhaps for 'any cats living in this house'. Then the words make a different statement:

CATS LIVING   THINGS THAT
IN THIS   HAVE COME IN
HOUSE   FOR THEIR SUPPER.

As always, the trick is not to stop at the surface, but to ask what the speaker means.
   Suppose I used 'All the cats that live in this house have come in for their supper' to say that (i) no such cats have *not* come in, and (ii) such cats exist – though for some reason I cannot pick any out specifically.

10   What diagram would represent this?

Finally: when we know that an individual is in one or the other of two sets, but not which one, we use a '?'.

This says 'Margaret Thatcher is a politician', but does not specify whether she is also a pop star.

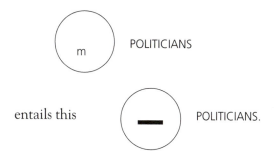

11 I have explained why this diagram entails this:

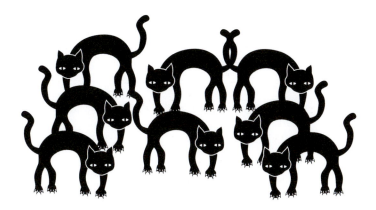

What diagram does the two-circle Margaret Thatcher one entail, and why?

12 Draw a three-circle diagram that says 'Aglavaine is a unicorn who may be black or white.'

Practice in using Venn diagrams

We can combine strokes and/or letters with shading, in the same diagram. This one contains the two statements 'No dogs are cats' and 'Paddy is one or the other, but not both':

and this adds the statement *Dogs and cats exist.*

Shading affects how we place our strokes, but we can still fit them in. (When you combine shading with other things, do the shading first. The other things must go in the space that is left.)

1   How would we place the letters and strokes if the shading were not there?
2   Use the diagram below to say 'All unicorns are white' and 'Some unicorns are not wild'.
    (Remember that we use *some A are B* to assert existence.)

UNICORNS

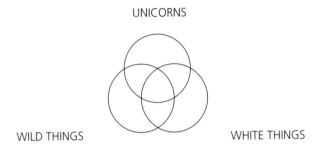

WILD THINGS   WHITE THINGS

3   Use three circles and a frame to illustrate the statement

'All men who wear bow ties are frivolous but cheerful, and some of them have wigs'.

Here are two more literary passages to practice on.

Alice's identity

Alice has eaten a piece of magic mushroom, which she was told would make her grow taller. In fact only her neck grows. It snakes up through the trees, past the nest of a terrified Pigeon.

> 'Serpent!' said the Pigeon.
> 'I –I'm a little girl' said Alice.
> 'A likely story! I suppose you'll be telling me next that you never tasted an egg!'
> 'I have tasted eggs, certainly…but little girls eat eggs quite as much as serpents do.'
> 'Why, then, they're a kind of serpent: that's all I can say.'
> (Lewis Carroll, *Alice in Wonderland*)

4 What is the Pigeon's conclusion about Alice, and what are her premises?

We can write this as a single three-premise argument; we'll need three general terms and one proper name. Premises and conclusion all have one of these forms:

All A are B
x is A

where A and B represent general terms and x a proper name.

5 Write the argument in this way, and draw a three-circle Venn to show whether it is valid or invalid. Explain how it shows this.

But we can express the argument in greater detail – to pick out exactly where it goes wrong – if we use syllogisms, as in the Kangaroo argument. We will need two. The first uses two of the Pigeon's premises; then its conclusion becomes a premise in the second, with the Pigeon's remaining premise.

6 Write the argument in this form. Now draw a Venn for each syllogism, to show the validity or invalidity of each step on its own. Explain how they show this.

(Another passage from
Joseph Heller's *Catch-22*.)

The war was still going on…No one seemed to notice but
Yossarian and Dunbar. And when Yossarian tried to remind
people, they drew away from him and thought he was crazy.
Even Clevinger, who should have known better but didn't, had
told him he was crazy…

'They're trying to kill me,' Yossarian told him calmly.

'No one's trying to kill you,' Clevinger cried.

'Then why are they shooting at me?' Yossarian asked.

'They're shooting at *everyone*,' Clevinger answered. 'They're
trying to kill everyone.'

'And what difference does that make?'

…Clevinger really thought he was right, but Yossarian had
proof, because strangers he didn't know shot at him with
cannons every time he flew up into the air to drop bombs on
them, and it wasn't funny at all.

*   *   *

Yossarian's original premises are:

(i) They're shooting at Yossarian

(ii) They're trying to kill the people they shoot at.

He has proof of the first, and the second seems obvious enough.
The logical form of each premise, and of Yossarian's conclusion, is
either *all A are B or x is A*.

7   Identify Yossarian's conclusion, and rewrite his argument in
    formulae that fit the Venn below.

8   Use this Venn to test it for validity, and explain how it does so.

PEOPLE THEY'RE
SHOOTING AT

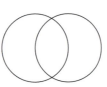

PEOPLE THEY'RE
TRYING TO KILL

y: Yossarian.

Yossarian is willing to agree with Clevinger that they are shooting at everybody (meaning everyone at the base camp). It makes no difference, he says: his conclusion is the same.

9 Suppose that instead of his original premises he assumes:

(i) They're shooting at everybody
(ii) They're trying to kill the people they shoot at.

What further (implicit) premise does he need to reach his conclusion? Is he right to assume it?

10 Rewrite this new argument in a form suitable for the Venn below, and use the Venn to assess it. Is the argument sound?

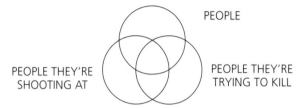

PEOPLE

PEOPLE THEY'RE
SHOOTING AT

PEOPLE THEY'RE
TRYING TO KILL

Clevinger seems to accept these premises, and yet to argue that Yossarian's conclusion is false.

11 What is Clevinger's conclusion, and does it really negate Yossarian's?
(*Hint*: when would 'They're shooting at everyone' be a reason for 'They're not shooting at *you*' ?)

12 In the answer to 11, you will find Clevinger's argument in a form that will suit a Venn. Draw it using these two circles and frame:

(You decide how to label the frame)

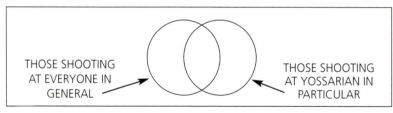

THOSE SHOOTING
AT EVERYONE IN
GENERAL

THOSE SHOOTING
AT YOSSARIAN IN
PARTICULAR

and assess the argument for soundness. Then explain the title that I gave to this passage.

(*Hint*: remember Miss Nightingale.)

 **This is the end of Part III.**

Part IV

You now know enough about the logic of sets to be getting on with. You should be able to recognise arguments which are based on it, and in Venn diagrams you have a way of showing whether or not these are valid. (This kind of thing always improves with practice, by the way: the more you use it, the better you will get.) The next section of the book is about logical proof, using rules of inference; and for this I shall go back to statement logic. After that (and some information about where the study of logic goes next) I stop. You will be ready for more formal courses if you want to go on with the subject, and able to deal with a wide range of arguments in ordinary life even if you do not.

Rules of inference (1)

Remember the good and bad news about truth-tables. In theory, we can always use them to check validity in truth-functional logic; but in fact we would often need a table so long or wide, or both, that no one who knew a better way would use that one. And there is a better way: a *proof*, using *rules of inference*. ('Infer' here means 'to work out logically'.) In truth-functional logic, our rules can be confirmed by truth-tables; but once we have seen that a rule is acceptable, we can use it without referring back.

Look at these arguments. They are all valid for the same reason.

I

> 'It's a plane – or a bird – or Superman!'
> 'Not Superman, darling. He's just a story.'
> 'Well, a plane or a bird then.'

II

'Ladies and gentlemen of the jury, you have heard from the victim's doctor that death could have been due either to gastro-enteritis from natural causes – to which she was prone – or else to poisoning by arsenic, whether accidental or deliberate. You have heard from the forensic officer that post mortem examination has eliminated all possibility of arsenical poisoning. Only one possibility therefore remains: the deceased met her end by gastro-enteritis due to natural causes.'

III

'Either he's telling the truth, or he's an extraordinarily good actor!'

'He IS an extraordinarily good actor then – because I know that he is lying.'

1   What are the premises of each argument, and what is its conclusion?

The reason all three arguments are valid is that they share a simple valid form. It is most obvious in the case of argument III (the Actor); but the other two have it as well, and so have many other forms. A familiar name for this kind of reasoning is 'process of elimination'. If we remember that we can take a disjunction in any order (so that for example 'It's a plane or it's a bird or it's Superman' is exactly equivalent to 'It's Superman or a bird or a plane') we can write the form

$$\begin{array}{l} \textbf{P or Q} \\ \textbf{Not P} \\ \hline \\ \textbf{Q.} \end{array}$$

2   Use a truth-table to show that this form is valid. You may choose either the full table ('full sweep' method) or the short-cut ('fell swoop').

Now look at these more complex logical forms. The first fits argument I (Superman) but not the others; the second fits argument II (the Jury) but not the others.

(i)	(ii)
(R or S) or T	(R or S) or T
Not T	Not (R or S)
———	———
R or S	T

Neither fits argument III (the Actor).

3   If we use (i) to analyse the Superman argument, what are R, S
    and T?
4   If we use (ii) to analyse the Jury argument, what are R, S and
    T?

(i) and (ii) are therefore valid for the same reason as the arguments:
they too share the Elimination form

P or Q
Not P
───────
Q.

In different ways, they are all *substitution instances* of this form.

5   What does form (i) substitute for P? And for Q?
6   What does form (ii) substitute for the Elimination form's
    second premise?
7   What does argument I (Superman) substitute for the
    Elimination form's conclusion?
8   What does argument II (the Jury) substitute for the Elimination
    form's first premise?
9   Write a substitution instance of the Elimination form, in which
    P is replaced by *if R then S*, and Q is replaced by *T or not R*.

If we test these longer forms by truth-table, the table will show
them to be valid. But it is tedious.

10 What is the validity-formula for form (i)? How many lines
    would a full table need?

With the long validity-formulae of (i) and (ii), even the 'fell swoop'
is tedious. But because these are substitution instances of a simpler
valid form, we can save ourselves the trouble. Any argument with

form (i) or (ii) will also have the Elimination form; and so it will be valid. Or to put it differently, any argument or argument-form which is a substitution instance of a simpler valid form is itself valid. It will not allow true premises and a false conclusion.

Once we understand this, we can use the simple form to establish a RULE OF INFERENCE, if it occurs often enough in argument to make this worthwhile. Reasoning by elimination is very common: most statement logic systems have this rule.

RULE 1. ELIMINATION (ELIM)

GIVEN P *or* Q and *not* P, we may conclude Q.

Here 'P *or* Q' is short for 'a statement of form P *or* Q' (etc.); and any statement whose form is a substitution instance of P *or* Q is a statement of form P *or* Q. ELIM is also called the rule of DISJUNCTIVE SYLLOGISM.

11 Which of the arguments below use ELIM?

I

Either Randolph is asleep or he's dead
Randolph is not asleep
_____

Randolph is dead

II

If Billy had come to play, Amanda would have bitten him
Amanda didn't bite Billy

Billy didn't come to play.

III

Either he has been crossed in love, or his feet hurt, or the man's
    just naturally bad-tempered
He's not a bad-tempered man

He has been crossed in love, or else his feet hurt.

12 In each argument that does, what are P and Q?

Rules of inference (2)

1   (*Revision*) Explain, using examples, what it is for

   (i) a formula to be a substitution instance of a *simpler* formula
   (ii) a formula to be a substitution instance of a *more complex* formula
   (iii)an argument-form to be a substitution-instance of a *simpler* argument-form
   (iv)an argument-form to be a substitution-instance of a *simpler* argument-form.

Another obvious candidate for a rule is the argument-form shared by these three:

I

If that malicious little creep sets foot in the house, I leave
He sets foot in the house

_____

I leave.

II

If the Snake is proud, he will accept
The Snake is proud

He will accept.

III

If the Snake accepts, he will die in the attempt, or he will live
    but fail, or he will succeed
He will accept

He will die in the attempt, or he will live but fail, or he will
    succeed.

2   What form is it? (Use the variables P and Q.)
3   What are P and Q in argument I?
4   What are P and Q in argument III?
5   Find a more detailed argument-form using variables P, Q, R and
    S, that fits argument III. Say what P, Q, R and S stand for in
    this form.
6   Show that this form is a substitution instance of the form
    referred to in question 2. What does it substitute for that form's
    P and Q?

The rule that this form exemplifies is commonly called
AFFIRMING THE ANTECEDENT, or MPP for short (from the
Latin *Modus Ponendo Ponens*. You need only remember the initials).

RULE 2.   AFFIRMING THE ANTECEDENT (MPP)

GIVEN *If P then Q* and *P*, we may conclude Q.

7   Explain how MPP 'affirms the antecedent'.

8   Use a truth-table (either 'full sweep' or 'fell swoop') to show that MPP is a valid rule of inference.

9   Are these argument-forms valid by MPP? (Never mind if they are valid for some other reason.) If so, what are P and Q in each?

<table>
<tr><td>

(i)

If (S or R) then T
S or R
───────────────

T
</td><td>

(ii)

If S then T
T
───────────────

S
</td></tr>
</table>

<table>
<tr><td>

(iii)

If S then T
Not S
───────────────

Not T
</td><td>

(iv)

If R then R
R
───────────────

R.
</td></tr>
</table>

10   This form is valid by MPP. Explain how the rule applies.

   If Q then P
   Q
   ───────────

   P.

11   Is this argument valid by MPP?

If Fang is a dog, he's a mammal
If he is a mammal, he is a vertebrate
If he is a vertebrate, he is an animal
Fang is a dog
────────────────────────────

Fang is an animal.

Both a valid argument and a valid argument-form may be shown to be valid by a PROOF.

In a proof, we list not just the premises and conclusion, but the steps in between. We number each line. When a line quotes a premise, we write PREMISE after it. For every other line, we give the rule according to which that step was reached, and the number(s) of the earlier line(s) from which it was derived.

A simple proof

1	If Fang is a dog, he's a mammal	PREMISE
2	If he is a mammal, he's a vertebrate	PREMISE
3	If he is a vertebrate, he's an animal	PREMISE
4	Fang is a dog	PREMISE
5	Fang is a mammal	1, 4 MPP
6	Fang is a vertebrate	2, 5 MPP.

7	Fang is an animal	3,6 MPP.

A proof of the related argument-form would begin:

1	If P then Q	PREMISE
2	If Q then R	PREMISE
3	If R then S	PREMISE …etc.

12 Say what P, Q, R and S stand for, and finish it off.

Rules of inference (3)

Our next rule – Denying the Consequent – is also known as MTT (from the Latin *Modus Tollendo Tollens*. Again you need only remember the initials).

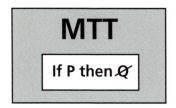

RULE 3. DENYING THE CONSEQUENT (MTT)

GIVEN two statements *If P then* Q and *Not* Q, we may conclude *Not P*.

The Billy and Amanda argument is valid by MTT.

If Billy had come to play, Amanda would have bitten him
Amanda didn't bite Billy

Billy didn't come to play.

1 What consequent is denied in that argument, and which part of the argument denies it?

2 The three arguments below use MTT. What are each argument's premises, and what is its conclusion? (In I and III, some of the argument is unspoken: spell it out.)

I

'If he's telling the truth, I'm a Dutchman.'

II

'Look, I'm not tired of life yet, and if I agreed to ride in that car of yours I'd have to be. So no, thanks!'

III

'He'd be here by now if he had caught the 3:10 train. He must have missed it.'

3 Are these argument-forms valid by MTT? If not, why not? If so, what do we substitute for P and Q in each case?

(i)	(ii)	(iii)
If S then R	If R then S	R or S
Not T	Not R	Not R
If R then T	———	———
———	Not S	Not S.
Not S		

4 Which of these is NOT valid by MTT? If it is not, explain why not.

I. All witches have cats   II. If you were a fish, you'd have feathers
   My Granny is a witch   You have no feathers
   ———   ———
   My Granny has a cat.   You're no fish.

III. If you're a frog you're not a sheep
    You are not a sheep
    ———
    You're a frog.

5 In any that are, what do we substitute for P and Q?
6 Show by truth-table ('fell swoop' or 'full sweep') that MTT is a
   valid rule.

Wall graffitto (Glasgow University, c. 1988)

A very obvious rule

When writing proofs, it is sometimes necessary to have rules that
state things so obvious we usually do not notice them. Look at this
argument-form, for example:

If S then not R
R

—————

Not S.

7 Is it valid by MTT?

If you got 7 right, you'll realise that before we can conclude *not S*,
we must show that R entails *not not R*.

8 What is the relation between R and *not not R*?

And this gives us our next rule.

RULE 4.   DOUBLE NEGATION (DN)

GIVEN *not not* P, we may conclude P, and vice versa.

Note the vice versa. *Not not P* does not merely entail *P*, it is entailed by it as well. It follows that if we want to show this rule's validity by a truth-table, our validity formula cannot be a conditional, which only expresses entailment. In this case we need the biconditional.

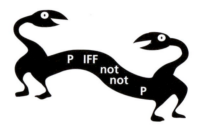

9   Use a 'full sweep' truth-table to show that DN is a valid rule.

10 Two of these are valid by rules you've had. Which are they, what rules do they use, and what is wrong with the remaining one?

(i)	(ii)	(iii)
If R then not Q	P or Q or R	If not P then not Q
Q	Not R	Not P
———————	—————	—————
Not R	P or Q	Not Q.

11 Here is a proof of (i) with the rules left out. Write in the correct rule for each line.

1	If R then not Q	PREMISE
2	Q	PREMISE
3	Not not Q	2 *rule?*

| 4 | Not R | 1, 3 *rule?* |

12 Write either a proof of (ii) or a proof of (iii).

Rules of inference (4)

Here are two more obvious rules, so obvious that normally we are not aware of using them. But they are still rules. We often need them in a formal proof. They spell out what we unknowingly take for granted: the kind of detail you must specify, for example, if you want to argue with a computer. And once we have spelled them out we can see that they are valid, which is not always true of unconscious reasoning.

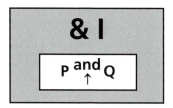

RULE 5. 'AND' INTRODUCTION (&I)

GIVEN P and Q, we may conclude P *and* Q.

Since 'AND' does not specify any order for its conjuncts, we need not spell out in our rule that we may conclude Q *and* P as well: of course we may.

1   Show by truth-table that &I is a valid rule.

'AND' INTRODUCTION (&I) says that if P is true, and Q is true, the conjunction *P and Q* is true. The next rule turns this round and says that if a conjunction is true, we know that any one conjunct is.

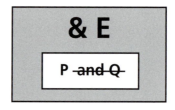

RULE 6.   'AND' ELIMINATION (&E)

GIVEN *P and Q*, we may conclude P.

We need not spell out that given *P and Q*, we may also conclude Q.

2   Use the term 'substitution instance' to explain why.

3   Show by truth-table that &E is a valid rule.

There will be more rules later. Meanwhile, here is some more practice in the rules you have had so far. To remind you, they are:

RULES 1– 6

1	ELIMINATION (ELIM):	GIVEN *P or Q* and *Not P*, we may conclude Q.
2	AFFIRMING THE ANTECEDENT (MPP):	GIVEN *If P then Q* and *P*, we may conclude Q.
3	DENYING THE CONSEQUENT (MTT):	GIVEN *If P then Q* and *Not Q*, we may conclude *Not P*.
4	DOUBLE NEGATION (DN):	GIVEN *Not not P*, we may conclude P, and vice versa.
5	'AND' INTRODUCTION (&I):	GIVEN P and Q, we may conclude *P and Q*.
6	'AND' ELIMINATION (&E):	GIVEN *P and Q*, we may conclude P.

('*P or Q*' is short for 'a statement of form *P or Q*' (etc); and any statement whose form is a substitution instance of *P or Q* is a statement of form *P or Q*.)

A proof in words

Proofs may be used on argument-forms as above, but also (remember) on the arguments themselves. You had a simple example in Chapter 38. Here is a slightly more complicated one. With the rules that you have had so far, and these premises:

> If your cat bites my cat, I'll put a spell on you
> If you cross my palm with silver, you'll win a prize at the flower show
> If I put a spell on you, your roses will die or your hens will stop laying
> If your roses die you won't win a prize at the flower show
> My cat chases yours and your cat bites my cat
> You cross my palm with silver

you can prove   YOUR ROSES WON'T DIE BUT YOUR HENS WILL STOP LAYING.

Here is the proof, but as before I have left out the rules.

4–12 Add them. (I have given you an example at the end, to start you off.)

1	If your cat bites my cat, I'll put a spell on you	PREMISE
2	If I put a spell on you, your roses will die or your hens will stop laying	PREMISE
3	If your roses die you won't win a prize at the flower show	PREMISE
4	If you cross my palm with silver, you'll win a prize at the flower show	PREMISE
5	My cat chases yours and your cat bites my cat	PREMISE
6	You cross my palm with silver	PREMISE
7	Your cat bites my cat	5 *rule?*
8	I'll put a spell on you	1,7 *rule?*
9	Your roses will die or your hens will stop laying	2,8 *rule?*
10	You'll win a prize	4,6 *rule?*
11	It's false that you won't win a prize	10 *rule?*
12	Your roses won't die	3,10 *rule?*
13	Your hens will stop laying	9,12 *rule?*

14	Your roses won't die but your hens will stop laying.	12,13 *rule?*

Here is a sample step:

Line 8 is derived from lines 1 and 7:

> 1 If your cat bites my cat, I'll put a spell on you
> 7 Your cat bites my cat
>
> ───────────────────────────────
>
> 8 I'll put a spell on you.

This has the form

If P then Q   **P: Your cat bites my cat**
P   **Q: I'll put a spell on you.**

─────────

Q

The rule that makes this step valid is therefore

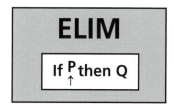

and the relevant line in the proof should read

8   I'll put a spell on you   1, 7 MPP.

How to analyse an argument step by step

The argument that we have just proved was already partly analysed. I had sorted out the premises and conclusion for you; and in writing the proof I supplied each step, including some that a normal human reasoner (unlike a computer) would not bother to spell out.

This means that it was not very like the arguments we usually meet. My next example is more realistic. The underlying thought is both valid and rather a simple piece of reasoning, easily proved; but it needs a good deal of untangling before we can start.

Sherlock Holmes instructs Watson

'How often have I said to you that *when you have eliminated the impossible, whatever remains, however improbable, must be the truth?* We know that he did not come through the door, the window, or the chimney. We also know that he could not have been concealed in the room, as there is no concealment possible. Whence, then, did he come?'
'He came through the hole in the roof?' I cried.
'Of course he did.'

(A. Conan Doyle, *The Sign of Four*)

In analysing an argument, it helps to start by identifying what the reasoning aims to prove.

1   Give Holmes's and Watson's (jointly reached) conclusion.

'How often have I said to you that...' is not part of Holmes' argument. It is there simply to underline the importance of his remark: 'When you have eliminated the impossible, whatever remains, however improbable, must be the truth'. If we substitute 'false' for 'impossible' this is equivalent to one of our rules of inference.

2   Which one?

That being so, this remark too is not a part of the argument. It describes the pattern of reasoning on which the argument depends.

Holmes's second sentence begins 'We know that', and again these words are not part of the argument: they are there in order to introduce certain things that 'we know' as a PREMISE.

3   What is the premise?

Holmes's third sentence:

> 'We know that he could not have been concealed in the room, as there is no concealment possible'

contains a complete subsidiary argument. This argument is valid, but not in statement logic. Its form is

P is not possible

Not P.

(Arguments whose validity depends on terms like 'possible' and 'necessary' are said to use *modal logic*.)

4   What is P?

Holmes takes the conclusion *not P* as a further premise in his main argument (again introducing it with 'We know'). So, for his main argument, he states two premises:

(1) The answer to question 3;
(2) the conclusion to his subsidiary argument.

If these were Holmes's (and Watson's) *only* premises, they would not support the final conclusion (your answer to question 1, if you got it right). In theory (1) and (2) could be true and this conclusion false – if the villain was never there at all, for example. But Holmes's first sentence suggests that he assumes a further premise which he does not state, no doubt because in the circumstances it seems obvious. Once we state that, the argument is valid.

5   What is this implicit premise?

Now we can try a proof. For simplicity, I shall use these letters to represent the simple statements:

D: He came through the door, the window or
    the chimney
R: He was concealed in the room
H: He came through the hole in the roof.

Note that these letters are abbreviations, not variables: D for the door/window/chimney statement, R for the room statement, and so on. Every step in the argument either is one of these statements, or it is a complex statement made out of one or more of them, plus one or more logical constants.

6   Explain the difference between using a letter as an *abbreviation* of this sort, and using one as a *variable* in an argument-form.

Using these abbreviations, how would you write

7   The argument's conclusion (= the answer to question 1)?
8   The first premise (= the answer to question 3)?

9   The second premise (= the answer to Holmes' subsidiary argument)?

10 The unstated premise (= the answer to question 5)?

When you formulate these, use brackets as you would in dealing with variables. If there are several forms that you might choose, pick one that will allow you to use your rule/s of inference correctly.
    The proof starts like this.

1.	*The answer to question 8*	PREMISE
2.	*The answer to question 9*	PREMISE
3.	*The answer to question 10*	PREMISE

To finish it, you need two more steps. The second of these is the answer to question 7. Both steps are reached by using the same rule (the one suggested by Holmes).

11–12 Finish the proof. (Here again are the rules, to remind you.)

RULES 1– 6

1	ELIMINATION (ELIM):	GIVEN *P or Q* and *Not P*, we may conclude Q.
2	AFFIRMING THE ANTECEDENT (MPP):	GIVEN *If P then Q* and *P*, we may conclude Q.
3	DENYING THE CONSEQUENT (MTT):	GIVEN *If P then Q* and *Not Q*, we may conclude *Not P*.
4	DOUBLE NEGATION (DN):	GIVEN *Not not P*, we may conclude P, and vice versa.
5	'AND' INTRODUCTION (&I):	GIVEN *P and Q*, we may conclude *P and Q*.
6	'AND' ELIMINATION (&E):	GIVEN *P and Q*, we may conclude P.

('*P or Q*' is short for 'a statement of form *P or Q*' (etc); and any statement whose form is a substitution instance of *P or Q* is a statement of form *P or Q*.)

Rules of inference (5)

You may recognise our next two rules: the Fox uses the first one several times, and his next-to-last step uses a telescoped version of the second.

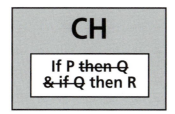

RULE 7. CHAIN RULE (CH)

> **GIVEN *If P then Q* and *If Q then R*, we may conclude *If P then R*.**

1   Show by truth-table ('fell swoop' method) that this is valid.

In Chapter 38 I gave you a proof of the Fang argument:

If Fang is a dog, he is a mammal
If he is a mammal, he is a vertebrate
If he is a vertebrate, he is an animal
Fang is a dog

Fang is an animal.

It used MPP (three times). But you could also use CH twice and MPP once.

2 Do it that way.
3 Which of these forms is valid by CH alone, or by CH plus another rule that you've had so far? (See the list at the end of Chapter 41.) In each case, say what formulae you would substitute for the chain rule's P, Q and R.

(i)	(ii)	(iii)
If P then Q	If (R or S) then P	If Q then (S or T)
If Q then R	Not P	If (S or T) then R
If R then S	——————	Q
——————	Not (R or S)	——————
S		R.

4 Write a proof of (iii).

Our next rule makes this reasoning valid:

> 'If I don't sit the exam I'll fail the course, and if I DO sit the exam I'll fail the course – so either way, I've had it!'

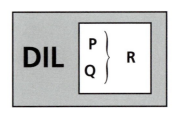

RULE 8. DILEMMA (DIL)

GIVEN *If P then R* and *If Q then R*, we may conclude *If (P or Q) then R*.

5 Test this rule's validity by truth-table.
6 What are P, Q and R in the Exam argument?

'Dilemma' is a word used in ordinary language, but typically only where R is an unpleasant consequence, as in the Exam argument. In such cases the speaker in the example is said to be impaled on

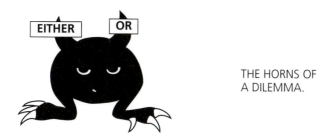

THE HORNS OF
A DILEMMA.

This is unfair to the mild-mannered DILEMMA of logic, where the consequence of *P or Q* may as easily be a nice one, as in

> 'I always get a penny when I go to see Grandpa. If I cry he gives me a penny to cheer me up, and if I don't cry he gives me a penny for being good!'

which uses MPP, CH and DIL to reach its conclusion.

7   What is the conclusion of the Grandpa Argument?
8   Here is a proof of it with bits left out. Fill them in.

When I go to see Grandpa:

1.	Either I cry or I don't cry	PREMISE
2.	If I cry I need cheering up	PREMISE
3.	If I need cheering up I get a penny from Grandpa	PREMISE
4.	*Step?*	2, 3 CH
5.	If I don't cry I'm good	PREMISE
6.	If I'm good I get a penny from Grandpa	PREMISE
7.	*Step?*	5, 6 CH
8.	*Step?*	4, 7 DIL

9.   *Step?*   1, 8 MPP.

(As usual the speaker does not put all this into words. But it is all there behind the surface, giving the structure that makes this reasoning valid.)

Still more about proofs

We can prove the Fang argument (and its related argument-form) in several ways. I have already suggested using MPP throughout, or CH twice and MPP once; we could also use CH once and MPP twice. The order of steps is also flexible: we can take them as we like, provided only that each step is either a premise, or derived from some earlier step/s by a valid rule. So far I have tended to list all the premises first, but in fact we seldom do this in a real argument. More often, the arguer first works something out from just one or two premises, then adds another premise and works out something more, and so on. For example, the Fang argument's premises are

If Fang is a dog, he is a mammal
If he is a mammal, he is a vertebrate
If he is a vertebrate, he is an animal
Fang is a dog

but instead of starting with them all, and/or in that order, we could write:

1.	Fang is a dog	PREMISE
2.	If Fang is a dog, he is a mammal	PREMISE
3.	Fang is a mammal	1,2 *rule?*
4.	If he is a mammal, he is a vertebrate	PREMISE
5.	If he is a vertebrate, he is an animal	PREMISE
6.	If he is a mammal, he is an animal	4, 5 *rule?*
7.	Fang is an animal.	3, 6 *rule?*

9   Fill in the rules.

Or we could start like this:

1. If Fang is a dog, he is a mammal   PREMISE
2. If he is a mammal, he is a vertebrate   PREMISE
1. If Fang is a dog, he is a vertebrate   1,2 CH
– etc.

Again if you remember earlier chapters, you will know that when we analyse arguments in real life, we usually have to supply implicit premises or steps. There may be several we could choose. The only thing we must not do is put words into someone's mouth which are *not* being taken for granted.

This gives us a lot of freedom. Look at Holmes and Watson again.

> 'We know that he did not come through the door, the window, or the chimney. We also know that he could not have been concealed in the room, as there is no concealment possible. Whence, then, did he come?'
>
>   'He came through the hole in the roof?' I cried.
>
>   'Of course he did.'

In the last chapter I said that the sentence beginning 'We know…' states a premise:

> 'He did not come through the door or window, or down the chimney.'

But I could say instead that it contains three premises:

> He did not come through the door
> He did not come through the window
> He did not come down the chimney

if I had any reason to list them singly. In that case of course I could not use the set of abbreviations that I first suggested:

D: He came through the door, the window or the chimney
R: He was concealed in the room
H: He came through the hole in the roof.

10 What would I need to change?

And I originally cut out the short argument, 'We also know that he could not have been concealed in the room, as there is no concealment possible', from the main argument, and assigned it the separate (modal logic) form

P is not possible
_____

Not P.

But I might instead have said that Holmes assumes the (obvious) premise, 'If no concealment is possible, then he was not concealed in the room' – as well as the premise that he states: 'There is no concealment possible'. I could then have included this argument as a step in the main one, using a slightly different proof:

1	He was concealed in the room or he came through the door, the window, the chimney, or the hole in the roof*	PREMISE
2	If there is no concealment possible, he was not concealed in the room*	PREMISE
3	There is no concealment possible**	PREMISE
4	He was not concealed in the room**	2, 3 MPP
5	He came through the door, the window, the chimney, or the hole in the roof*	1, 4 ELIM
6	He did not come through the door, the window, or the chimney**	PREMISE

_____

7	He came through the hole in the roof**	5, 6 ELIM.

*Unspoken but assumed.   **Spoken.

If I want to use letters for simple statements, I can keep my original D, R and H; but I need one more letter to cope with my new premise. Make it P.

11 What statement is P?

12 Write the proof given above, replacing statements by the letters I have just suggested.

(Since you are using letters, be sure to include brackets where they are needed. Whenever you could bracket in several ways, choose whichever allows you to apply the rules in the way I have given.)

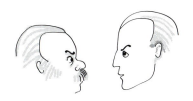

More about equivalence rules

Rules of this kind can be misused in circular arguments, which prove nothing. You should recognise our next one. I used it in Chapter 4, when I introduced the argument:

> 'Women who get raped ask for it.'
> 'What do you mean?'
> 'Well if they didn't they wouldn't get raped, would they?'.

I pointed out that this has the logical form

If not Q then not P

If P then Q

and is VALID, but only because it is circular: a premise and conclusion of this form state exactly the same thing in different ways.

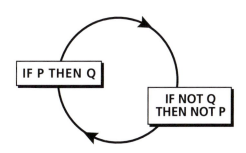

Therefore if the conclusion needs to be proved, so – for identical reasons – does the premise.

This is true wherever we have an equivalence rule. In DN for example we can conclude P from *not Not P* and vice versa, just because they say the same thing in different ways. And just as the Rape argument is circular, so is any DN argument with the form

Not not P	or	**P**
———————		———————
P		**Not not P.**

Note that the conclusion is not *identical* to the premise in these forms. If it were, such circular arguments would be less persuasive than – sometimes – they are. That is why I defined a circular argument in Chapter 4 as one where *we cannot know that one or more of the premises is true, unless we already know that the conclusion is.* This covers both identity and equivalence.

Circular arguments are valid but useless. But we have already seen in the case of DN that saying the same thing in another way can be useful within a longer proof. For example if I have two premises

> 1. P
> 2. If Q then not P

I cannot directly conclude *not Q* from them by MTT, though it is obvious that (informally) *not Q* follows. But if I substitute *not not P* for P, I can.

Our next rule is useful in much the same way as DN.

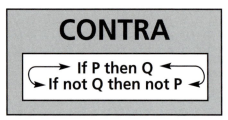

RULE 9. CONTRAPOSITION (CONTRA)

> **GIVEN *If P then Q*, we may conclude *If not Q then not P*, and vice versa.**

1 Explain why this argument-form is a substitution instance of CONTRA:

If not P then not Q
_____

If Q then P.

2 Show by truth-table that CONTRA is valid. (Remember that this is an equivalence rule, not just a rule of one-way entailment. Construct your validity-formula as you did for DN.)

3 Which of these is valid by CONTRA, or by CONTRA plus another rule? (Wherever CONTRA is used, say what replaces P and Q in the rule.)

(i)
If (P or Q) then P
Not P
_____
Not (P or Q)

(ii)
If R then (S and T)
_____
If (S and T) then R

(iii)
If P then (Q or R)
Not P
_____
Not (Q or R)

4 One of them is also valid without CONTRA, by a different rule. Write a proof of each version.

Now another equivalence rule. You may remember this:

(a) They can't climb trees or jump this high.

(b) Eventually they will get tired or bored.

5   Give the most detailed form of (a) in statement logic. Say what replaces each variable.

6   At least one of these is equivalent to the negation of (a). Which?

   (i) They can climb trees or jump this high.
   (ii) They can climb trees and they can jump this high.
   (iii)It's false that they can't climb trees or jump this high.

If you got the answer right, you have an intuitive understanding of our next rule.

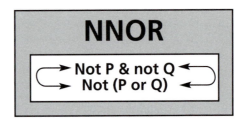

RULE 10. NEITHER/NOR RULE (NNOR)

GIVEN *Not P and not Q*, we may conclude *Not (P or Q)*, and vice versa.

7   Show by truth-table that NNOR is a valid rule.

It is clear enough, when you think about it, that the two forms in NNOR are equivalent. 'I didn't see hide nor hair of him' = 'I didn't see hide of him AND I didn't see hair of him'; and 'You can't get it for love nor money' = 'You can't get it for love, AND you can't get it for money'. But beginners in logic often think that *not P and not Q* should be equivalent to *not (P AND Q)* rather than *not (P OR Q)*.

The remedy (as always) is to study examples until you see the light.

8   Show by truth-table that *Not (P and Q)* is NOT equivalent to *not P and not Q*.

9   Find an example to show this: that is, find a pair of statements P and Q, such that *not (P and Q)* is TRUE when *Not P and not Q* is FALSE, or vice versa.

Another mistake beginners often make is to expect *Not (P or Q)* to be equivalent to *not P or not Q*.

10   Show by truth-table that *Not (P or Q)* is NOT equivalent to *not P or not Q*.

11   Find an example to show this: a pair of statements P and Q, such that *not (P or Q)* is TRUE when *not P or not Q* is FALSE, or vice versa.

The negation of (b) is, 'It is not the case that eventually they will get tired or bored'.

12   If P is 'Eventually they will get tired', and Q is 'Eventually they will get bored', what is the logical form of this statement? Could we use NNOR on it?

More about proofs

You now have ten rules of inference. (I shall give you fifteen altogether.) Before we go on, here are some general remarks on how to use them.

RULES 1–10

1	ELIMINATION (ELIM)	GIVEN *P or Q* and *Not P*, we may conclude Q.
2	AFFIRMING THE ANTECEDENT (MPP)	GIVEN *If P then Q* and *P*, we may conclude Q.
3	DENYING THE CONSEQUENT (MTT)	GIVEN *If P then Q* and *Not Q*, we may conclude *Not P*.
4	DOUBLE NEGATION (DN)	GIVEN *Not not P*, we may conclude *P*, and *vice versa*.
5	'AND' INTRODUCTION (&I)	GIVEN *P* and *Q*, we may conclude *P and Q*.
6	'AND' ELIMINATION (&E)	GIVEN *P and Q*, we may conclude *P*.
7	CHAIN RULE (CH)	GIVEN *If P then Q* and *If Q then R*, we may conclude *If P then R*.
8	DILEMMA (DIL)	GIVEN *If P then R* and *If Q then R*, we may conclude *If (P or Q) then R*.
9	CONTRAPOSITION (CONTRA)	GIVEN *If P then Q*, we may conclude *If not Q then not P*, and vice versa.
10	NEITHER/NOR RULE (NNOR)	GIVEN *Not P and not Q*, we may conclude *Not (P or Q)*, and vice versa.

('*P or Q*' is short for 'a statement of form *P or Q*' (etc.); and any statement whose form is a substitution instance of *P or Q* is a statement of form *P or Q*.)

Proof strategy

When you start to use proofs, it often happens that you can follow a proof when someone else does it, but if asked to prove something by yourself, you cannot. Eventually you will develop an eye for which steps and rules will get you from a set of premises to a given conclusion; but until you do, a useful piece of advice is:

WORK FROM BOTH ENDS
and
START BACKWARDS.

First, identify your conclusion.

Sometimes it will be specified: 'Given the following premises, prove that P'. But if you are analysing a passage in ordinary language, you may need to start by deciding what exactly the speaker aims to prove. Or you might want to show which of several conclusions follow from your premises: see the Agent argument below. In that case, you will need to think about each possible conclusion in turn, until you find one you can prove. Once you have found it, you can rule out any other that is incompatible.

When you have identified a conclusion, look at its logical form and ask 'What rule might give me this, as my final step?' That will show you some possible final steps: DIL, for example, gives conclusions with the logical form *if (P or Q) then R*, CH gives conclusions whose form is *if P then R* – and so on.

Next, identify all your premise/s, and consider their logical form. Will any one or two of them, plus a rule, give you your conclusion in a single step? If not, could you get it if you worked out just one more step? ('I've got *if R then P* as a premise, so I could get P if I had R', and so on.)

If no path from premises to conclusion seems clear, do your premises lead anywhere that *might* be useful? For example if one of them has the form *if P then Q*, and Q might help, look for P; or else for something that would give you P, like *P or R* plus *not R*…Sooner or later, light will dawn.

Here is an example to work through, with a heavy hint at every stage.

Who is the agent?

Suppose we have 1–4 as premises. Can we validly discover who (apart from Dimitri) is a secret agent?

1. Either Hank is a secret agent, or Lily is.
2. If Lily is a secret agent, Hank knows it.
3. If either Dimitri knows it or Hank knows it, the CIA know it.
4. The CIA don't know it.

There are four possibilities:

        (a) Hank is an agent and Lily is not
        (b) Lily is an agent and Hank is not
        (c) They both are
        (d) Neither is.

But it is clear from Premise 1 that at least one of them must be, so we can disregard (d).

It is possible that our four premises will not allow us to prove (a), (b) or (c).

1   Is it also possible that they might allow us to prove more than one of these?

Who is the agent?

2   (a), (b) and (c) are all conjunctions. Which of our ten rules might we therefore use to get one of them, as our final step?
3   Could we get to (a), (b) or (c) in a single step, given these premises? If so, how?
4   Could we conclude (a), (b) or (c) from one of our premises, plus *one* further statement? If so, which conclusion can we get, and what further statement do we need? (Your answer should be 'Yes' for Premise 1.)

Now look at our premises: do any suggest a path we might take to get that extra statement? (Premise 4 is nice and short: start with that.)

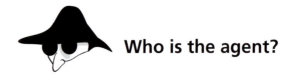 **Who is the agent?**

5   Can we combine Premise 4 with any other, to get a statement that might be useful? If so, which? (We can. Study the list of rules for one whose premises have the right form.)
6   What can we do with the step we have just reached?
    (Again, compare the premises given in our rules with this step's logical form. One of the equivalence rules looks promising.)

If you got question 6 right, you are now just two steps away from a conclusion. (Look back at your answer to question 4. If you got it right, the next step is obvious.)

7   Can we find a rule that leads from question 6's answer, to a statement of who is NOT an agent?
    (Yes, we can.)

And now we know THAT –

8   What two final steps give us the answer to –

Who is the agent?

Write out the whole proof in words, from start to finish.

As you get used to formulae, you will find it easier to write proofs using letters for the simple statements, and giving each step the form of a wff. This makes it easier to see the proof's logical form. So, for practice:

9 Using the letters below (and no others), give the premises and the conclusion of the argument you have just proved.

    H: Hank is a secret agent
    L: Lily is a secret agent
    K: Hank knows that Lily is a secret agent
    D: Dimitri knows that Lily is a secret agent
    C: The CIA know that Lily is a secret agent.

You might have proved it differently, however.

 ## *Another way*

Suppose that instead of suggesting that you start with Premise 4, I hinted that you might transform Premise 3 into something that will help.

10 How, and by which rule?
    ('Transform' suggests an equivalence rule.)

Assuming you got that right:

11 What useful step can we get from your answer to 10, plus another premise? (We are now back on the same path as before, but it took one step longer.)

12 Write out this new proof from start to finish, but use letters to stand for simple statements, and give each step the form of a wff. (Use the letters given above, and no others.)

Rules of inference (7)

Our next rule is another equivalence rule: the second De Morgan's rule (the first was NNOR). Like NNOR, it spells out some useful things about 'not', 'and' and 'or'.

1   What is this statement's most detailed form (in statement logic)?

'The spreckle's not twigging or the crack-shot's not delivering enough power – possibly both.'

2   What is the one state of affairs that it says is NOT the case?
3   Find a statement of form *not P or not Q* that says the same as 'You haven't got chickenpox AND measles!'.
4   Which three states of affairs could make this false?

'She's an angel –   and she loves me!'

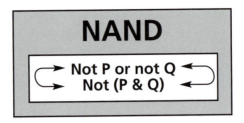

If you got these right, you understand the principle of our next rule.

RULE 11. NOT-BOTH RULE (NAND)

> **GIVEN *not P or not Q*, we may conclude *Not (P and Q)*, and vice versa.**

5   Show by truth-table that NAND is a valid rule.

Like NNOR, NAND is clear enough when you think about it, using examples like those I've just given. But again beginners in logic sometimes find it tricky.

6   Which of these is valid by NAND, or by NAND plus another rule? (Wherever NAND is used, say what replaces NAND's P and Q.)

(i)	(ii)	(iii)
Not (Q and R)	Not (R or Q)	If Q then (R and S)
R	———————	Not R or not S
———————	Not Q	———————
Not Q		Not Q

7   Write a proof of one that uses NAND.

You know the equivalence stated in our next rule. You've shown it by truth-table, in Chapter 28 (question 11). We need the rule because the others in our system – as in other systems that have them – use only the logical constants 'and', 'or', 'if-then' and 'not'.

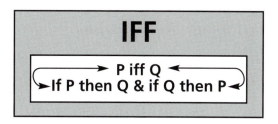

RULE 12: BICONDITIONAL RULE (IFF)

GIVEN *P Iff Q,* we may conclude *If P then Q* and *If Q then P,* and vice versa.

Since the conjuncts of *if P then Q and if Q then P* may be taken in either order, we need not spell out that we may also conclude *if Q then P and if P then Q:* of course we may.

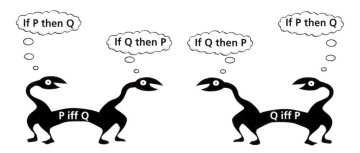

8–12 Here is a proof that Ginger the cat is not of Irish descent, since he can't join the Red-Headed League (see Chapters 28 and 29). Fill in the missing bits.

1	Ginger can join the Red-headed League if and only if he has red hair and is of Irish descent	PREMISE
2	*Step?*	1, IFF
3	*Step?*	2, &E
4	Ginger can't join the Red-headed League	PREMISE
5	It's false that he has red hair and is of Irish descent.	3, 4 MTT
6	*Step?*	5 NAND
7	Ginger has red hair	PREMISE
8	It's false that Ginger lacks red hair	*7 Rule?*

9	Ginger is not of Irish descent.	*Lines?* ELIM.

Proof strategy again

I have now given you these rules.

RULES 1– 12

1	ELIMINATION (ELIM):	GIVEN P *or* Q and *not* P, we may conclude Q.
2	AFFIRMING THE ANTECEDENT (MPP):	GIVEN *if P then* Q and P, we may conclude Q.
3	DENYING THE CONSEQUENT (MTT):	GIVEN if P then Q and *not* Q, we may conclude *not* P.
4	DOUBLE NEGATION (DN):	GIVEN *not not* P, we may conclude P, and vice versa.
5	'AND' INTRODUCTION (&I):	GIVEN P *and* Q, we may conclude P *and* Q.
6	'AND' ELIMINATION (&E):	GIVEN P *and* Q, we may conclude P.
7	CHAIN RULE (CH):	GIVEN *if P then* Q and *if Q then* R, we may conclude *if P then* R.
8	DILEMMA (DIL):	GIVEN *if P then* R and *if Q then* R, we may conclude if (P *or* Q) *then* R.
9	CONTRAPOSITION (CONTRA):	GIVEN *if P then* Q, we may conclude *if not Q then not* P, and vice versa.
10	NEITHER/NOR RULE (NNOR):	GIVEN *not* P *and not* Q, we may conclude *not (P or* Q), and vice versa.
11	NOT-BOTH RULE (NAND):	GIVEN *not* P *or not* Q, we may conclude *not (P and* Q), and vice versa.
12	BICONDITIONAL RULE (IFF):	GIVEN P *iff* Q, we may conclude *if P then* Q and *if Q then* P, and vice versa.

('P or Q' is short for 'a statement of form P or Q' (etc.); and any statement whose form is a substitution instance of P or Q is a statement of form P or Q.)

Before I add the final three, here is some more practice in what you already have.

Suppose you are given three premises, whose forms are

If (T or S) then not Q
If not Q then R
If Q then R.

1   What if anything can you prove from these, singly or together, and rules 1–2?

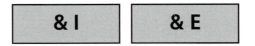

2   What if anything can you prove from them, singly or together, and rules 3–4?

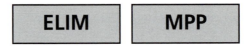

3   What if anything can you prove from them, singly or together, and rules 5–6?

4   What if anything can you prove from them, singly or together, and rules 7–8?

5   What if anything can you prove from them, singly or together, and rules 9–10?

6   What if anything can you prove from them, singly or together, and rules 11–12?

7   Which two rules would you need to prove *if ((T or S) or Q) then R* from these premises? Write the proof.

WORK FROM BOTH
ENDS
and
START BACKWARDS.

Our original three formulae were

If (T or S) then not Q
If not Q then R
If Q then R.

8   Can you prove *not Q* from these premises? If so, how? If not, why not?

9   Which of the formulae below, added to those above, would give you R?

T or S
Not Q
(T or S) or Q
Q.

We can assume premises like these only if they are given: they are contingent, and so could be false. On the other hand if we could find a *necessarily true* formula that would also allow us to conclude R, given our original three premises, we would always be justified in assuming it.

10 Find a necessarily true formula that would do, and write the proof. (*Hint*: look at the answer to question 4.)

Finally, suppose that instead of the premises given above, you have just this one:

(If P then (not R or not Q)) and P.

and you want to prove *not R or not Q*.

11 Can it be done? (*Hint*: This is a conjunction. What rule/s apply to a premise of that form?)
12 Now construct a formula from which you could prove *Not R or not Q* in just *one* step, using one of our rules. (The form of *Not R or not Q* should make the answer obvious.)

Where rules come from

There is no fixed set of rules that every statement-logic system must have, though some (like MPP) seem indispensable. As always, the idea is to balance convenience against economy. Convenience depends on what kind of argument you will be wanting to analyse. Some systems contain the following rule, for example:

GIVEN P, we may conclude *P or Q*.

1   Show by truth-table that this is valid.

But although it can help in a formal proof, this rule is not much used in day-to-day argument. So I left it out. On the other hand, I have included rules that we do not strictly need, when they follow lines of thought we often use. For instance, we can prove this argument-form by MTT:

If P then Q
Not Q

Not P.

But we could also use CONTRA + MPP:

1	If P then Q	PREMISE
2	Not Q	PREMISE
3	If not Q then not P	1 CONTRA

| 4 | Not P | 2,3 MPP. |

So in theory, we do not need MTT if we have the other rules. But MTT is not only quicker, it reflects a very common way of thinking: the argument based on a counterfactual (what is not the case; what did not happen):

If she had caught that train, she'd be here by now...

If he's telling the truth, I'm a Dutchman...

If she loves me she would have written...

When we want to analyse real arguments step by step, in a form as close as possible to the arguer's thought, MTT is therefore useful.

My aim is to help you assess ordinary reasoning, not to study any one system. So don't feel tied to my set of rules, unless you are answering questions in this book which are based on them. If you can show by truth-table that an inference is valid, and you need it (or a substitution instance of it) for a proof, make it a rule if it suits you: design your own system. Just make *sure* that it's valid. And make every rule as simple as possible. Your test by truth-table will then be no more laborious than necessary; and your rule will have more substitution instances, so it will apply more widely.

For example, suppose you recognise intuitively that this argument-form is valid:

(P or Q) and (Q or S)

If (P or Q) then (Q or S).

You would like to include it in a proof; but you do not see how to do so by any rule/s your system allows.

2 Which of these should you test by truth-table, to justify a rule that will help you?

(i)	(ii)	(iii)
(P or Q) and (Q or S)	P and (Q or S)	P and Q
If (P and Q) then (Q or S)	If P then (Q or S)	If P then Q

3 Test it, and explain why this shows it to be a valid rule.
4 Would this be a possible rule? Why, or why not?

 **GIVEN *P or Q*, we may conclude P.**

Our next rule seems so obvious that you may wonder why we need it. We assume it without thinking – but for that very reason, it's worth spelling out that we can justify it.

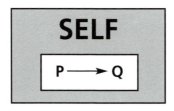

RULE 13. SELF-ENTAILMENT (SELF)

GIVEN P, we may conclude P.

In other words, every statement entails itself.

5 Show by truth-table that SELF is a valid rule.

A different kind of rule

So far my rules have referred simply to what we may conclude when we are given certain individual statements – sometimes one, as in &E ('GIVEN *P and Q*, we may conclude…'), sometimes a pair, as in MPP ('GIVEN *if P then Q* and *P*, we may conclude…'). My two final rules are different. They refer to whole arguments, and so may need some introduction. The first is RAA, short for REDUCTIO AD ABSURDUM ('reaching an absurd conclusion').

The principle behind RAA is: if I make an assumption and what follows from it (validly) is absurd, my assumption must be wrong. 'Absurd' here means 'necessarily false'.

6   (*Revision*) If a valid argument has a false conclusion, what do we know about its premise/s?

One statement that has to be false is a self-contradiction, whose form is *R and not R*. (Or *P and not P*; but when I give you the rule I shall need the letter P for something else.)

7   (*Revision*) Show by truth-table that a statement of this form is never true.

It is important to remember the difference between surface and logical form here. A sentence can look like *R and not R* and still make a true statement:

'Do you agree with the saying "My enemy's enemy is my friend"?'
'Well, I do and I don't'

– but only because looks can mislead. Here for example, 'I don't' does not in fact negate what 'I do' states. 'I do and I don't' means 'I agree in some respects, but not in others'. Its real form is not *R and not R*.

8   What is its form? It has three in statement logic, from the simplest to the most complex: give them all.

A valid argument cannot have a false conclusion and true premises. So if we have a set of premises, and from them we VALIDLY derive a conclusion whose real form is *R and not R*, there is no question about it:

This gives us a possible rule:

GIVEN a set of premises entailing *R and not R*, we may conclude that at least one premise is false.

But that is not very precise. Consider these premises:

1. Everything has a cause
2. Causes can't go back forever
3. If causes can't go back forever, there was a First Cause
4. If there was a First Cause, not everything has a cause.

9 Use them to prove a statement whose form is *R and not R*. Make your R 'Everything has a cause'.

Since we can prove a contradiction from them, our 'rule' tells us that 1, 2, 3, 4, or more than one of them, is false; but it cannot tell us which. A more useful rule applies when we have reason to accept all our premises as true *except one*, which we want to test. We can test it by assuming it not as something given, but hypothetically. An hypothesis is something we only accept on probation, 'for the sake of argument'.

('AN hypothesis' is not a misprint, although the 'h' is spoken, as in 'horse'. It's traditional. 'A hypothesis' is now used too; but I shall write 'an' to get you used to it. The plural of 'hypothesis' is 'hypotheSES'.)

If we can prove a self-contradiction from premises that we know are true *and* our hypothesis, we know that

And that gives us our rule.

RULE 14. REDUCTIO AD ABSURDUM (RAA)

GIVEN a set of premises whose conjunction is P: if adding a further premise Q allows us to derive *R and not R*, we may conclude *Not Q*.

Suppose for example that we accept the three premises

1. Everything has a cause
3. If causes can't go back forever, there was a First Cause
4. If there was a First Cause, not everything has a cause

but want to test the truth of:
2. Causes can't go back forever.

We can prove that 2 is false by RAA:

1.	Everything has a cause	PREMISE
2.	*Causes can't go back forever*	*PREMISE**
3.	If causes can't go back forever, there was a First Cause	PREMISE
4.	If there was a First Cause, not everything has a cause	PREMISE
5.	If causes can't go back forever, not everything has a cause	3,4 CH
6.	Not everything has a cause	2, 5 MPP
7.	Everything has a cause and not everything has a cause	1, 6 &I

8.	IT IS NOT THE CASE THAT causes can't go back forever	2, 7 RAA.

(1–7 are proof A in my answer to question 9; B would also do.)

When we have reached the conclusion 'IT IS NOT THE CASE THAT causes can't go back forever', we are no longer assuming premise 2: that hypothesis now takes its proper place as a statement which must be FALSE, given premises 1, 3 and 4.

Now suppose that we accept premises 2, 3 and 4, but want to test 1: 'Everything has a cause'. Here is a proof by RAA that 1 is false. (For variety I have used a different contradiction.) I have left some bits out.

10   Fill them in.

1.	*Everything has a cause*	*PREMISE**
2.	Causes can't go back forever	PREMISE
3.	If causes can't go back forever, there was a First Cause	PREMISE
4.	If there was a First Cause, not everything has a cause	PREMISE
5.	There was a First Cause	*2, 3 rule?*
6.	It's false that not everything has a cause	*line/s? DN*
7.	There was no First Cause	*4, 6 rule?*
8.	There was a First Cause and there was no First Cause	*line/s? rule?*

9.	IT IS NOT THE CASE THAT everything has a cause	1, 8 RAA.

*Hypothesis.

In a proof, RAA shows that an assumption is false.

11 Could you also use it to show that a statement is true? How, or why not?

One final point: the set of premises (P) to which RAA refers may contain any number, including 0. In that case we are only justified in concluding *Not Q* if Q is absurd in itself.

12 Prove by RAA that the statement 'I am a poached egg and I am not a poached egg' is false. (Say which statements replace RAAs P, Q and R.)

More about RAA

We can test RAA by truth-table; but since RAA works differently from rules 1–13, we get its validity-formula in a different way. Still, we can see at once that its consequent must be *not* Q.

1   Why?

The antecedent of our validity-formula should sum up the conditions in which RAA says we may validly conclude this.

RULE 14. REDUCTIO AD ABSURDUM (RAA)

> **GIVEN a set of premises whose conjunction is P: if adding a further premise Q allows us to derive R *and not* R, we may conclude *not* Q.**

First: RAA applies when, and only when, we derive *R and not R* as described above. So, whatever other form/s such arguments have, they will all have the form:

P
Q
_____

R and not R.

This is clearly invalid. But RAA also specifies that *R and not R* is *validly* derived. So any argument to which RAA applies must have not only this form but some valid form as well. This valid form will spell out P and/or Q in greater detail, showing that the argument cannot have true premises and a false conclusion. We can ignore any case where this is not so.

RAA also specifies that we are GIVEN the set of premises whose conjunction is P: these premises are true. So P is true: we can ignore any case where P is false.

In just these circumstances, *not* Q must follow – or RAA is not a valid rule.

The formula we should test is therefore

If (if P and Q then (R and not R)) then not Q.

But we need not consider every line of this formula's truth-table: as I have just explained, RAA's conditions apply only to certain cases. We can ignore lines 5–8 for a start.

	P	Q	R	If (if P and Q then (R and not R)) then not Q
(1)	T	T	T	
(2)	T	T	F	
(3)	T	F	T	
(4)	T	F	F	
(5)	F	T	T	
(6)	F	T	F	
(7)	F	F	T	
(8)	F	F	F	

2 Why?

3 Find two more lines that we can ignore, and explain why.

4 Fill in the truth-values for the remaining lines, and explain how they show that RAA is a valid rule.

5 Which of these is valid by RAA, alone or plus other rule/s? If it is, say what RAA's P and Q would be.

(i)	(ii)	(iii)
Not Q	P or Q	P
———————	———	———
Not (Q and P)	P and Q	P or Q.

Remember that an argument-form lists only GIVEN premises: those that entail the argument's conclusion. To find the hypothesis we are testing by RAA (if there is one), look first for a negative conclusion. RAA's conclusion *not Q* is a negation, and RAA's Q is the hypothesis being tested. But remember too that when a proof uses RAA and other rules, RAA may not always give the final step. So the argument's conclusion does not *have* to be a negation.

6 Write a proof of each valid form.

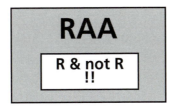

One final rule

I shall introduce this in an exercise which will also give you more practice in analysing an argument step by step.

Gussie's problem (1)

Gussie Fink-Nottle, an amateur naturalist, is too shy to propose to Madeline Bassett…

'Do you know how a male newt proposes, Bertie? He just stands in front of the female newt vibrating his tail and bending his body in a semicircle. I could do that standing on my head. No, you wouldn't find me grousing if I were a male newt.'
    'But if you were a male newt, Madeline Bassett wouldn't look at you. Not with the eye of love, I mean.'
    'She would, if she were a female newt.'
    '…Well, if she were a female newt, you wouldn't be in love with her.'
    'Yes I would, if I were a male newt.'
    A slight throbbing about the temples told me that the discussion had reached saturation point.
                    (P.G. Wodehouse, *Very Good, Jeeves*)

The story implies two things we may take as GIVEN:

(i) If Gussie loves Madeline and can propose to her, he will

and (since nothing stands in the way of Madeline accepting Gussie – she's not against marriage, or married to somebody else):

(ii) If Madeline loves Gussie
     and Gussie proposes,
     Madeline will accept.

Gussie's first speech boils down to a claim whose form is *if P then Q*.

7   Choose statements from the list below to replace P and Q, and say what this claim is.

 Gussie *can* propose to Madeline
Gussie *does* propose to Madeline
Madeline accepts Gussie
Gussie loves Madeline
Madeline loves Gussie
Gussie is a male newt
Madeline is a female newt.

8   Bertie objects, with a statement whose form is *if P then not Q*. What statements from the list replace P and Q here? (Are they the same P and Q as before?)

Gussie's reply to this has the form *if (P and Q) then R*.

9   Which statements from the list replace P, Q and R?

Bertie's next objection has the same form as his first one.

10 What are P and Q here?
11 Gussie's reply has the same form as *his* last remark. Once again, choose statements from the list to replace P, Q and R.
12 There are two pairs of incompatible statements in this conversation. Which are they?

To be be continued.

Gussie's problem (2)

'Do you know how a male newt proposes, Bertie? He just stands in front of the female newt vibrating his tail and bending his body in a semicircle. I could do that standing on my head. No, you wouldn't find me grousing if I were a male newt.'

'But if you were a male newt, Madeline Bassett wouldn't look at you. Not with the eye of love, I mean.'

'She would, if she were a female newt.'

'…Well, if she were a female newt, you wouldn't be in love with her.'

'Yes I would, if I were a male newt.'

A slight throbbing about the temples told me that the discussion had reached saturation point.

(P.G. Wodehouse, *Very Good, Jeeves*)

In the end, Bertie accepts Gussie's view of the case; and once we drop his objections, we have five statements that we can take as GIVEN, that is as premises. They are:

(i) If Gussie loves Madeline and can propose to her, he will
(ii) If Madeline loves Gussie and Gussie proposes, Madeline will accept
(iii) If Gussie were a male newt, he could propose to Madeline
(iv) If Gussie were a male newt and Madeline were a female newt, Madeline would love Gussie
(v) If Gussie were a male newt and Madeline were a female newt, Gussie would love Madeline.

Bertie and Gussie could use these to prove that Madeline will accept Gussie, IF ONLY they had one more premise, a conjunction of two simple statements in this list:

Gussie *can* propose to Madeline
Gussie *does* propose to Madeline
Madeline accepts Gussie
Gussie loves Madeline
Madeline loves Gussie
Gussie is a male newt
Madeline is a female newt.

1   What is the missing premise? Call it (vi).

Premise (vi) is not GIVEN: in Gussie's world it is false. This is Gussie's problem. But in a better world it might be true…

2–5 Assume it hypothetically, and fill in the gaps of this proof. The rules you'll need are among the first six, at the head of Chapter 38.

1.	If Gussie loves Madeline and can propose to her, he will	PREMISE (i)
2.	If Madeline loves Gussie and he proposes, Madeline will accept	PREMISE (ii)
3.	If Gussie were a male newt, he could propose to Madeline	PREMISE (iii)
4.	If Gussie were a male newt and Madeline were a female newt, Madeline would love Gussie	PREMISE (iv)
5.	If Gussie were a male newt and Madeline were a female newt, Gussie would love Madeline	PREMISE (v)
6.	*[Answer to question 1]*	*PREMISE (vi)* *
7.	*Gussie loves Madeline*	5, 6 *rule?*
8.	*Step?*	4, 6 MPP
9.	Gussie is a male newt	6 *rule?*
10.	Gussie can propose to Madeline	3, 9 *rule?*
11.	*Step?*	7, 10 &I
12.	Gussie will propose to Madeline	*lines?* MPP
13.	Madeline loves Gussie and Gussie will propose	8, 12 *rule?*

14.	Madeline will accept	*lines?* MPP.

*Hypothesis

And probably they would live happily ever after.

But in a world where we do not know that statement (vi) is true – or where we know that it is false – all that this proof can tell us is that, given what we are given, IF Premise 6 were true, then Madeline would accept Gussie.

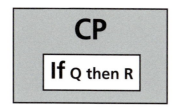

And this illustrates our final rule.

RULE 15. CONDITIONAL PREMISE (CP)

> **GIVEN a set of premises whose conjunction is P: if adding a further premise Q allows us to derive R, we may conclude *If Q then R*.**

In Gussie's world we cannot use our proof to show that Madeline will accept Gussie. A necessary premise is only hypothetical. But at least we can use our proof plus CP to get step 15 below.

13. Madeline loves Gussie and Gussie will propose	8, 12 *Rule?*
14. Madeline will accept	*Steps?* MPP

---

15. IF [*premise 6*] THEN Madeline will accept	6, 14 CP.

This conclusion no longer depends on our assuming the hypothetical Premise 6. Instead it gives that hypothesis its proper role as the antecedent of a conditional we *can* prove, given what we are given.

6 (*Revision*) We have proved that in Gussie's world, where statements (i)–(v) are true, Madeline would accept Gussie IF (vi) were true. We also know that in Gussie's world (vi) is false. Does it follow that Madeline will not accept Gussie? Use the terms 'necessary condition' and/or 'sufficient condition' to explain why, or why not.

7 How does what happens to our hypothesis here differ from what would happen to it with RAA?

We can test CP by truth-table as we tested RAA. CP says that

GIVEN a set of premises whose conjunction is P: if adding a further premise Q allows us to derive R, we may conclude *If Q then R.*

When we derive R from P plus an hypothesis Q, we have an argument with the form

$$\begin{array}{c} \mathbf{P} \\ \mathbf{Q} \\ \hline \mathbf{R.} \end{array}$$

CP applies only where this is valid: that is, some more detailed form shows that if the argument's premises are true, so is the conclusion. So CP only fits cases where the validity-formula *if P and Q then R* is TRUE. And since P is given, P is also true. In a case like this the truth of CP's conclusion *if Q then R* must follow, or CP is not a valid rule.

The validity-formula that we should test is therefore

If (if P and Q then R) then if Q then R.

Its consequent, *if Q then R*, is what CP says we may conclude; its antecedent, *if P and Q, then R* states the conditions in which we may conclude it. And so – as with RAA – we need not consider every line of this formula's truth-table: CP's conditions do not apply to them all. For a start, as with RAA, we can ignore lines (5)–(8), where P is false. When P is the conjunction of premises that we are given, we know P is true.

	P	Q	R	If (if P and Q then R) then if Q then R
(1)	T	T	T	
(2)	T	T	F	
(3)	T	F	T	
(4)	T	F	F	
(5)	F	T	T	
(6)	F	T	T	
(7)	F	F	T	
(8)	F	F	F	

8 What other line/s can we ignore, and why? For the lines that remain, supply the missing truth-values and explain why these show that CP is a valid rule.

9 CP allows us to infer a conditional statement. Does this mean that the conclusion of any argument that uses CP will be a conditional?

These argument-forms are valid by CP plus other rules. In each case CP gives the final step, so you will have no trouble deciding what hypothetical premise their proofs assume. (If you got question 9 right you will realise that this is not always the case.)

(i)	(ii)	(iii)
P or Q	P and Q	P or Q
If P then S	If P then S	If P then R
———————	———————	———————
If not S then Q	If R then S	If (if Q then R) then R.

10–12 Write a proof of each.

Proof strategy (3)

RULES (THE FULL LIST)

1 ELIM: GIVEN *P or Q* and *not P*, we may conclude Q.

2 MPP: GIVEN *if P then Q* and P, we may conclude Q.

3 MTT: GIVEN *if P then Q* and *not Q*, we may conclude *Not P*.

4 DN: GIVEN *not not P*, we may conclude P, and vice versa.

5 & I: GIVEN P *and* Q, we may conclude P *and* Q.

6 &E: GIVEN P *and* Q, we may conclude P.

7 CH: GIVEN *if P then Q* and *if Q then R*, we may conclude *if P then R.*

8 DIL: GIVEN *if P then R* and *if Q then R*, we may conclude *if (P or Q) then R.*

9 CONTRA: GIVEN *if P then Q*, we may conclude *if not Q then not P*, and vice versa.

10 NNOR: GIVEN *not P and not Q*, we may conclude *not (P or Q)*, and vice versa.

11 NAND: GIVEN *not P or not Q*, we may conclude *not (P and Q)*, and vice versa.

12 IFF: GIVEN *P iff Q*, we may conclude *if P then Q and if Q then P*, and *vice versa.*

13 SELF: GIVEN P, we may conclude P.

14 RAA: GIVEN a set of premises whose conjunction is P: if adding a further premise Q allows us to derive *R and not R*, we may conclude not Q.

15 CP: GIVEN a set of premises whose conjunction is P: if adding a further premise Q allows us to derive R, we may conclude *if Q then R.*

('P or Q' is short for 'a statement of form P or Q' (etc.); and any statement whose form is a substitution instance of P or Q is a statement of form P or Q.)

Suppose (as before) that you are given three premises, whose forms are

If (T or S) then not Q
If not Q then R
If Q then R.

1   What if anything could you prove from these, singly or together, and rule 13?

2   What if anything could you prove from them, singly or together, and rule 14?

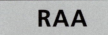

3   What if anything could you prove from them, singly or together, and rule 15?

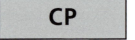

Given the answer to questions 2 and 3:

4   Would you always need &I to prove something by RAA?
5   What can be proved using CP and SELF and any single premise you like?

Suppose you want to prove R from one or more of the premises at the top of this page. You could do it by DILEMMA plus MPP, if you took the logical truth Q *or not* Q as an extra premise. It's always safe to assume a logical truth.

1. If not Q then R   PREMISE
2. If Q then R   PREMISE
3. Q or not Q   PREMISE
4. If (Q or not Q) then R   1,2 DIL

---

5. R   3,4 MPP.

But here I am asking you to keep to the three premises that I specified. You may use another premise hypothetically: that is only temporary, and your conclusion does not depend on its truth. But you must not take anything else as GIVEN, even if it is logically true.

6   (*Revision*) Why does your conclusion not depend on a premise, if you assume it hypothetically?

RAA suggests a proof strategy here.

7   What is it?

On the other hand, you could use *Q or not Q* if you proved it first. RAA will let you do that, without any premise being given at all.

8   Prove *Q or not Q* by RAA.
    (*Hint*: remember the Poached Egg argument in Chapter 47 – plus the fact that *Q or not Q* is a necessary truth.)

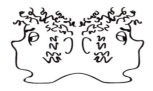

Practice with RAA

'Offend the Fatal Four and you die! To speak of roses to Giulio is to offend the Four, as is any reference at all to violets. Looking too long at Wang's moustache is to offend the Four, if you wear a moustache yourself. Wear an emerald in Lucy's presence, and you offend the Four. Mention wasps to Anastasia and you offend the Four, unless you smile as you speak.'

Each of the five sentences in this warning makes a statement with the logical form *if P then Q*.

9   Rewrite them, using only the letters below and the constants of statement logic. (You will need others besides 'if-then'.) For each, say what replaces P and Q.

    A: You mention wasps to Anastasia
    D: You die
    F: You offend the Fatal Four
    G: You speak of roses to Giulio
    L: You wear an emerald in the presence of Lucy
    M: You wear a moustache
    S: You smile as you speak
    V: You refer to violets
    W: You look too long at Wang's moustache.

Now suppose that, smiling as you speak, you mention wasps and violets to Anastasia.

10 Derive a statement from this that you can write using letters given above, plus logical constant/s.

11–12 With your answer to 10 as a premise, and others from your answer to question 9, prove by RAA that you die.

Practice with CP

At the end of Chapter 14 I promised to prove that I should use induction, for these reasons:

(a) I want to make reliable predictions and general statements.
(b) If induction is a reliable method, I can: what I have not experienced will be like what I have (if what I have experienced is a good sample). If induction is not reliable, I cannot.
(c) If I bet that induction is not reliable, I lose out either way. If I am right, there is no chance of basing predictions or general statements on experience; if I am wrong there is a chance, but I do not take it.
(d) If I bet that induction is reliable and I am *wrong*, I lose again. But this bet also gives me a chance to win, which the other does not. For if I am *right*, reliable general statements and predictions are possible, using induction.

(a) gives us the premise:

'I want to make reliable predictions and general statements'

and surely we can assume:

'If I want to do this and it requires induction, I should use induction'.

(b), (c) and (d) yield:

'If I use induction and it's reliable, I'll make reliable predictions and general statements'

'If I use it and it's not reliable, I won't make reliable predictions and general statements'

'If I don't use it, I won't make reliable predictions and general statements'.

And

'Either I use induction and it's reliable; or I use it and it's not; or I don't use it'.

is a logical truth: it covers all the possibilities.

This gives us six likely premises. In fact we need only five; but the sixth has its uses too, as you will see. I suggest that we take the five that we need in the following order. Starting with:

1. Either I use induction and it is reliable; or I use it and it is not; or I do not use it.
2. If I use it and it is not reliable, I will not make reliable predictions and general statements
3. If I do not use it, I will not make reliable predictions and general statements

we can prove (in 10 steps) that using induction is necessary if I am to make reliable predictions or general statements. Then if we add two more:

11. If I want to make reliable predictions and general statements, and this requires induction, I should use induction
12. I want to make reliable predictions and general statements

we can prove (at step 14) that I should use induction. We

do not need 'If I use induction and it's reliable, I'll make reliable predictions and general statements'.

It will be clearer if we use letters to stand for simple statements:

> U: I use induction
> P: I make reliable predictions and general statements
> R: Induction is reliable
> S: I should use induction
> W: I want to make reliable predictions and general statements.

1–8 Complete the proof below. (The full list of rules is at the start of Chapter 50.)

PROOF 1

1.	(U and R) or ((U and not R) or not U)	PREMISE
2.	If (U and not R) then not P	PREMISE
3.	If not U then not P	PREMISE
4.	If ((U and not R) or not U) then not P	*lines?* DIL
5.	P*	PREMISE*
6.	Not not P	5 *rule?*
7.	Not ((U and not R) or not U)	*lines?* MTT
8.	U and R	1,7 *rule?*
9.	U	8 *rule?*
10.	If P then U	5,9 CP
11.	If W and (if P then U) then S	PREMISE
12.	W	PREMISE
13.	W and (if P then U)	*lines? rule?*

14.	S	*11,13 rule?*

*Hypothesis.

(It is important that S does not rely on the truth of P. At step 10, this hypothesis is given its proper role: the antecedent of a conditional. It is the conditional that we prove, and on which our conclusion S relies.)

For this first proof we don't need the premise *if U and R then P* ('If I use induction and it's reliable, I'll make reliable predictions and general statements'). But we can use it to reach another conclusion which explains, in a single statement, *why* I should use induction: namely that induction, if reliable, is both necessary and sufficient for reliable predictions and general statements. Until step 8 this proof is the same as the first (and again we assume P hypothetically at step 5). Then it takes a different course.

9–10   Fill in the blanks.

PROOF 2

1.	(U and R) or ((U and not R) or not U)	PREMISE
2.	If (U and not R) then not P	PREMISE
3.	If not U then not P	PREMISE
4.	If ((U and not R) or not U) then not P	*lines?* DIL
5.	P*	PREMISE*
6.	Not not P	5 *rule?*
7.	Not ((U and not R) or not U)	*lines?* MTT
8.	U and R	1,7 *rule?*
9.	If P then (U and R)	5, 8 CP
10.	If U and R then P	PREMISE
11.	(If P then (U and R)) and if U and R then P	9, 10 *rule?*

---

12. P iff (U and R)   11 *rule?*

*Hypothesis.

11–12 Explain informally why neither the conclusion of Proof 1 nor that of Proof 2 guarantees that induction is reliable.

A final practice argument

Here is a final argument for you to analyse step by step, using the techniques you have learned in this section. It contains twenty-four questions: a double dose.

Why the Foundation won

The Foundation – a state far away on the edge of the Galactic Empire – has just escaped conquest by the Empire because Riose, the attacking Imperial General, was recalled and executed. Ducem Barr, an ally of the Foundation, explains why the Foundation could not lose.

> 'Look at the situation. A weak general could never have endangered us, obviously. A strong general during the time of a weak Emperor would never have endangered us either, for he would have turned his arms toward a more fruitful target (events have shown that three-fourths of the Emperors of the last two centuries were rebel generals). So it is only the combination of strong Emperor and strong general that can harm the Foundation; for a strong Emperor cannot be dethroned easily, and the strong general is forced to turn outwards, past the frontiers.
>
> But, what keeps the Emperor strong? It's obvious. He's strong, because he permits no strong subjects. Riose won victories, so the Emperor was suspicious. So [Riose] was recalled, and accused, condemned, murdered. The Foundation wins again.

Why, look, there is not a conceivable combination of events that does not result in the Foundation winning. It was inevitable, whatever Riose did, whatever we did.'

(Isaac Asimov, *Foundation and Empire*)

'Riose won victories, so the Emperor was suspicious. So [Riose] was recalled, and accused, condemned, murdered', is not part of the main argument: it merely cites Riose as an example of the general point Barr wants to make. So we should leave it out of the proof.

1   What is the general point that Barr wants to make?
    (*Hint*: he wants to argue that something is the case *whatever may happen*. This something is the conclusion of his argument.)

We can put every step in Barr's main argument in terms of logical constants and three simple statements:

> The emperor is strong
> The general is strong
> The Foundation is conquered.

2   What disjunction does Barr implicitly assume, to cover whatever may happen? And does it do this? Put it in the form described above. (*Hint*: look at the eventualities that he discusses in turn.)

Like Holmes' argument in Chapter 41, Barr's main argument depends on subsidiary arguments: two, this time. I give them below. Their conclusions become premises in the main argument.

SUBSIDIARY ARGUMENT I

'A strong general during the time of a weak emperor would never have endangered us either, for he would have turned his arms toward a more fruitful target (events have shown that three-fourths of the Emperors of the last two centuries were rebel generals).'

SUBSIDIARY ARGUMENT II

> 'But, what keeps the emperor strong? It's obvious. He's strong, because he permits no strong subjects.' [The conclusion is implicit.]

To express these arguments, we must add three more simple statements:

> The general attacks the Foundation
> The general attacks the emperor
> The emperor permits strong subjects.

3 What is the conclusion of argument I? Give it first in Barr's words, then in the form I described above.
4 What is the implicit conclusion of argument II? Put it in the form described above.

(Remember that both these conclusions become premises in the main argument.)

5 Here is a proof of argument I. Fill in the missing bits.

1. If the general is strong and the emperor is not,
   the general attacks the emperor   PREMISE
2. If the general attacks the emperor, he does
   not attack the Foundation   PREMISE
3. Step?*   PREMISE
4. If the general attacks the emperor, the
   Foundation is not conquered   2, 3 CH

───

5. *Your answer to question 3.*   *line/s? rule?*

*This is implicit: an obvious assumption.

6 Which of Barr's words give us this argument's first two premises?
7 Here is a proof of argument II. Fill in the missing bits.

1. If the emperor is strong, he permits no strong
   subjects   PREMISE
2. *Step?**   PREMISE

---

3. *Your answer to question 4**   *line/s? rule?*

*These are implicit. Again premise 2 is an obvious assumption.

8   Which of Barr's words give us this argument's first premise?

Barr states one premise of his main argument explicitly.

9   What is his explicit premise? Give it first in Barr's words, then in the form I described above. (*Hint*: look again at the eventualities that he discusses.)

10–18   Fill in the missing bits of the main proof. (Remember to use the form I described above.)

1. *Answer to question 2*   PREMISE
2. *Answer to question 9*   PREMISE
3. *Answer to question 3*   PREMISE
4. *Step?**   *PREMISE*
5. *Answer to question 4*   PREMISE
6. The emperor is strong   4, &E
7. *Step?**   5, 6 *rule?*
8. The general is strong   4, &E
9. *Step?**   7, 8 &I
10. *Step?**   4, 9 RAA
11. Either the general is not strong, or the general   1, 10 *rule?*
    is strong and the emperor is not
12. If either the general is not strong, or the general   2, 3 *rule?*
    is strong and the emperor is not, the Foundation
    is not conquered

---

13. *Answer to question 1.*   *lines?* MPP.

*Hypothesis.

19–20 Rewrite the argument using these letters for statements, and giving each step the form of a wff.

> E: The Emperor is strong
> G: The General is strong
> C: The Foundation is conquered

21–24 Now rewrite the two subsidiary arguments using letters for statements, giving each step the form of a wff. You'll need to add these letters:

> F: The general attacks the Foundation
> A: The general attacks the emperor
> S: The emperor permits no strong subjects.

 This is the end of Part IV.

Epilogue

In this book, I give you many of the basic tools for sound reasoning. Most introductions to logic cover the same things to some extent, but move more quickly through the early stages: they start with a short discussion of validity, say something about Venns, and use truth-tables (and/or other diagrams like the semantic tableau) to introduce truth-functions. As I do, they include proofs in statement logic. Typically they call this logic 'sentential' or 'propositional'; for why I call it 'statement logic' instead, see Chapter 6. They usually then go on at least as far as quantified logic, which I do not. They also use symbols for the truth-functional constants, where I use words: 'Q v (P → R)' for example instead of 'Q or (if P then R)'. Symbols are necessary at the later stages; but in this very introductory book I avoid them for two reasons.

The first is that though some beginners find them useful (and enjoy them), they are something extra to learn at a stage where you should really be thinking about the ideas they stand for: ideas which 'and', 'or', etc. express perfectly well, once you know that in logic these are truth-functional. (People who use symbols in writing still *say* 'and' and 'or'.) And they give basic logic a 'mathematical' look which puts some beginners off, unnecessarily.

This is misleading. The skill of basic logic is linguistic: understanding what arguments in messy, elliptical language mean and translating them into something clearer. Instead of calling the logic that we normally use for sound reasoning mathematical, we would do better to say that mathematics is logical: it uses, studies and extends certain features of sound reasoning, in a special way. (I hope that by now you immediately see the difference between 'All logic is mathematics' and 'All mathematics is logic'.) The only abstract sign that we really need in basic logic, I think, is the variable.

The study of logical form as such – abstracted from argument in practice – is mathematical. Here the connection with ordinary language is often remote, and (obviously) you need special symbols. Quantified logic, which follows statement (or 'propositional') logic in most courses, is a middle ground: it is still relevant to argument in practice, but it is more abstract in form. It combines the logic of sets with that of statements, in a single system. I do not cover this, because my approach is the same as many logic textbooks. Here written words are possible in theory, but would be impossibly unwieldy – like using words to write arithmetic.

My second reason is that there is no one definitive set of symbols. Here are some that you might find.

Not P	~P	– P	¬ P	$\overline{P}$
P and Q	P.Q	PQ	P∧Q	P & Q
P or Q	P v Q	P ⋁Q	PQ	
If P then Q	P ⊃Q	P → Q		
P iff Q	P≡Q	P ↔ Q	P~Q	

Why learn one lot (unnecessarily) when – if you do more formal logic – your next book may use another?

You will also find a different approach to proof, at later stages. In the logic of everyday life we derive our conclusions mainly from *premises* which we suppose are true, but which are not necessary truths. More rigorous systems may draw conclusions only from *axioms* held to be self-evident – as few and simple as possible, for security. Or we may take nothing at all as given, and prove not conclusions as such but *sequents*: what a formula or a set of formulae entail if assumed. A sequent in statement logic might be 'P *and* Q and *if* P *then* R together entail R'. Using '→' for 'if-then' and '&' for 'and', we would write this 'P & Q, P→R ‖– R'. The ‖– sign is called a 'gatepost', and proofs of this kind are called 'natural deduction'.

And you may learn about the logic of relations – concepts like 'is bigger than', 'is located between' and so on – or modal logic: the relation between statements with forms like *P is necessary* and *P is possible*. These can be useful in assessing arguments for soundness. But one must stop somewhere; and the commonest unsound arguments – the kind that trip us up again and again, unless we are careful – lie within a narrower range, the one I discuss in this book.

In the bibliography that follows, I list several formal logic textbooks, which will take you at least as far as quantification, and a couple that concentrate on more informal aspects of argument and of language generally. The other references are to any philosophical books I happened to mention in the text.

Bibliography

Some introductions to formal logic

Hodges, W. (1977) *Logic*, Harmondsworth: Penguin Books.

Lemmon, E.J. (1961) *Beginning Logic*, Cambridge, MA: Harvard University Press.

Quine, W.V.O. (1974) *Methods of Logic* (3rd edn) London: Routledge & Kegan Paul.

Salmon, W. (1984) *Logic*, Englewood Cliffs, NJ: Prentice-Hall.

Shaw, P. (1981) *Logic and its Limits*, Oxford: Oxford University Press.

Tomassi, P. (1999) *Logic*, London: Routledge.

(There are many others.)

Background/informal logic

Fischer, A. (1988) *The Logic of Real Arguments*, Cambridge: Cambridge University Press.

Flew, A. (1975) *Thinking about Thinking*, London: Fontana.

Thouless, R.H. and Thouless, C.R. (1930) *Straight and Crooked Thinking*, London: Hodder & Stoughton.

Philosophical books and authors mentioned in the text

Aristotle (syllogistic logic): for a general account see W.D. Ross (1930) *Aristotle*, London: Methuen.

Descartes, R. (the *Cogito*): *Discourse on Method* and *Meditations on First Philosophy*, both in E. Haldane and G.R.T. Ross (1969) *The*

Philosophical Works of Descartes, vol. I, Cambridge: Cambridge University Press.

Harré, R. (1981) *Great Scientific Experiments*, Oxford: Phaiden Press.

Hume, D. ('Hume's Fork') *An Enquiry Concerning Human Understanding*, ed. L. Selby-Bigge, (1955) Oxford: Oxford University Press; (induction): A *Treatise of Human Nature*, ed. L. Selby-Bigge (1958) Oxford: Oxford University Press.

Plato (account of a statement): *Sophist*; ('simples') *Theaetetus*, both translated in E. Hamilton and H. Cairns (1961), *The Collected Dialogues of Plato*, New York: Pantheon Books.

Popper, K. (1972) *Conjectures and Refutations*, London: Routledge & Kegan Paul.

Quine, W.V.O. (1961) 'Two Dogmas of Empiricism', in (1961) *From a Logical Point of View*, Cambridge, MA: Harvard University Press.

Rosenberg, J. (1978) *The Practice of Philosophy*, Englewood Cliffs, NJ: Prentice-Hall.

Strawson, P.F. (1952) *Introduction to Logical Theory*, London: Methuen.

Wittgenstein, L. (1953) *Philosophical Investigations*, Oxford: Blackwell.

Answers to Chapter 1

1 (i) 'Everyone who has a Rolls Royce is rich' and 'My Granny
        has a Rolls Royce'.
   (ii) 'My Granny is rich.'

2 You cannot do it without denying one or both premises. For
   example, Granny's Rolls may have been abandoned in a field
   for thirty-five years, and Granny's hens (her only source of
   income apart from a small potato patch) live inside it. (Second
   premise TRUE, first premise FALSE). Or Granny is too poor to
   own a bicycle, much less a car. (Here the first premise could be
   either TRUE or FALSE, for all we know; but the second is definitely FALSE.)

3 (i) 'Beggars wear rags' and 'Uncle Marley wears rags'.
   (ii) 'Uncle Marley is a beggar'.

4 Example: It is true that beggars (often) wear rags; they cannot
   afford anything better. Uncle Marley, however, is a miser with
   bags of gold under the floor. He wears rags because he cannot
   bear to spend money on clothes, and if people think he is a
   beggar they will not try to rob him.

5 VALID. If you don't see why, check the descriptions of 'valid'
   on page 2 and 'invalid' on page 3: IF the premises were true
   instead of false – if insects *did* have eight legs and spiders *were*
   insects, not arachnids – then spiders would have eight legs. It's
   inevitable.

6   YES. But if it has, we can no longer be sure of a true conclu-
    sion. Example: the Granny argument. See 2 above: when either
    premise is false (or they both are), the speaker has not proved
    that her Granny is rich: something like the other cases
    described could be true instead. It could still be the case that
    her Granny is rich, of course – but for other reasons.

7   YES – but only if it has one or more false premises. Example:
    the same.

8   YES. But in that case the conclusion is not proved by the argu-
    ment. If true, it is true for some other reason/s than those given
    in the premises. Example: the Spider argument.

9   NO. An argument like that must be invalid. Example: the
    Uncle argument.

10 Something like: 'A valid argument is one whose form does not
    allow true premises and a false conclusion' or perhaps: 'A valid
    argument is one whose form guarantees a true conclusion, IF
    the premises are true'.
    (I shall use the first, but they come to the same thing.)

11 An invalid argument is one whose form ALLOWS true
    premises and a false conclusion.
    Important: this does not mean that an invalid argument must
    have them. It is invalid simply because its form does not rule
    this possibility out.

12 Wait and see.

1   YES. The logical order is

Beggars wear rags   or   Uncle Marley wears rags
Uncle Marley wears rags   Beggars wear rags
_____   _____

Uncle Marley is a beggar.   Uncle Marley is a beggar.

2   NO. The Spider argument's statements are in their logical order.

3   The Spider argument's first premise claims that ALL insects have eight legs, i.e. belong to an eight-legged species. (Another way of putting this would be, 'All *normal* insects have eight legs.')

4   Its second premise claims that ALL spiders are insects. (In this case – if the premise were true – even abnormal spiders would be insects; so confusion cannot arise.)

5   In the Uncle argument, the sense of 'Beggars wear rags' is not clear: it could mean all beggars or typical beggars (compare 'normal insects') or most or possibly many beggars. In some contexts it could just mean some beggars, but this is unlikely here: I doubt if a normal listener would consider it.

   If what is being claimed were really that ONLY beggars wear rags, or ALL AND ONLY, the Uncle argument would be valid after all. But this is not what the words normally mean; and if I claimed it is what I did mean, you could legitimately accuse me of misleading language.

   (The imprecision of 'Beggars wear rags' can help to mask the argument's invalidity: we are left with a feeling that some general connection is being made between rags and beggars, without being clear which, so we cannot be sure which form of argument we should be assessing.)

6   Harold kept saying, 'Well, the fact is…'.
7   Anyone who keeps saying, 'Well, the fact is…' is lying.
8   Whenever *Harold* keeps saying, 'Well, the fact is…', he is lying.
9   Anyone who keeps saying, 'Well, the fact is…' is lying

Harold kept saying, 'Well, the fact is…'
_____

Harold was lying.   (VALID)

10   Whenever *Harold* keeps saying, 'Well, the fact is…', he is lying.
     Harold kept saying, 'Well, the fact is…'
_____

Harold was lying.   (VALID)

11   It might be either, 'Anyone who is proud would accept or (more specifically), 'If the Snake is proud, he will accept'.

12   Either   Anyone who is proud would accept
                   The Snake is proud
                   _____

                   The Snake will accept

     or

                   If the Snake is proud, he will accept
                   The Snake is proud
                   _____

                   He will accept.

1–9   The ones you already knew:

(A)   'The Snake is proud.'
Assumed without argument.

(B)   'If the Snake is proud, he will accept.'
Assumed without argument.

(C)   'The Snake will accept.'
Worked out from (A) and (B). It is then used as a premise towards a new conclusion.

The rest:

(D) 'If the Snake accepts, then either he will die in the attempt, or he will live but fail, or he will succeed.'
Assumed without argument.

(E)   'Either the Snake will die in the attempt, or he will live but fail, or he will succeed.'
Worked out from (C) and (D). It is later used as a premise towards a new conclusion.

(F)   'If the Snake dies in the attempt, the Fox will have no rival and can persuade the band that further tests are a waste of time.' Assumed without argument.

(G) 'If the Snake lives but fails, he will lose face and leave for distant parts.' Assumed without argument.

(H) 'If the Snake loses face and leaves for distant parts, the Fox will have no rival and can persuade the band that further tests are a waste of time.' Assumed without argument.

(I)   'If the Fox has no rival and can persuade the band not to set a test, he will soon become Captain, without having to steal the Eye.' Assumed without argument.

(J)   'If the Snake succeeds, it will become impossible for the Fox to steal the Eye, and the vengence of the Priests of Zorro will destroy the Snake.' Assumed without argument.

(K) 'If it becomes impossible for the Fox to steal the Eye and the vengence of the Priests of Zorro destroys the Snake, the Fox will soon become Captain, without having to steal the Eye.' Assumed without argument.

(L)   'If the Snake dies in the attempt, or lives but fails, or succeeds, the Fox will soon become Captain, without having to steal the Eye.' Worked out from (F) through (K).

(M) 'Whatever happens, the Fox will soon become Captain, without having to steal the Eye.'
Worked out from (E) and (L).

10 If everything the Fox assumes without argument is true, YES.
(M) is true if (E) and (L) are.
(L) is true if (F)–(K) are; and (F)–(K) are assumed without argument.
(E) is true if (C) and (D) are. D is assumed without argument.
(C) is true if (A) and (B) are. A and B are assumed without argument.

11 YES. 'Valid' means just what we have shown: that if an argument's premises are true, its conclusion must be.

12 A valid argument is one whose form will not allow a false conclusion, if the premises are true. A sound argument is a valid argument whose premises *are* true.

Answers to Chapter 4

1   y: Either the mother or the son, but this time whichever is *not* speaking.

2   The premises:

$$\text{All A are B or C}$$
$$\underline{\text{x is neither B nor C}}$$

will get us as far as the conclusion: **x is not A.**

3   *Implicit or suppressed premises*, because they are unspoken.

4   Because it can never have true premises. The ground-shifter starts from one position, then shifts to a new one that contradicts it. Here, for example, if the first premise, 'I was in the next county', is true, the second (unstated) premise, 'Well in fact I was not. I was here' must be false: 'I was not…' contradicts 'I was….' And so it goes on, every time the ground is shifted (or the goalposts moved).

5   See the answer to question 5 in Chapter 1. Just because a ground-shifter's premises cannot all be true, the argument can never have the forbidden combination: TRUE premises and FALSE conclusion. And this is due to its form: what the ground shifting is about does not matter. It therefore fits our definition of 'valid'.

6   You need true premises in order to prove anything.

7   'It wasn't me' could mean various things, each of them not a premise, but the conclusion of some stage in the argument. What it means would then change as the ground shifts: 'It wasn't me in the pub', 'It wasn't me that got into a fight with the man' – etc. Or we could take it as a general disclaimer: 'I was not the guilty party'. This would fit every stage. We cannot be sure which interpretation is best because the arguer does not say.

8   P: Women 'ask for it'.
    Q: Women get raped.

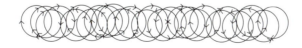

9   Only if its premise is true. What do *you* think?

But even when a circular argument's premises are true, it cannot prove a conclusion whose truth we did not know already. The rule:

A valid argument proves nothing, unless its premises are true.

says only that a valid argument cannot prove anything UNLESS it has true premises (i.e. is sound); it does not say that if it has them, this means we can always use it to establish a new truth.

10–11   Two words used persuasively in this definition of 'abortion' are: (i) 'murder'; (ii) 'child'.

(i) 'Murder' means *wrongful* killing. Anyone who does not oppose abortion should therefore query the definition of it as murder.

(ii) 'Child' typically means a young human being *after* birth. You might accept (because you have this sense in mind) that killing a child is always murder, and then (because it is true in *some* sense that an unborn child is a child) feel forced to agree that it is murder to kill an embryo or foetus, even though you don't agree really. Here you should challenge the definition of abortion as killing a child in the sense of 'child' *you* meant, when you agreed that killing a child is murder. (Another fallacy may be involved here: *equivocation*. I shall say more about that later.)

As it stands, the passage is not an argument but a statement. But it might be used as an abbreviated argument, with the implicit conclusion, 'Abortion is always wrong'.

12 What are 'the *true* needs and interests of its rank and file members'? The phrase 'perhaps as determined by somebody else' begs an important question: what if democracy requires that people be free to determine their *own* needs and interests? (The author says that this defines a paternalistic sense of 'democracy'; but many people would say that paternalism is – by definition – undemocratic.)

1–2 These are up to you.

3 'She died for Cause X' misses the point, if we are trying to decide whether it is right or not: the cause's own merits are what counts (even if it has had no martyrs at all; even if it was totally unpopular). In the argument:

She died for Cause X

Cause X is right

the premise could easily be true and the conclusion false (think of all the martyrs there have been to opposing causes, so that both could not be right).

4 Again, up to you.

5 The premise could easily be true and the conclusion false (again, think of all the authorities who disagree).

6 P may be replaced by whatever statement the arguer wants to conclude. In the first example, x may be replaced either by the name of whichever authority the arguer is invoking, or an identifying description.

7 The first: remember what the point of passing a student's work or failing it is. (The second premise might be false too; but the arguer would normally only think there is any hope in an appeal to pity when it was true).

8 Because it spells out why the person appealed to might feel sorry for the arguer.

9 The perfectly valid **If P then Q**
P

Q.

10–12 Once again, these are up to you.

1   See the rest of the chapter.
2   'Your feet hurt.'
3   That your feet hurt.

4   Obviously if I ask, 'Does your nose itch?' and you nod, you are not stating that your feet hurt but that your nose itches. And if you are practising gestures in front of the mirror and you nod (first haughtily, then with a charming smile) your nods are not stating anything at all.

5   Over to you.

6   Only (iv) and (v), which – as normally used – mean the same (and so, when used in a statement, would state the same thing about the same numbers). 'Granny' means 'grandmother', and a grandmother is the mother of *either* your mother or your father, so (i), (ii) and (iii) have different senses (and obviously do not share a sense with any of the rest). Again (vi) does not share a sense with any of the others: it means something about days in the week and they do not.

7   'Belonging to the speaker' (or writer or singer, etc.).

8   'At the time of speaking' (or writing, etc.).

9   They are all about the (real or unreal) state of affairs *your being rich*.

10   There could be many ways of putting it: 'Is two plus two equal to four?', 'Do two and two make four?', 'Is four the sum of two and two?' and so on. What they all do, however, is ask whether $2+2=4$.

11   No, for the same reasons that it cannot make a statement.

12   If in doubt, re-read Chapter 1. And maybe Chapter 2. Perhaps 3, 4 and 5 as well...

1   They are valid because their forms will not allow true premises and a false conclusion. But to prove something, an argument must have true premises as well as a valid form; and when our premises are incompatible, they can never all be true. When we argue in a circle our premises may be true but we cannot know they are, unless we already know that the conclusion is. So we cannot use the argument to show this.

2   The meaning of the terms '2', '+', '=' and '4'.

3   1+1=2 is about counting. If you correctly count one rabbit (of either sex) and then another, you will find there are two. What happens when you put two rabbits together in a hutch is not relevant here.

4   If a statement's meaning makes it necessarily false, that same meaning plus the meaning of 'Not' ('It is not the case that') make its negation logically true.

5   (i) TRUE because of the meaning of the general form, 'If A is/are bigger than B, then B is/are smaller than A'.

    (iii) TRUE because 'cat' means a kind of animal.

    (iv) TRUE because of the meaning of its form: A *is* A.

    (v) FALSE because 'cat' and 'mouse' mean *different* kinds of animal.

    (vii) TRUE for the same reason (i) is.

    The truth-values of (ii), (vi) and (vii) depend not on meanings but on fact.

6   (iv) Two others depend partly on the repetition of 'cats' and 'mice', but this is not enough on its own: see the next answer.

7   (i) and (vii): 'A is bigger than B' means the same as 'B is smaller than A'. So these have the form *if Bs are smaller than As then Bs are smaller than As*, or more simply (where 'P' stands for any statement) *if P then P*.

    (iv): A cat is a kind of animal, so (iv) has the form *an AB is a B*. 'A' stands for whatever distinguishes cats from other kinds.

8   (v) has an underlying form that makes it false: *some Bs that are not As, are As*. Even if we do not define them more precisely, competent English speakers who know both words will agree that 'cat' means an animal that is NOT a mouse, and vice versa.

(vi) has repetition both on the surface and in its underlying form, but it leaves the matter open.

9 (i) and (iv) guarantee truth; (ii) guarantees falsity; (iii) leaves it open.

10 It is not overtly analytic because on the surface there's no repetition. But when we are speaking of natural numbers, 'even' means 'evenly divisible by two' and 'odd' means 'not evenly divisible by two'. So the underlying form is *every A is B or not B*, which guarantees truth.

11 It is still true. Dithering is a way of not agreeing.

12 For sound argument, premises need not be true in all possible worlds, only in this one (unless your conclusion is about all possible worlds). If we have reason to believe that it is true in this one, it is a good premise.

1 When its logical form makes it necessarily true.
2 The philosophical study of knowledge and belief.
3 Sheep on the one hand; the rest of the world on the other.
4 Since these features are compatible, animals which have them might exist. On the other hand, nothing about them requires that such an animal *must* exist.
5 When it describes unicorns in a way that denies conditions we have agreed are necessary. ('That's a griffin, not a unicorn.')

6 (i) Being an animal is necessary for being a sheep, but not sufficient. A sheep must be an animal; but a goat is an animal too.
    (ii) Being a ram is sufficient for being a sheep, but not necessary. A ram must be a sheep; but a ewe is a sheep too.

7 For example   (i)   being an animal
                (ii)   having a tail
                (iii) having cloven hooves.

8 We would have to know whether these conditions could all be true together. If they can't, the animal is impossible.
9 Yes, if the creature in the story does not have features which could not occur together. If *any* such unicorn could exist, unicorns are possible; and if so, 'unicorns exist' is contingent.
10 Not if it is possible that there might have been *nothing*.
11 No. 'All cats have lungs' is *at least* empirically true: we have learned that from the cats of this world. What is in doubt is whether it is also logically so (so that to understand the meaning of the word is enough for us to know it without any experience of cats, and know it about all possible worlds).
12 When you shout it.

Answers to Chapter 9

1 'Thing(s) you buy from Happy Ed'.
2 'A rich person'/'rich people' (as appropriate).
3 x .
4 Form shared by the Wolf, Great-Aunt and Rabbit arguments:

No A is B
x is not B
———————
x is A.

5 B.
6 x.
7 Remember that a form is invalid if it *allows* an argument to have true premises and a false conclusion: it need not guarantee this. So to show that a form is invalid, you need an example where this is actually the case. If Annabel is a non-vegetarian schoolgirl, argument (1) would do; if she happens to be a wolf, (1) is still invalid – but because the conclusion is true, it does not show this. Or imagine that 'Real men don't keep rabbits' is true* and so is 'Colonel Carruthers doesn't keep rabbits'. He is a racehorse as it happens, and horses don't keep rabbits. If argument (3) were valid, it would then inevitably have a true conclusion. Does it?
8 'I leave.'
9 P: It can go wrong.
   Q: It will [go wrong].
10 P: The Snake is proud.
   Q: He [the Snake] will accept.
11 Yes. Any argument with this form must have a true conclusion, if its premises are true.

12 **If not P then Q**
   Not Q
   ———————
   Not P.

   P: You are an elephant.

---

* To the Editor, *RABBIT-FANCIERS' GAZETTE*: No, of course I'm not saying it's true. I'm just asking you to *imagine* that it is.

1 The forms are different in just one way: the second has *not Q* where the first has Q. We can replace Q in an argument form by *any* statement. So in the first form we could replace Q by a statement begining with 'not': for example by whatever, in the second form, we represent by *not Q*. But we could also replace Q by a statement that doesn't begin with 'not'. So arguments whose premises do not contain a 'not' will also fit the first form. In the second form, you cannot avoid 'not' in your two premises: the form itself requires them.

2 (1) NO. This argument has not got the (invalid) first form:

If P then Q
Q
_____
P.

Instead it has the VALID form:

If P then Q   P: You're bigger than a goat
P   Q: You're bigger than a flea.
_____

Q.

(2) YES, this argument has the first form. (P and Q are as above.)

(3) YES. (How sad that it is invalid.)
        P: She loves me
        Q: She doesn't love him.

3 (1) NO, this argument has not got the second form:

If P then not Q
Not Q
_____
P.

The answer to question 2 gives its real form.

(2) Again NO. The answer to question 1 explains why.

(3) YES, this argument has the second form.

P: She loves me
Q: She loves him.

4   It shares with ALL four-premise arguments the simplest form:

P
Q
R
S
―
T

with a single letter for each whole premise, and one for the whole conclusion.

5   'An elephant'.

6   (For example) they don't begin 'If you are an elephant', as all arguments of this form must.

7   An ARGUMENT must have at least one premise, followed by 'therefore' or some equivalent term, and a conclusion. Premises and conclusion must all be statements. The Ant, Frog and Insect examples are like this. (But some of the necessary elements of an argument may often be implicit, or disguised by the words' surface form.)

An argument FORM fits more than one argument, and it can do this only by not being a complete argument itself: it has gaps. When these are filled by the right kind of term, you get an argument.

8   You can get really silly ones for this. For example:

All wolves are carnivores
Casimir is a sheep
_____
Casimir is a carnivore

A: wolves
B: carnivores
C: sheep
X: Casmir.

9   NO. If you still think an invalid argument can't have a true conclusion, go back to Chapter 1.

10 Only argument A6 has the form A*:

X is sometimes F

X: The Elephant
F: Afraid of Mice.

It could be the case that X is always F.

A5 is not far off it. Its premise fits A*, but not its conclusion. It has the form:

X is sometimes F

X is always F.

A4 has one premise too many, and again the wrong conclusion: 'is' is not the same as 'could be'. Its form is:

X is sometimes F
X is not G or H

X: The Elephant
G: Guided by Experience
F: Afraid of Mice

X is always F.

H: Guided by Reason.

11 NO. The relevant argument with form A** would be

Paintings are sometimes forgeries.
The existence of forged paintings does NOT depend on there
    being some paintings that are not forged

It could be the case that all paintings are forgeries.
(The conclusion is false, but so is the second premise.)

**Remember that even if
an argument's form is
valid, false premises can
lead you astray.**

12 If 'could' means 'could, for all we know', YES.

Answers to Chapter 11

1 This form fits every two-premise argument. That includes invalid ones: those that either do, or could, have true premises and a false conclusion. For example:

> P Once upon a time, in a faraway castle, there lived a princess who was really a fox
>
> Q 2+2=4
>
> ---
>
> R Jean-Paul Sartre's account of bad faith has a certain novelistic plausibility, but is ultimately incoherent.

(If you think THAT'S valid, you need help!)

The Granny argument is valid not because it has this form, but because it also has a valid one – in fact, several.

2 I never said that *all* a valid argument's forms must be valid. In fact, they can't be: as we have seen, every argument has a simplest form – F1 in this case – that will fit all the arguments, valid or invalid, which have the same number of premises. If among its several forms an argument has even one that is valid, this is enough to guarantee that the argument – because of that one form – cannot have true premises and a false conclusion.

3 They all do.

4 They all are (unlike F1).

5 NO – impossible. Each of these forms (F2–F5) guarantees a true conclusion from true premises. An invalid argument does not guarantee this.

6 (F4). F1 does not show the argument's validity, and (F2), (F3) and (F5) are unnecessarily limited. (F2) is limited to the rich, (F5) to Rolls Royce owners, and (F3) to Granny and nobody else, as in

All pensioners are wrinkled   and   All witches have cats
My Granny is a pensioner   My Granny is a witch

My Granny is wrinkled   My Granny has a cat.

7   (F1), (F6) and (F7) fit the Snake Argument. (F4) does not.

8   (F6) and (F7): neither of these could have true premises and a false conclusion.

9   P: The Snake accepts.
    Q: The Snake either dies in the attempt, or he lives but fails, or he succeeds.
    (The surface differences between 'accepts' and 'will accept' (and so on) do not affect the argument's logical form. We know that the Fox is referring to the future throughout.)

10 YES. If the argument has this (valid) form, we know that the conclusion must be true if the premises are. So, the argument itself is valid.

11 Like Step 1, Step 2 also has the invalid form (F1).

12 P: The Snake accepts.   R: The Snake lives but fails.
    Q: The Snake dies in the attempt. S. The Snake succeeds.

    YES, it is valid: any argument of this form must have a true conclusion if its premises are true.

Answers to Chapter 12

1 (F1) P: If the Snake is proud, he accepts
              Q: The Snake is proud
              R: The Snake accepts.

Again, the surface difference between 'accepts' and 'will accept' (and so on) does not affect the logical form.

      (F6) P: The Snake is proud
              Q: The Snake accepts.

      (F7) A: Proud creature/s
              B: Those who accept (or someone who will accept)
              x: The Snake.

2 P, Q, etc. are holes we fill with statements. Typically we express a statement in a sentence, such as 'The Snake is proud' or 'If the Snake is proud, he will accept'.

3 x, y, etc. are holes we fill with *referring terms*, that pick out the subjects of our speech. These are *individuals*: the word/s for them include names like 'Lilia Cleghorn' or descriptions like 'The Snake', which picks out one special snake (the character in our story); or pronouns like 'he' or 'they'.

4 A, B etc. are holes to be filled by *general terms* that describe kinds of things: for example 'proud' or 'a bad bargain'.

    (Treat the italicised words in 2–4 as technical terms. You will meet them again.)

5 No. The premises could be true and the conclusion false: some of the things Happy Ed sells might be good value even if the van was not.

6 No: I have already said they are the same argument. All that matters for validity is whether or not the premises – whatever their order – could be true and the conclusion false; and this will obviously be the same for both.

7 x: My van
    A: Things (or a thing) bought from Happy Ed
    B: Bad bargains/a bad bargain.

The difference between 'bad bargains' and 'a bad bargain' (and so on) does not affect the logical form.

8   (i) is a statement; (ii) is a general description; (iii) identifies an individual; (iv) is a general description.

9   (i), (iii) and (iv) are malforms. The logical constant 'if...then...' requires statements, so the variables should be P, Q, etc., not x, y (which should be filled with terms like 'Uncle Marley' that identify individuals) nor A,B (which should be filled with general descriptions like 'bad bargains').

10   *x is A.* 'All the world' refers to the *whole* world: an individual.

11   The gaps in (i) '*if you are...you are not a sheep*' and (ii) '*if you are an elephant you are not...*' are like the A, B variables. We fill them with general terms, standing for kinds of thing: 'elephants/an elephant', 'boots/a boot', 'numbers/ a number' and so on. Such statements have the forms (i) *if you are A you are not a sheep* and (ii) *if you are an elephant you are not A*. The words 'If you are...you are not a sheep' and 'If you are an elephant you are not...' could however also be used to make statements whose forms have a different type of variable: (i) *if you are x you are not a sheep* and (ii) *if you are an elephant you are not x*. Here the gap – or variable – would instead be filled by a term that identifies an individual: for example, 'If you are *Princess Anne* you are not a sheep' or 'If you are an elephant you are not *the Eiffel Tower*'.

It would not make sense however to replace the blanks with whole statements (try it). So these words could not be used to say anything whose form is (i) *if you are P you are not a sheep* or (ii) *if you are an elephant you are not P*.

12   In Rosenberg's statement-forms X *is sometimes F* and *it could be the case that* X *is always F*, his variable X, like my own lower-case x, is filled by a term that refers to one or more individuals: 'my senses' and 'God'. His F is the A-type of variable, since its fillings – '(things that are) mistaken' and '(things that) allow me to be mistaken' – are general terms, describing kinds of things.

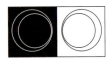

1   A is 'able to have one messy side, while still being perfect' (or words to that effect).

2   The fallacy of using the same term in different senses, at different points of your argument. (See Miss Nightingale's argument in Chapter 10.)

3   If you use the valid form, the argument – here and in answers 4 through 6 – will be

> The world is perfect (or imperfect) in the way a tapestry is
> A perfect tapestry can have one messy side
> _____
> The world can be perfect though it has one messy side.

The first premise states an unfortunate analogy for your purpose. An all-powerful creator could do better than a world that is perfect on only one side; and, if totally good, would choose to. If these premises are true, you have proved a conclusion incompatible with what you want to argue. Luckily for you, the analogy is also unsupported, so we have no reason to suppose that the first premise is true.

4   The conclusion is compatible with what you want to argue. If true, it would explain how perfection in the world – as in a tapestry – might still require an imperfect side; so it is not an unfortunate analogy for your purposes. You are unlucky that it is unsupported.

5   This is an unfortunate analogy for your purpose. A tapestry-weaver aims for perfection with limited ability; by contrast an all-powerful God will only underachieve by choice. It is just as well for your argument that the analogy is unsupported. (It is also unlikely, if this is your idea of God, that you would *want* to claim the world was perfect: its apparent imperfection probably inspired the idea.)

6   Tapestries have weavers, and you want to argue that the world does not. On the other hand, you are not arguing that the world is like a tapestry in having a weaver, but simply in being perfect although it has one messy side. So if for some reason you wanted to argue that the world might be perfect, it would not be an unfortunate analogy for your purposes – just useless

because unsupported. What is not clear is why, if you are an atheist, you should want to argue any such thing.

7   In the argument:
>   'A law implies a lawgiver. Now the Universe is full of laws – the law of gravitation and many others; hence it follows that the Universe has a lawgiver'

y is 'a state' and A is 'having lawgivers / a lawgiver'.
8   They both have laws (of a kind).
9   Miss Nightingale is only justified in assuming that the Universe has descriptive laws. These are not the kind that require a lawgiver. The Universe will be like a state with respect to (having or lacking) a lawgiver only if both have *prescriptive* laws.

10   They share the invalid form A*

> **X is sometimes F**
> _____
> **It could be the case that X is always F.**

11   Rosenberg claims that when we fill x in the form

> **x is like y with respect to A**
> **y is A**
> _____
> **x is A**

with 'arguments I and II', y is 'argument III' and A is 'invalid'. Argument III is

> **Paintings are sometimes forgeries**
> _____
> **It could be the case that paintings are always forgeries.**

12   The fact that arguments I, II and III share an invalid form is not enough to make them invalid. For that, they must be alike in not having any *valid* form. III does not; but I think that if we are fair to Descartes', he would probably say that in I and II he assumes an implicit premise which gives them the valid form

A**   X is sometimes F

X's being F does NOT depend on X's sometimes
being non-F

___

It could be the case that X is always F.

If so, Descartes' arguments are like III in various ways, but not with respect to validity.

1   Arguing in a circle; assuming as a premise the conclusion you claim to prove. (It does NOT mean prompting or raising a question.)

2   It is too sketchy to need careful dissection. You could just reject the analogy: 'PEOPLE ARE NOT EGGS!'. You could re-use it: 'Well, you don't make an omelette by wasting them!' or some of it: 'It's human beings you'll be beating up, not eggs'. You could ask for clarification in a way that shows up its callousness: 'You see other people's lives as eggs, do you?' (since it is not clear exactly what I am comparing to the eggs). You could find a counter-analogy – an equally familiar one if possible (bull in a china shop?)…and so on.

   (Analogies like this – where I do not spell out that it is one, but expect you to see that it is – are *metaphors*.)

3   Invalid form: **x is like y**
                      y is A
                      _____

                      x is A.

   Valid form:
                      x is like y with respect to (being or not being) A
                      y is A
                      _____

                      x is A.

4   x: These future eggs (or 'The set of these future eggs', since x typically represents an individual).
    y: (The set of) all the eggs I have known.

5   In version 1 of the Egg argument, A represents 'things that shatter harmlessly'.

6   (i) is an argument by analogy. (ii) reasons validly from a general statement about a whole, to one about a part of that whole.

7   x: (the set of) all eggs.
    y: see the answer to 4.
    A: see the answer to 5.

8   The conclusion is also a premise; so if it is false, at least one premise is false. The form of a circular argument therefore will not allow true premises with a false conclusion. An argument of this form proves nothing, because if the conclusion needs proving, so does at least one premise.

9 Encouraging or inspiring further enquiry (and discovery. Archimedes's cry of 'Eureka!' when he discovered his Principle – meaning 'I've found it!' – comes from the same Greek root).

10 When two statements are incompatible, they cannot both be true (though they can sometimes both be false).

11 (i) Not testable. This is a necessary truth, which experience could never falsify. (It is therefore too general to tell us anything about what it is to be an egg.)

(ii) Not testable. If something is undetectable by any process, how could you ever prove that it was or was not there?

(iii) Testable: an egg that did not explode would falsify this.

(iv) This is not testable if such phantasies occur, and are repressed, when the child is too young to tell anyone. Any method that the analyst *thinks* will make a patient recall such a thing is suspect, since it could just as easily encourage the patient to imagine having imagined it. It's not as if the memory were of a real event, which somebody might have recorded.

(v) As an explanation of why eggs break, it's bogus: 'fragile' just means 'breakable'. You do not need to test it to see that the so-called 'cause' is not one. You can test the part that says hen's eggs break, of course.

(vi) This one is interesting. It looks testable; but if that means it is falsifiable by experience, then no, it is not. So long as fresh eggs exist, any one of them might be a counter-example. And on the other hand if you thought you had found a counterexample, how could you know? It would have to be an egg that stayed fresh *forever*.

You can only know that a law like (vi) is true or false if you know it is *true*, by enumeration. That is not possible here: even if hens became extinct, and we had kept track of all the eggs there ever were, we would not know if those that met other ends – in omelettes say – would eventually have gone bad.

12 2 in 10, which is the same as 1 in 5.

1 Logical constant: Any element of a statement or argument (besides 'therefore') which it shares with others of the same logical form. Example: 'If-then' in a statement of the form *if P then Q*.

Variable: A letter in a formula, representing a hole to be filled by the appropriate kind of word or phrase. Example: P and Q in the formula *if P then Q*. (Here the appropriate fillings would be whole statements.)

2 **If P then Q**   P: (i) The Snake is proud
   P   (ii) The Snake accepts
   ─────────   Q: (i) The snake accepts
   Q   (ii) The Snake dies in the
                                     attempt or he lives but fails or
                                     he succeeds.

3 *Randolph argument*
   P: Randolph is asleep or Randolph is dead
   R: Randolph is dead.

   Measles argument
   P: It's measles or these are fleabites
   R: These are fleabites.

4 P: It's measles.
   P appears twice in the valid form: once in each premise.

5 P: Randolph is asleep
   Q: Randolph is dead.

6 **P or Q**   The logical constants are 'or' and 'not'.
   Not P
   ─────
   Q.

7 **P**   This form shows no connection between the
Q   statements it lists as premises and conclusion. So it
—   gives no reason why the conclusion should be true
R   whenever the premises are.

But when an argument-form shows us that a premise or conclusion is *complex*, and that a simpler statement within it turns up elsewhere in the argument, we may find a connection, and therefore a reason, as in

P or Q   P: Randolph is asleep
Not P   Q: Randolph is dead.

————

Q

8 The statement-logic forms of 'If I had measles I'd have a fever, and I haven't' are:

(i) **P**   P: If I had measles I'd have a fever, and I haven't;

(ii) **P and Q**   P: If I had measles I'd have a fever
Q: I haven't a fever

(iii) **(If P then Q) and R**   P: I have measles
Q: I have a fever
R: I haven't a fever

(iv) **(If P then Q) and not Q**   P: I have measles
Q: I have a fever.

9 They are all COMPLEX except (C).
10 (A) has the constant 'if-then'; (B) has 'not'; (D) and (E) have 'and'.

11 (A): That malicious little creep sets foot in the house.
      I leave.

   (B): All insects have wings.

   (D): All the world's a stage
       All the men and women are merely players.

   (E): All witches have cats
       My Granny is a witch.

12 Only the form all statements share, just because they are statements: P.

Answers to Chapter 16

1   P: You will meet the Witch
    Q: You will meet the Goblins
    R: You will die.

2   Wff: (i) **P.**

    Malforms:

    (ii) **If Q and R**   'If-and' is not a logical constant. Try
                            replacing letters with statements; you
                            will get nonsense.

    (iii) **P and R or Q**   Ambiguous. We should add brackets to
                            show whether we mean *P and (R or Q)*
                            or *(P and R) or Q*.

    (iv) **P and R, or Q**   This makes sense, but we do not use
                            commas in statement logic. It should
                            be *(P and R) or Q*.

3   Wff: (iii) **P and (R or Q)**

    Malforms:

    (i) **A or B**   Wrong kind of variable. Our present
                            system uses P, Q, R, etc., to be filled by
                            statements. (I use A, B, etc. in another
                            system, as variables to be filled by
                            general terms.)

    (ii) **P (and R or Q)** 'And' and 'or' should join pairs of
                            complete statements, not statements
                            plus extra bits, with forms like *(and R
                            or Q)*. Try replacing letters with state-
                            ments: you will get nonsense.

4   The gaps in 'If-then-' must be filled with single, complete state-
    ments. *If P or Q then R* satisfies this condition in just one case:
    P or Q must represent a single (complex) statement filling the
    first gap, R a statement filling the second. *If P or Q then R* will
    then yield an unambiguous statement whenever we replace P,
    Q and R by (shorter) statements. So it is a wff.

    (If brackets make its structure easier to see, we can bracket
    it: *If (P or Q) then R* is also a wff. But this is not necessary.)

5   Without brackets, it's ambiguous between *if P then (R or Q)* and *(if P then R) or Q*. We want the second, where the brackets correspond to the dash in my original statement.

6   Five. When a wff represents a complex formula, its main constant is called the MAIN CONNECTIVE, unless the main constant is 'not'. ('Not' does not connect two formulae but negates a single one: see question 12.) The main connective joins the two formulae that (with this constant) make the whole.

Of our five possibilities, two have the first 'and' as their main connective:

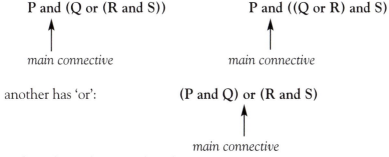

P and (Q or (R and S))   P and ((Q or R) and S)

main connective   *main connective*

another has 'or':   **(P and Q) or (R and S)**

main connective

and two have the second 'and':

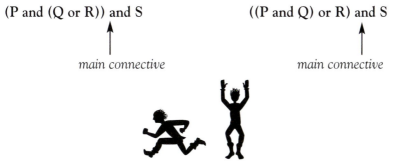

(P and (Q or R)) and S   **((P and Q) or R) and S**

main connective   *main connective*

7   Malform: (i) **(((((P and Q) or R).**
It has two more right-facing brackets than it should. Brackets must be in pairs, each pair enclosing a complete formula (i.e. a wff).

Wff: (ii) **(((P and Q) or R))**
(P and Q) or R is a wff. So *((P and Q) or R)* is also a wff: its outer brackets enclose *(P and Q) or R*. And so *(((P and Q) or R))*, whose outer brackets enclose *that* wff, is a wff as well.

367

8 The two outer pairs in (ii) are unnecessary. Remove them and you have *(P and Q) or R*, which is exactly equivalent to (ii).

9 Malforms:
   (i) **If P then Q and R**   It is ambiguous between *(if P then Q) and R* and *if P then (Q and R)*.
   (ii) **P (or Q) and R.**   Brackets must enclose a whole formula, which *or Q* is not.
   Wff: (iii) **P and P.**   No problem. It is logically equivalent to P.

10 No, it's an argument-form. Its premises and conclusion are wffs.

11 (i) **If P then (Q and R)**   (ii) **If (P and Q) then R**.

12 (i) The first 'not' in *not not P* negates *not P*. The second 'not' negates *P*.
   (ii) 'Not' negates *P or R*.
   (iii)'Not' negates *P*. If we want to make it negate *P or R*, we'll have to write formula (ii) instead.

1 YES: 'If-then'.

2   P: The Snake dies in the attempt
    Q: The Snake lives, but fails
    R: The Snake succeeds.

3 'The Fox soon becomes Captain, without having to steal the Eye.' It is implicit. (So we could put it in various ways, e.g. 'take the test' instead of 'steal the Eye'. The only thing we must be careful not to do is put words into the Fox's mouth which he does not clearly intend.)

4 An argument needs at least two statements – premise and conclusion – related by 'therefore', which is not itself a statement, but relates statements. (If there are several premises, the argument will of course have more than two statements.)

5 'The Fox will have no rival, and can easily persuade the band that further tests are a waste of time.'

6   P: The Snake dies in the attempt. (As the answer to 2.)
    R: The Fox will soon become Captain, without having to steal the Eye (=the Snake's final conclusion: not as in the answer to 2).

7 YES: no argument of this form could have true premises and a false conclusion.

8   P: The Snake lives but fails
    Q: The Snake loses face and leaves at once for distant parts
    R: The Fox has no rival and can easily persuade the band that further tests are a waste of time
    S: The Fox soon becomes Captain, without having to steal the Eye.

9 It is valid. We can represent the same premises and conclusion as two successive arguments, where the conclusion of the first is used as a premise in the second:

If P then Q	and	**If P then R**
If Q then R		**If R then S**
————		————
If P then R		**If P then S**

and we have already decided that this form cannot have true premises and a false conclusion.

10 YES, it's valid: it has the same valid form as Step 3.

   P: The Snake steals the Eye
   Q: Nobody else can steal it
   R: The Fox doesn't have to steal it.

11 YES, it's valid: it has the same valid form as Step 4.

   P: The Snake steals the Eye
   Q: The priests of Zorro soon destroy him
   R: The Fox is soon the only candidate
   S: The Fox soon becomes Captain

12 **If P then Q**   P: The Snake steals the Eye
   If P then R   Q: The Fox doesn't have to
   ―――――――――――――
   If P then (Q and R).   R: The Fox soon becomes Captain.

   YES, it is valid. (How could a conclusion of this form be false if
   the premises were true?)

1   When they identify a subject or subjects, and say something about it or them.

2   (i) YES. This states, 'Hansel is a child AND Gretel is a child'.
    (ii) NO. Here 'and' does not link two independent statements, one about Hansel and the other about Gretel, which we claim are both true. It states a relation between Hansel and Gretel, and its form is simple, not complex. We could rewrite it without 'and' either as 'Hansel is Gretel's brother' or as 'Gretel is Hansel's sister'.

3   NO, if this means 'Paul and Evangeline are married to each other' as usually it would. Then it is like (ii) above: we could rewrite it without 'and' either as 'Paul is Evangeline's husband' or 'Evangeline is Paul's wife'. But YES, if it just means 'Paul is a married man *and* Evangeline is a married woman' – as it might for example in the answer to 'How many of our school friends are married now?' (The words 'Paul and Evangeline are married' are therefore ambiguous in a way that those of (ii) are not. If I want to say that Hansel is *a* brother, not necessarily Gretel's, and Gretel is *a* sister, not necessarily Hansel's, I would not say 'Hansel and Gretel are brother and sister'.)

4   (i) **P, although Q**   YES.
    (ii) **P but Q**   YES.
    (iii) **P instead of Q** NO. This claims that P is true, but Q is false.
    (iv) **P as well as Q**   YES.
    (v) **Not only P but Q** YES.
    (vi) **If P then Q**   NO. This says nothing about the actual truth of P or Q.

    (i) and (ii) suggest that there's something unexpected about P and Q being true together. (iv) might suggest we already knew that Q, but P is a bit less obvious; (v) suggests the reverse. But each says that both P and Q are true; so, in statement logic, we would replace each by *P and Q*.

    ('If-then' is a logical constant in its own right: see Chapter 22.)

5 The first 'and'. It connects 'I fell down and I broke my leg' and 'I howled'.

6 The second 'and' connects 'I broke my leg' and 'I howled'.

7 There are twelve possibilities in all, since the order of variables doesn't matter with 'and'. They are:

P and (Q and R)   P and (R and Q)   (P and Q) and R
(P and R) and Q   Q and (P and R)   Q and (R and P)
(Q and P) and R   (Q and R) and P   R and (P and Q)
R and (Q and P)   (R and P) and Q   (R and Q) and P.

These all mean exactly the same: any statement of this form is true when P, Q and R are all true; otherwise it is false.

8 (i) **If (Q and R) then P**   NO. It represents an 'if-then' statement. (Its component *Q and R* represents a conjunction.)

  (ii) **(P or Q) and R**   YES. The conjuncts are *P or Q* and R.

  (iii) **(P and R) or Q and R)**   NO. It represents an or-statement or disjunction. (*P and R* and *Q and R* represent conjunctions.)

9 YES. What its conjuncts are depend on how you bracket and order the component statements. They could be:

(i) The witch has turned Oscar into gingerbread
     The witch has turned Ludmilla, Fritz and Clara into gingerbread

or

(ii) The witch has turned Oscar and Ludmilla into gingerbread
     The witch has turned Fritz and Clara into gingerbread

or

(iii)The witch has turned Oscar, Ludmilla and Fritz into gingerbread

The witch has turned Clara into gingerbread

or

(iv)The witch has turned Ludmilla and Clara into gingerbread

The witch has turned Oscar and Fritz into gingerbread … etc.

10 (i) negates *P or Q*.

(ii) means the same as *(Not P) or Q*: it states that either *Not P* is true, or *Q* is, or they both are.

11–12 (a) 'Not all wolves are carnivores.'

(Equivalent to 'It is false that all wolves are carnivores'. Do not confuse this with 'NO wolves are carnivores'.)

(b) 'Someone can/could stay up a tree forever.'

(Equivalent to 'It is false that no one can stay up a tree forever'. 'Someone' means 'at least one person, perhaps more'.)

(c) 'Branches never break.'

(Equivalent to 'It is false that branches sometimes break'.)

(d) 'No animals are unfriendly' *or* 'All animals are friendly'.

(Both equivalent to 'It is false that some animals are not friendly'.)

(e) 'They CAN climb trees or jump this high.'

(Equivalent to 'It is false that they can't climb trees, or jump this high'. Not the same as 'They can climb trees AND jump this high'.)

(f) 'They will neither get tired eventually, nor eventually get bored'.

(Equivalent to 'It is false that eventually they will get tired or bored'.)

1 Look at this truth-table: it lays out all possible combinations (true or false) of P and Q. In line 1 both are true, in line 2 P is true and Q is false – etc. (There will be more about truth-tables in Chapter 20.)

	P	Q	P or Q
(1)	T	T	T
(2)	T	F	T
(3)	F	T	T
(4)	F	F	F

When *P or Q* is inclusive (meaning *P and/or Q*), *P or Q* is false when – and only when – both P and Q are false: line 4.

	P	Q	P or Q
(1)	T	T	T
(2)	T	F	T
(3)	F	T	T
(4)	F	F	F

2 **P or Q and not (P and Q)**
   P: You may have won a trip to the Bahamas (in our Prize Draw).
   Q: You may have won £10,000 (in our Prize Draw).

   Since *P or Q* would mean 'You may have won a trip to the Bahamas or you may have won £10,000 *or both*', we need a formula that adds 'and NOT both' – in other words adds *NOT (P and Q)*. (Remember that *P and Q* means BOTH are true, not just one of them.)

3 P: Applicants for language courses must have some knowledge of French
   Q: Applicants for language courses must have some knowledge of German.

375

4   We can analyse '2 is either even or odd' as '2 is even or 2 is odd'. So yes, it has the logical form *P or Q*. Since 2 is even, the statement is true in the manner of line 2 in the truth-table: P true, Q false.

	P	Q	P or Q
(1)	T	T	T
(2)	T	F	T
(3)	F	T	T
(4)	F	F	F

5   All of them. In each case, the statement is false when, and ONLY when, P, Q and R are all false.

6   *(P or Q) or R* for example; or *R or (P or Q)*...and so on..

7

(i) **If (Q or R) then P:**   NOT a disjunction. Its main connective is 'if-then'. (The formula that follows the 'if' is a disjunction.)

(ii) **(P and Q) or R:**   Yes, a disjunction. The disjuncts are *(P and Q)*, and R.

(iii) **(P or Q) and not (P and Q):**   NOT a disjunction. Its main connective is 'and'. (The first of its two conjuncts is a disjunction.)

8   It's TRUE, because one disjunct is true (the one spoken by the truthful yellow Martian).

Since it is a disjunction, its form is *P or Q*: the true disjunct ('Spligs are dddivyptu') replaces Q. So it is true in the manner of line 3 of the truth-table for P or Q:

	P	Q	P or Q
(1)	T	T	T
(2)	T	F	T
(3)	F	T	T
(4)	F	F	F

9 'Quorflogs are spppingle AND spligs are dddivyptu' is false. It would be true if, and only if, both conjuncts were true; but the first (since it is spoken by a lying green Martian) is false.

10 Since 'Quorflogs are spppingle' is false, its negation, 'Quorflogs are NOT spppingle', is true.

11 In common usage if I say, 'I hit him and he hit me', I normally mean that I hit him first, whereas if I say 'He hit me and I hit him' I mean that he hit me first. The truth and falsity of these two statements therefore depends on something more than the mere truth or falsity of 'He hit me' and of 'I hit him': we have to consider the order in which they occur. But when 'and' is a logical constant, only truth-values count. The order in which the two conjuncts occur is irrelevant, and any meaning that depends on this order is lost.

12 If the statements 'He hit me' and 'I hit him' are both true, then 'I hit him and he hit me' is true, and so is 'He hit me and I hit him'. If either 'He hit me' or 'I hit him' is false, or if both are, 'I hit him and he hit me' is false, and so is 'He hit me and I hit him'.

Answers to Chapter 20

1 Lines 2 and 3.

	P	Q	P and Q
(1)	T	T	T
(2)	T	F	F
(3)	F	T	F
(4)	F	F	F

2 Line 4.

	P	Q	P and Q
(1)	T	T	T
(2)	T	F	F
(3)	F	T	F
(4)	F	F	F

3 See Chapter 19, question 1.

4–5 There are only two possibilities.

	P	not P
(1)	T	F
(2)	F	T.

6

	Q	Q or Q
(1)	T	T
(2)	F	F.

7   R can be either true or
    false when Q is true:

	P	Q	R
(1)		T	T
(2)		T	F

    and either true or false
    when Q is false.

	P	Q	R
(3)		F	T
(4)		F	F

And this combination can
occur when P is true:

	P	Q	R
(1)	T	T	T
(2)	T	T	F
(3)	T	F	T
(4)	T	F	F

and again when P is false.

	P	Q	R
(5)	F	T	T
(6)	F	T	F
(7)	F	F	T
(8)	F	F	F

8   It will be TRUE when *P and Q* is false, and FALSE when *P and
    Q* is true.

9   (i) **P and Q**   P: Quorflogs are NOT spppingle
                              Q: Spligs are NOT dddivyptu
    (ii) **Not P and not Q** P: Quorflogs ARE spppingle
                              Q: Spligs ARE dddivyptu
    (iii) **P and not Q**   P: Quorflogs are NOT spppingle
                              Q: Spligs ARE dddivyptu
    (iv) **Not P and Q**   P: Quorflogs ARE spppingle
                              Q: Spligs are NOT dddivyptu.

10–11 You have drawn the table for (i) before. Here are the tables for the others.

(ii)

	P	Q	Not P	and	not Q
(1)	T	T	F	F	F
(2)	T	F	F	F	T
(3)	F	T	T	F	F
(4)	F	F	T	T	T

(iii)

	P	Q	P	and	not Q
(1)	T	T		F	F
(2)	T	F		T	T
(3)	F	T		F	F
(4)	F	F		F	T

(iv)

	P	Q	Not P	and	Q
(1)	T	T	F	F	T
(2)	T	F	F	F	F
(3)	F	T	T	T	T
(4)	F	F	T	F	F

12 Stage One

	P	Q	(P or Q)	and not (P and Q)
(1)	T	T	T	T
(2)	T	F	T	F
(3)	F	T	T	F
(4)	F	F	F	F

Stage Two

	P	Q	(P or Q)	and not	(P and Q)
(1)	T	T	T	F	T
(2)	T	F	T	T	F
(3)	F	T	T	T	F
(4)	F	F	F	T	F

Stage Three

	P	Q	(P or Q)	and	not	(P and Q)
(1)	T	T	T	F	F	T
(2)	T	F	T	T	T	F
(3)	F	T	T	T	T	F
(4)	F	F	F	F	T	F

1 Line 1. These particular disjuncts could not be true together. 'I have EXACTLY a million pounds' means that I have a million, neither more nor less; so it entails 'I do NOT have more than a million pounds'.

2 Q: I have LESS than a million pounds.

3 Line 3. P is 'I have EXACTLY a million pounds' and this is false; so if *P or Q* is true, it can only be because Q is true.

	P	Q	P or Q
(1)	T	T	T
(2)	T	F	T
(3)	F	T	T
(4)	F	F	F

The real world ⟶ (3)

4 In a better world, the statement could be true because I had exactly a million. Then P would be true and Q false, as in line 2. In a better world still, I might have MORE than a million pounds. In that case – with this P and this Q – line 4 would fit the facts, and *P or Q* would be false.

	P	Q	P or Q
(1)	T	T	T
(2)	T	F	T
(3)	F	T	T
(4)	F	F	F

Two other (better) possible worlds. ⟶ (2), (4)

And again, line 1 is impossible for this particular P and Q: they are incompatible. 'I have EXACTLY a million pounds' means that I have a million, neither more nor less. This entails 'I do NOT have less than a million pounds', so both could not be true.

5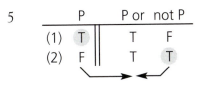

There is a true disjunct in each line, so in each line *P or not P* is TRUE.

6 There is a false conjunct in each line, so in each line *P and not P* is FALSE.

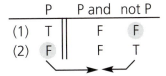

7 P: I have a million pounds
Q: I do not have a million pounds.

8 No. *P and Q* and *P or Q* are both contingent forms, as their truth-tables show. We need to know more than these forms say: namely, that this particular Q negates this particular P.

9 YES. One necessarily true form is enough to show that a statement is necessarily true.

10 NO. *Every* statement has at least one contingent form: P. Many have more than one. If a statement is necessarily true or false, its contingent form/s are simply not detailed enough to show this.

11 YES. One necessarily false form is enough to show that a statement is necessarily false.

12 Given the answers to 9 and 11, OBVIOUSLY NOT. No statement is both true and false.

Answers to Chapter 22

1   (i) P: You are a fish   (ii) P: You are a fish
       Q: You have fins   Q: You have feathers.

2   (i) Something like: 'If China is bigger than France, it's bigger
       than Switzerland'.
       P: China is bigger than France   (TRUE)
       Q: China is bigger than Switzerland.   (TRUE)

3   (ii) Something like: 'If Switzerland is bigger than China, it's
        bigger than France'.
        P: Switzerland is bigger than China   (FALSE)
        Q: Switzerland is bigger than France.   (FALSE)

    (iii)Something like: 'If France is bigger than China, it's bigger
        than Switzerland'.
        P: France is bigger than China   (FALSE)
        Q: France is bigger than Switzerland.   (TRUE)

4

	P	Q	If P then Q
(1)	T	T	T
(2)	T	F	F
(3)	F	T	T
(4)	F	F	T

5   'If you were a fish, you would have feathers' is TRUE for mate-
    rial implication. Since P ('You are a fish') and Q ('You have
    feathers') are both false, it fits line 4 of the truth-table above.

6   Stage One

	P	Q	Not (P and not Q)
(1)	T	T	F
(2)	T	F	T
(3)	F	T	F
(4)	F	F	T

Stage Two

	P	Q	Not (P and not Q)		
(1)	T	T		F	F
(2)	T	F		T	T
(3)	F	T		F	F
(4)	F	F		F	T

Stage Three

	P	Q	Not	(P and not Q)	
(1)	T	T	T	F	F
(2)	T	F	F	T	T
(3)	F	T	T	F	F
(4)	F	F	T	F	T

If P then Q and *not (P and not Q)* have identical truth-values.

	P	Q	If P then Q
(1)	T	T	T
(2)	T	F	F
(3)	F	T	T
(4)	F	F	T

7 (i) is a conditional statement.
    Antecedent: Pigs can fly.
    Consequent: I'm a Dutchman.
  (ii) is a conditional statement.
    Antecedent: I'll come to the party.
    Consequent: Sally can babysit.
  (iii) is NOT a conditional statement, in spite of its surface form. It does not mean 'If Sally can babysit, then I don't know'; it means 'I don't know whether or not Sally can babysit'.
  (iv) is NOT a conditional statement. It has an antecedent ('You're going to the library') but instead of a consequent – which like the antecedent must be a statement – it has a request. Requests have no truth-value.
  (v) is NOT a conditional statement. It has an antecedent ('You can't be good') but instead of a consequent it has a command or instruction. Commands, like requests, have no truth-value.
  (If in doubt about any of this, look again at Chapter 6.)

8 (i) is a conditional.
       Antecedent: *Q or R*
       Consequent: *P.*
   (ii) is NOT a conditional. Since its main connective is 'and',
        it's a conjunction. (Its first conjunct is a conditional.)
   (iii) is a conditional.
       Antecedent: *If P then R* (also a conditional)
       Consequent: *Q.*

9 Stage One

	P	Q	R	If (Q or R) then P
(1)	T	T	T	T
(2)	T	T	F	T
(3)	T	F	T	T
(4)	T	F	F	F
(5)	F	T	T	T
(6)	F	T	F	T
(7)	F	F	T	T
(8)	F	F	F	F

Stage Two

	P	Q	R	If (Q or R)		then	P	
(1)	T	T	T	T			T	T
(2)	T	T	F	T			T	T
(3)	T	F	T	T			T	T
(4)	T	F	F	F			T	T
(5)	F	T	T	T			F	F
(6)	F	T	F	T			F	F
(7)	F	F	T	T			F	F
(8)	F	F	F	F			T	F

10 Stage One

	P	Q	R	(If P then Q) and R
(1)	T	T	T	T
(2)	T	T	F	T
(3)	T	F	T	F
(4)	T	F	F	F
(5)	F	T	T	T
(6)	F	T	F	T
(7)	F	F	T	T
(8)	F	F	F	T

386

Stage Two

	P	Q	R	(If P then Q)	and	R
(1)	T	T	T	T	T	T
(2)	T	T	F	T	F	F
(3)	T	F	T	F	F	T
(4)	T	F	F	F	F	F
(5)	F	T	T	T	T	T
(6)	F	T	F	T	F	F
(7)	F	F	T	T	T	T
(8)	F	F	F	T	F	F

And in case you did the table for (iii):

Stage One

	P	Q	R	If (if P then R) then Q
(1)	T	T	T	T
(2)	T	T	F	F
(3)	T	F	T	T
(4)	T	F	F	F
(5)	F	T	T	T
(6)	F	T	F	T
(7)	F	F	T	T
(8)	F	F	F	T

Stage Two

	P	Q	R	If (if P then R)	then	Q
(1)	T	T	T	T	T	T
(2)	T	T	F	F	T	T
(3)	T	F	T	T	F	F
(4)	T	F	F	F	T	F
(5)	F	T	T	T	T	T
(6)	F	T	F	T	T	T
(7)	F	F	T	T	F	F
(8)	F	F	F	T	F	F

11 (i) Antecedent: You're a bird   (FALSE)

     Consequent: You're not reading this   (FALSE).

     By strict implication the whole conditional is TRUE, because birds cannot read. By material implication, the whole conditional is TRUE: see line 4 of the table.

	P	Q	If P then Q
(1)	T	T	T
(2)	T	F	F
(3)	F	T	T
(4)	F	F	T

(ii) Antecedent: You're a bird   (FALSE)
    Consequent: You ARE reading this   (TRUE)
    By strict implication the whole conditional is FALSE, because birds cannot read. By material implication, the whole conditional is TRUE: line 3 of the table.

	P	Q	If P then Q
(1)	T	T	T
(2)	T	F	F
(3)	F	T	T
(4)	F	F	T

(iii) Antecedent: Today is Monday
    Consequent: Tomorrow is Tuesday.
    (Both TRUE or both FALSE, depending which day you read this.)
    Tuesday always follows Monday, so by strict implication (iii) is always TRUE. By material implication the whole conditional again is always TRUE: true as in line 1 if today is Monday, true as in line 4 if it is any other day.

	P	Q	If P then Q
(1)	T	T	T
(2)	T	F	F
(3)	F	T	T
(4)	F	F	T

(iv) Antecedent: Today is Monday
      Consequent: Tomorrow is Thursday.

(These have three possible pairs of truth-values, depending which day you read this.)

Since Thursday never follows Monday, by strict implication (iv) is always FALSE. But by material implication, if it is Monday, the antecedent is TRUE and the consequent FALSE; so the whole conditional is FALSE, as in line 2.

	P	Q	If P then Q
(1)	T	T	T
(2)	T	F	F
(3)	F	T	T
(4)	F	F	T

And if it is not Monday, the antecedent is FALSE: the consequent may then be TRUE (if it is Wednesday) or FALSE (if it is any other day). Either way, by material implication the whole conditional is TRUE, as in line 3 or line 4.

	P	Q	If P then Q
(1)	T	T	T
(2)	T	F	F
(3)	F	T	T
(4)	F	F	T

12 It is contingent. The table shows that it can be either false (line 2) or true (lines 1, 3, and 4).

Answers to Chapter 23

1   Randolph argument I: YES. The conclusion could not be false if the premises are true.

Randolph argument II: NO. This form does not *guarantee* a false conclusion when the premises are true: since 'or' means 'and/or', Randolph might be asleep (as premise 2 states) and dead as well, for all that it tells us. (Did you fail to see this possibility because in fact nobody is both asleep and dead? If so, you were thinking about the argument's content, not its form; and only form counts in validity.) But it allows one. He could – as in fact he would – also be asleep and alive.

2   YES, it is valid. Form: **If P then not Q**

If Q then not P.

3   Something like:

If I weigh more than 1000 pounds, I weigh more than 100 pounds	(TRUE)
I don't weigh more than 1000 pounds	(TRUE)
I don't weigh more than 100 pounds.	(FALSE)

'I' refers here to the writer of this book. If we do not know who I am, we cannot assign a truth-value to premise no. 2, nor to the conclusion. A hippo or a mouse might be speaking. Remember this whenever you give an example containing an indexical. It is also true for names whose bearer we do not know. 'De Gaulle was bigger then Napoleon' does not need an extra note because, as they are normally used, these names refer to people we know about; but 'Smith is bigger than Jones' will not do unless you add some background ('Smith is a hippo and Jones is a mouse'). By contrast, premise no.1 is always true, if the words are used in their usual sense: it is analytic.

4   A formula is the logical form of a statement. When it is contingent, statements with that form may be either true or false. A contingent *conditional* is one that allows, but does not require, a true antecedent and a false consequent.

When a contingent conditional is an argument's validity-formula, the argument's form allows, but does not require, true premises and a false conclusion. So when a validity-formula is CONTINGENT, the related argument is INVALID.

Example: Randolph argument II – see the answer to question 12.

Warning: do not call the argument itself 'contingent' or the validity-formula 'invalid'. Only single statements or formulae – statement-forms – are contingent or necessary, and single statements are never arguments. An argument needs at least TWO statements (premise and conclusion) plus a 'therefore'. For the same reason, only arguments and argument-forms can literally be invalid. We do sometimes speak of a 'valid conclusion', but this is just short for 'conclusion of a valid argument'.

5   When a formula is necessarily false, statements with that form cannot be true. When a conditional is necessarily false its form guarantees a true antecedent and false consequent. This happens only when the antecedent is *necessarily* true – with a form like *P or not P* – and the consequent necessarily false. When this conditional is an argument's validity-formula, the argument *must* have a false conclusion when its premises are true: you will never get a true conclusion by accident.

6 It is valid. Take the simplest necessarily true conditional, *if P then P*: related argument-form

$$\frac{P}{P.}$$

When P is true, the formula cannot have a false consequent, and when P is false, it cannot have a true antecedent. And the related argument-form cannot have a true premise and a false conclusion.

	P	If P then P
(1)	T	T
(2)	F	T

7   P: Randolph is asleep   Q: Randolph is dead.
8   *(P or Q) and not P.*

9   *If (P or Q) and not P then Q.* We do not need more brackets because this is not ambiguous; but if it makes the form clearer, feel free to put some round the whole antecedent: *if ((P or Q) and not P) then Q.*

10 Stage One

	P	Q	If (P or Q)	and	not	P	then	Q
(1)	T	T	T	F	F			T
(2)	T	F	T	F	F			F
(3)	F	T	T	T	T			T
(4)	F	F	F	T	T			F

Stage Two

	P	Q	If (P or Q)	and	not	P	then	Q
(1)	T	T	T	F	F			T
(2)	T	F	T	F	F			F
(3)	F	T	T	T	T			T
(4)	F	F	F	F	T			F

Stage Three

	P	Q	If (P or Q)	and	not	P	then	Q
(1)	T	T	T	F	F	**T**		T
(2)	T	F	T	F	F	**T**		F
(3)	F	T	T	T	T	**T**		T
(4)	F	F	F	F	T	**T**		F

The line of Ts under the main connective shows that the argument's validity-formula is a necessary truth. So, for the reasons given in the answer to question 6, the related argument is VALID.

Randolph

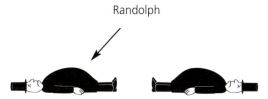

Line 3: a world where the premises of Randolph Argument I are true.

11 *If (P or Q) and P then Q.* Again, add brackets for readability if you like: *if ((P or Q) and P) then Q.*

12 Stage One

	P	Q	If (P or Q)	and	P	then	Q
(1)	T	T	T		T		T
(2)	T	F	T		T		F
(3)	F	T	T		F		T
(4)	F	F	F		F		F

Stage Two

	P	Q	If (P or Q)	and	P	then	Q
(1)	T	T	T	T	T		T
(2)	T	F	T	T	T		F
(3)	F	T	T	F	F		T
(4)	F	F	F	F	F		F

Stage Three

	P	Q	If (P or Q)	and	P	then	Q
(1)	T	T	T	T	T	**T**	T
(2)	T	F	T	T	T	**F**	F
(3)	F	T	T	F	F	**T**	T
(4)	F	F	F	F	F	**T**	F

The F under the main connective in line (2) shows that when P is true and Q is false, the formula *if (P or Q) and P then Q* will be false. Since this is the validity-formula for Randolph argument II, the argument will have true premises and a false conclusion if ever P ('Randolph is asleep') is true but Q ('Randolph is dead') is false.

Line 2: a world where the premises of Randolph Argument II are true.

1 Stage One

		P	Q	If (if P then not Q) then if Q then not P				
(1)		T	T	T	F		T	F
(2)		T	F	T	T		F	F
(3)		F	T	F	F		T	T
(4)		F	F	F	T		F	T

Stage Two

		P	Q	If (if P then not Q) then if Q then not P						
(1)		T	T	T	F	F		T	F	F
(2)		T	F	T	T	T		F	T	F
(3)		F	T	F	T	F		T	T	T
(4)		F	F	F	T	T		F	T	T

Stage Three

		P	Q	If (if P then not Q) then if Q then not P							
(1)		T	T	T	F	F	**T**	T	F	F
(2)		T	F	T	T	T	**T**	F	T	F
(3)		F	T	F	T	F	**T**	T	T	T
(4)		F	F	F	T	T	**T**	F	T	T

2 For example:
    If ((((if P then Q) and (if Q then R))
    and (if R then S)) and P
    then S.

3 Sixteen lines, because it has four variables.

4 (i) WRONG. Formulae are not valid: only arguments are. (See the answer to question 4, Chapter 17).
    (ii) RIGHT.

5–11(i) WRONG.

	P	Q	If P then Q
(1)	T	T	T
(2)	T	F	F
(3)	F	T	T
(4)	F	F	T

(ii) RIGHT.

(iii) WRONG. It is false if the antecedent is true; but if the antecedent is false, the statement is TRUE.

	P	Q	If P then Q
(1)	T	T	T
(2)	T	F	F
(3)	F	T	T
(4)	F	F	T

(iv) RIGHT.

(v) WRONG. A necessarily false validity-formula tells you that the related argument *must* have a false conclusion when the premises are true. It is enough if it *could*. So the right thing to say is, 'When an argument is invalid, its validity-formula is either contingent or necessarily false'.

(vi) WRONG. A valid argument can have several forms, and some may not be detailed enough to show that it is valid. For example, any argument with the validity-formula you tested for question 1 will have not only the valid form you tested:

If P then not Q

———————————

If Q then not P

but also the simple, invalid form $\dfrac{P}{Q.}$

(vii) RIGHT. One valid form is enough to make an argument valid. So an invalid argument cannot have such a form.

(viii) WRONG: see (vi). If an argument-form is too simple to show the argument's validity, its validity-formula is contingent. *If P then Q* – the validity-formula for $\dfrac{\mathrm{P}}{\mathrm{Q}}$ – is an example.

(ix) WRONG: see the answer to (v). It could also have a validity-formula that was necessarily false.

12 (i) Antecedent true, consequent false: Shrdlu the Liar is speaking. (Truth-table for *if P then Q*, line 2.)

(ii) Antecedent *necessarily* false, consequent false: Truthful Qwertyuiop is speaking. (Truth-table for *if P then Q*, line 4.)

(iii) Antecedent *necessarily* true, consequent true: Truthful Qwertyuiop is speaking. (Truth-table for *if P then Q*, line 1.)

(iv) Antecedent true, consequent true: Truthful Qwertyuiop is speaking. (Truth-table for *if P then Q*, line 1.)

(v) Antecedent false, consequent true: Truthful Qwertyuiop is speaking. (Truth-table for *if P then Q*, line 3.)

1 **Not ((P or Q) and not Q) and not P.**

2 Lines 3 and 4, both of which posit the false state of affairs, 'You are a fish'.

	P	Q	If P then Q
(1)	T	T	T
(2)	T	F	F
(3)	F	T	T
(4)	F	F	T

3 'If sharks are not snails then 2+2=7' is FALSE. (Line 2 of the truth-table for *if P then Q.*)

4 (i) 'If sharks are not snails then sharks are snails' is FALSE (line 2).
   (ii) 'If sharks are snails then sharks are not snails' is TRUE (line 3).

5 You will need arguments with true premises and a false conclusion. For example (assuming, Reader, that you are not a dog, but human):

If P then Q	If you are a dog, then you have bones	(T)
Q	You have bones	(T)
P	You are dog	(F)

If P then Q	If you are a dog, then you have bones	(T)
Not P	You are not a dog	(T)
Not Q	You do not have bones	(F)

If P then Q	If you are dog then you have bones	(T)
If Q then P	If you have bones then you are a dog	(F).

6 No. One example is enough to show that a form *can* have true premises and a false conclusion: i.e. it is invalid. But it is valid only if *no* example can have them. We cannot show this simply by giving examples, because the list of possible examples is endless.

7 Stage One

	P	Q	If	(if P then Q)	and	P	then	Q
(1)	T	T		T				T
(2)	T	F		F				T
(3)	F	T		T				F
(4)	F	F		T				F

Stage Two

	P	Q	If	(if P then Q)	and	P	then	Q
(1)	T	T		T	T	T		T
(2)	T	F		F	F	T		F
(3)	F	T		T	F	F		T
(4)	F	F		T	F	F		F

Stage Three

	P	Q	If	(if P then Q)	and	P	then	Q
(1)	T	T		T	T	T	**T**	T
(2)	T	F		F	F	T	**T**	F
(3)	F	T		T	F	F	**T**	T
(4)	F	F		T	F	F	**T**	F

8 **If P then S**   P: The Snake dies in the attempt
   If Q then S   Q: The Snake lives but fails
   If R then S   R: The Snake succeeds
   If (P or Q) or R   S: The Fox soon becomes captain
   then S*   without having to steal the Eye.

* or *if P or (Q or R) then S* – etc.

9   **If P then Q**   P: The Snake dies in the attempt, or
     P   lives but fails, or succeeds
     ————   Q: The Fox soon becomes captain
     Q.   without having to steal the Eye

10   **If (P or Q) or R then S**   P, Q, R and S as in the answer to 8.
    (P or Q) or R
    ————————
    S.

11   Validity-formula for Step 7:

        **If ((if P then S and if Q then S) and if R then S)
then if ((P or Q) or R) then S.**

  There are of course several ways you could bracket this.

12   Since there are four variables, the table for this would need sixteen lines.

1   A (logically) necessary truth is a statement whose form will not allow it to be false. It will have at least one underlying formula which is analytic. When this is a formula in statement logic, a truth-table will show that it is so: whatever the truth-values of its variables, the formula will come out TRUE.

2   *If P then (Q and R)*. Since this is a conditional, when it is false its antecedent P must be true: a material conditional is false just when its antecedent is true and its consequent false.

3   For the same reason, when *if P then (Q and R)* is false, *Q and R* must be false. When *Q and R* is false, either *Q* is false, or *R* is, or both are.

4   Three: in a full table they would be lines (2), (3) and (4).

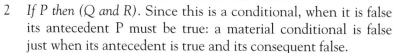

P Q R If (if P then Q and if P then R) then if P then (Q and R)

(2) T	T	F		*T?*		*F?*	T	F	F
(3) T	F	T		*T?*		*F?*	T	F	F
(4) T	F	F		*T?*		*F?*	T	F	F

5   'And' is the main connective of the antecedent *if P then Q and if P then R*. (Its conjuncts are the premises in the argument we are testing.)

6   *If P then Q and if P then R* must both be true. This means that P must be false, and/or both Q and R true.

7   NO, we have not. In lines (2) and (4), the truth-values of P and R make *if P then R* false; so the antecedent of the whole formula is false, and the formula is TRUE.

P Q R If (if P then Q and if P then R) then if P then (Q and R)

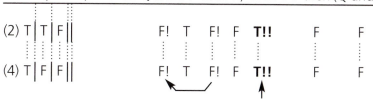

(2) T	T	F		F!	T	F!	F	**T!!**	F	F
(4) T	F	F		F!	T	F!	F	**T!!**	F	F

And in lines (3) and (4), the truth-values of P and Q make *if P then Q* false, with the same result.

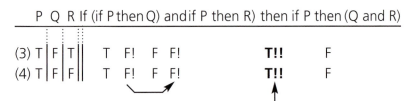

So there is no line where the validity-formula is false; and the argument is VALID.

8 **If (if P then Q and if Q then R) then if P then R.**

9 Its consequent must be false. Since this consequent is *if P then R*, P must be true and R false. There are two possibilities: lines (2) and (4) of the full table. (You needn't bother with line numbers when using this method: this is just for your information.)

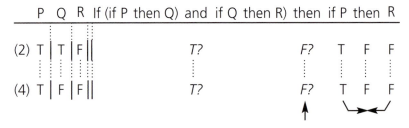

10 NO: there is no such line. The formula's antecedent *if P then Q and if Q then R* must be true; so *if P then Q* must be true, and also *if Q then R*.

But in line (2), the truth-values of Q and R make *if Q then R* false. So the antecedent is false, and the whole validity-formula is TRUE.

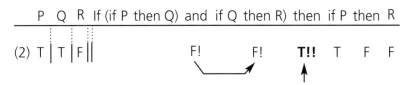

And in line (4), the truth-values of P and Q make *if P then Q* false, with the same result.

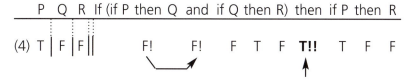

The argument-form that we are testing is VALID.

11 The validity-formula is *if (if P then R and if Q then R) then if (P or Q) then R* and as always – to make it false – we need a true antecedent and a false consequent. If the consequent is false, P or Q is true and R is false. P or Q can be true in three different ways, so we have three possibilities. (They correspond to lines 2, 4 and 6 of the full table.)

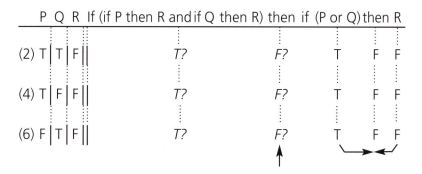

But the formula's antecedent must also be true. In lines (2) and (6) the truth-values of Q and R make *if Q then R* false, so the antecedent is FALSE:

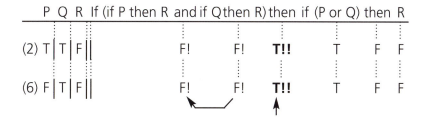

and in line (4) the truth-values of P and R make *if P then R* false, with the same result.

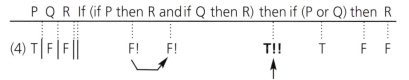

So YES, we have now shown (by truth-tables) that the Fox's whole argument is valid.

12 His reasoning was valid, but it was not sound: the premise, 'Once the Snake has stolen the Eye, the possibility of MY doing so cannot arise' was false. This allowed a false conclusion – and so it turned out.

1   The table says that whenever *P iff Q* is true, P and Q have the same truth-value, and whenever *P iff Q* is false, they do not. The value for the whole formula is therefore T for line (1) where both are true and T for line (4) where both are false. It is F for lines (2) and (3), where the truth-values of P and Q differ.

2   They are identical.

	P	Q	P iff Q
(1)	T	T	T
(2)	T	F	F
(3)	F	T	F
(4)	F	F	T

	P	Q	Q iff P
(1)	T	T	T
(2)	T	F	F
(3)	F	T	F
(4)	F	F	T

3   P: You have red hair
     Q: You can join the Red-Headed League.

4   NO. Other things might also make you eligible, like being a red-haired member's relation or having grey hair that used to be red.

5   YES, he can. 'You' in a context like this (where no limitation is specified) should apply to *any* 'you' including Ginger, and

> If you have red hair you can join the Red-Headed League
> You have red hair
> _____
> You can join the Red-Headed League

is of course valid. If the League starts out by stating this IF-rule and then changes the requirements to keep out cats, it is guilty of ground-shifting.

6   YES. In the ONLY-IF case, *only* red-haired candidates are allowed.

7   Any of three forms would do. 'You can join the Red-Headed League ONLY IF you have red hair' means the same as

    (i) 'If you do NOT have red hair, you can NOT join the Red-Headed League': logical form *if not P then not Q*

or   (ii) 'You CAN'T join the Red-Headed League WITHOUT having red hair': logical form *not (Q and not P)*

or   (iii)'If you CAN join the Red-Headed League, you HAVE red hair': logical form *if Q then P.*

8   NO. If the ONLY-IF rule is all we know, we do not know that the IF-rule holds ('You can join IF you have red hair'). All we know is that without red hair, you cannot. Think of 'You will win the Lottery ONLY IF you buy a ticket.' True: you will never win if you do not. But that does not mean you will win if you do. (For another example, see the answer to question 10.)

9   We do not know, because we do not know whether the IF-rule holds. A necessary condition like red hair may be one of several.

'Sorry. You seem to be unaware of our further rule: TO JOIN THE RED-HEADED LEAGUE YOU MUST BE OF IRISH ORIGIN. You are a Persian cat.'

red

The Secretary of the League

10   When the rule is 'You can join the League IFF you have red hair AND are of Irish origin':

    (i) is FALSE. The IF-rule here is 'You can join the League if you have red hair AND are of Irish origin'.

    (ii) is TRUE. Two ONLY-IF rules now hold, and this is one of them. The other is 'You can join the League ONLY IF you are of Irish origin'.

    (iii)is FALSE, because (i) is false. (iii) is equivalent to the conjunction of (i) and (ii).

11 Here are some parallels with the Uncle definition: you can think of others.

Suppose that P is 'The argument is valid', and Q is 'The argument's form will not allow true premises and a false conclusion'. Then if I say merely

(i) 'An argument is valid IF its form will not allow true premises and a false conclusion',

this is inadequate for two reasons.

First, it does not distinguish 'valid argument' from wider terms. Something is also *an argument* if it is an argument whose form will not allow true premises and a false conclusion; and it is *a linguistic entity*; and it is *not a teapot*; and it *exists*. These are not what I set out to define. And second, although it specifies one sufficient condition for validity, if you did not know what 'valid argument' meant you might think other conditions would do as well. ('If *you* say it, Your Majesty, it is valid!') This is not the case.

And if I say merely

(ii) 'An argument is valid ONLY IF its form will not allow true premises and a false conclusion'

I fail to distinguish 'valid argument' from narrower terms. An argument can only be a *valid syllogism* (a valid three-line argument) if its form will not allow true premises and a false conclusion; or a valid argument *about liberty*; or a valid argument *stated by Her Majesty* – and so on. But when I say

(iii) 'An argument is valid IFF its form will not allow true premises and a false conclusion'

I define 'valid argument' exactly.

12 Two statements are strictly equivalent if they have the same truth-value *because of what they state*; they are materially equivalent if they merely have the same truth-value. The first clearly guarantees the second. But the second does not guarantee the first, because it could also be true for some other reason. For example, *being stated by a truthful Martian* guarantees that two statements have the same truth-value (namely, 'true'), irrespective of what they state.

Answers to Chapter 28

1   (ii) and (iii). Both say that red hair is necessary for joining the Red-Headed League'. (i) does not.

2   NO. Other things may be necessary too (see the answer to 4).

3   YES. 'Sufficient' means *enough*.

4   NO. Red hair is no longer enough: you need to be of Irish origin too.

5   It is necessary, but not sufficient. The Irish rule is a *further* rule. You still need red hair.

6   *Possibly* O'Reilly can join: he meets the only necessary conditions that we have heard of. But the Secretary has not said that these are all: for all we know, he could require something else:

'And furthermore, you must be able to dance a jig.'

– and so on indef initely:

'And cavorting about on four legs won't do, you must do it bipedally.'

etc.

(As it turns out, there are no more requirements: red hair and Irish origin are sufficient. But so far the Secretary has not said so.)

7   *If not Q then not P*, or if you want a shorter formula, *if P then Q*. They are logically equivalent, but I think the first is closer to how we might naturally put it.

8   NO. The Secretary, remember, is not a fox. He fits the requirements in another way.

9   (v), (vi) and (vii). None of the others says enough.

10 Stage One

	P	Q	If P then Q	and if not P then not Q	
(1)	T	T	T	F	F
(2)	T	F	F	F	T
(3)	F	T	T	T	F
(4)	F	F	T	T	T

Stage Two

	P	Q	If P then Q	and	if not P	then	not Q
(1)	T	T	T		F	T	F
(2)	T	F	F		F	T	T
(3)	F	T	T		T	F	F
(4)	F	F	T		T	T	T

Stage Three

	P	Q	If P then Q	and	if not P	then	not Q
(1)	T	T	T	T	F	T	F
(2)	T	F	F	F	F	T	T
(3)	F	T	T	F	T	F	F
(4)	F	F	T	T	T	T	T

They are equivalent.

	P	Q	P iff Q
(1)	T	T	T
(2)	T	F	F
(3)	F	T	F
(4)	F	F	T

11

	P	Q	If P then Q	and	if Q then P
(1)	T	T	T	T	T
(2)	T	F	F	F	T
(3)	F	T	T	F	F
(4)	F	F	T	T	T

They are all equivalent.

12　(i) YES.

(ii) NO.

(iii) NO.

(iv) YES.

(v) NO. It is sufficient, but not necessary.

(vi) NO. It is necessary, but not sufficient.

(vii) You are a mother IFF you are a female parent.

(viii) You are a grandmother IFF you are the mother of a parent.

1   (1) All animals in this house are cats.
    (2) All moon-gazing animals are suitable for pets.
    (3) All animals I detest are animals I avoid.
    (4) All carnivores are night-prowling.
    (5) All cats are mouse-killers.
    (6) All animals that take to me are in this house.
    (7) No kangaroo is suitable for a pet.
    (8) All mouse-killers are carnivores.
    (9) All animals that do not take to me are animals I detest.
    (10) All animals that prowl at night are moon-gazing.

2   (i) CATS UNICORNS

    (ii) As (i): they are equivalent.

    (iii) CATS UNICORNS

3   All *animals* that are neither cats nor unicorns.

4   (i) and (iii): as above.

    (ii)
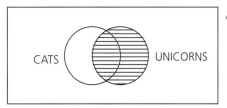

5   A statement P entails another statement Q iff Q is true when-
    ever P is. And clearly P is true whenever *P and R* is: that is how
    conjunctions work. So Q is also true whenever *P and R* is, i.e. *P
    and R* entails Q. (In this case P will also have the form *all A are
    B* and Q the form *there is at least one A*.)

6   GENIUSES   MAD THINGS

7   ANIMALS IN
THIS HOUSE   CATS

8   1.   Anything that is neither a cat, a unicorn nor a genius
      2.   Cats that are neither unicorns nor geniuses
      3.   Cats that are unicorns but are not geniuses
      4.   Cat-geniuses that are also unicorns
      5.   Cat-geniuses that are not unicorns
      6.   Unicorns that are neither geniuses nor cats
      7.   Unicorn-geniuses that are not cats
      8.   Geniuses that are neither unicorns nor cats.

9   A: Animals in this house
     B: Cats
     C: Mousekillers.

10   ANIMALS IN THIS HOUSE

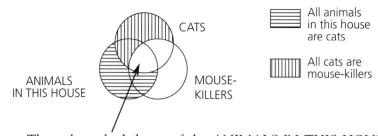

The only unshaded part of the ANIMALS IN THIS HOUSE circle falls within the MOUSEKILLERS circle. So the diagram shows that *no cats are NOT mousekillers* – which is what we mean by 'All cats ARE mousekillers'. The argument is VALID.

11–12 You have shown that all the animals in this house are mousekillers. Make this the first premise of syllogism 2. To go with it, you could in theory choose either premise (6) – with 'animals in this house' as your middle term – or (8), with the middle term 'mousekillers'. But my list of suggested premises leaves (6) out: I would rather use it later. So you should choose (8): 'All mousekillers are carnivores'; and again choose alternatives to (6) in the three steps that follow.

(But wherever 'animals in this house' is a possible middle term, you *could* use (6). If you would like more practice, try other routes when you have finished doing the puzzle my way.)

SYLLOGISM 2

All the animals in this house are mousekillers (conclusion to 1)
All mousekillers are carnivores   (premise 8)

_____

All the animals in this house are carnivores.

Middle term: MOUSEKILLERS.
Diagram: as for syllogism 1, with different sets.

Diagram 2

As before, once we put our premises into the diagram by shading it, we can see that the conclusion follows: the only part of the ANIMALS IN THIS HOUSE circle that is still unshaded falls within the CARNIVORES circle. So *all the animals in this house are carnivores*, and the argument is VALID.

SYLLOGISM 3

All the animals in this house are carnivores   (conclusion to 2)
All carnivores are night-prowlers   (premise 4)

_____

All the animals in this house are night-prowlers.

Middle term: CARNIVORES.

Diagram: as for syllogisms 1 and 2, with different sets.

Diagram 3

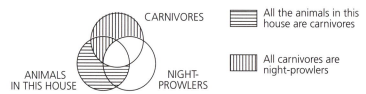

When we have shaded in the premises, the only part of the ANIMALS IN THIS HOUSE circle that is still unshaded falls within the CARNIVORES circle. So all the animals in this house are carnivores, and the argument is VALID.

SYLLOGISM 4
All the animals in this house are night-prowlers   (conclusion to 3)
All night-prowlers are moon-gazers   (premise 10)
_____

All the animals in this house are moon-gazers.

Middle term: NIGHT-PROWLERS.
Diagram: as for syllogisms 1, 2 and 3, with different sets.

Diagram 4

The pattern should be familiar now. We can see from diagram 4 that all the animals in this house are moon-gazers, so the argument is VALID.

SYLLOGISM 5

| All the animals in this house are moon-gazers | (conclusion to 4) |
| All moon-gazers are suitable for pets | (premise 2) |

All the animals in this house are suitable for pets.

Middle term: MOON-GAZERS.
Diagram: the same again, with different sets.

Diagram 5

The diagram shows that all the animals in this house are suitable for pets, so the argument is VALID.

1   B. The middle term is shared by both premises. It is the link between these premises, and allows us to conclude something new from them. (It drops out of the conclusion.)

2 SYLLOGISM 6
All the animals that take to me are animals in   (premise 6)
this house
All the animals in this house are suitable for pets (conclusion to 5)
_____

All animals that take to me are suitable for pets.

Middle term: ANIMALS IN THIS HOUSE.
Diagram: as before, with different sets.

Diagram 6

When we shade in the premises we see that all animals that take to me are suitable for pets, so the argument is VALID.

3   (7): 'No kangaroos are suitable for pets'. Our other premise is 'All animals that take to me are suitable for pets', and (7) has one of the same terms: no other premise has. So (7) gives us a middle term for syllogism 7: no other premise does.

4 B. The argument-form is   **All A are B**
                              No C is B (or *No B is C*)
                              No C is A (or *No A is C*).

5 A: Animals that take to me
   B: Animals that are suitable for a pet
   C: Kangaroos.

6 SYLLOGISM 7
All animals that take to me are suitable for pets   (conclusion to 6)
No kangaroos are suitable for pets   (premise 7)

No kangaroos are animals that take to me.

Middle term: ANIMALS THAT ARE SUITABLE FOR PETS.
Diagram: A new one for a change.

Diagram 7

When we draw in both premises, the intersection of the
KANGAROOS circle and the ANIMALS THAT TAKE TO
ME circle is completely shaded. This means that the set of
KANGAROOS THAT TAKE TO ME is empty, i.e. 'No
kangaroos are animals that take to me'. The argument is
VALID.

7 Premise (9). Add it to the conclusion of syllogism 7 and we can
   validly infer that *all kangaroos are animals I detest*. But once
   again, we'll need a different form of argument and diagram: see
   the next three questions.

8 They refer to four sets: ANIMALS THAT TAKE TO ME,
   ANIMALS THAT DO NOT TAKE TO ME, ANIMALS I
   DETEST and KANGAROOS. The first two sets are clearly
   related, but are not the same.

9   Everything within the frame but outside the circle of ANIMALS THAT DO NOT TAKE TO ME:

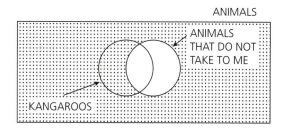

10 *Diagram 8A*

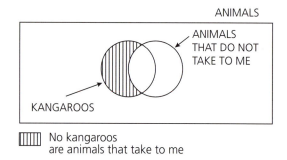

We shade the KANGAROOS circle where it lies outside the circle of ANIMALS THAT DO NOT TAKE TO ME. Once we do this, we can see that no kangaroos are NOT animals that do not take to me. This is the same (in our system) as 'ALL kangaroos ARE animals that do not take to me'.

11 SYLLOGISM 8

All kangaroos are animals that do not
take to me   (from conclusion to 7)
All animals that do not take to me are
animals I detest   (premise 9)
───────────────────────────────

All kangaroos are animals I detest.

Middle term: ANIMALS THAT DO NOT TAKE TO ME.
Diagram: as so often before, with different sets. The argument is VALID.

Diagram 8B

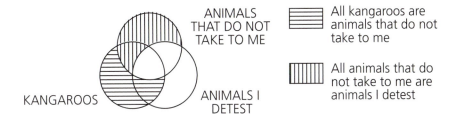

All kangaroos are animals that do not take to me

All animals that do not take to me are animals I detest

And finally…

12 *The diagram*

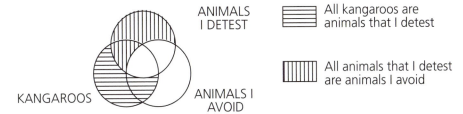

All kangaroos are animals that I detest

All animals that I detest are animals I avoid

Same form of diagram as above: the syllogism is VALID.
Middle term: ANIMALS I DETEST.

THE SYLLOGISM:
    All kangaroos are animals I detest   (conclusion to 8)
    All animals that I detest are animals I avoid   (premise 3)
    _____

All kangaroos are animals I avoid…

…or

I ALWAYS AVOID KANGAROOS.

Answers to Chapter 31

1   NO, it does not (unless we add something that asserts existence, which you have not learned how to do yet). These diagrams

just mention various sets, without saying anything about them. The first mentions GEESE (inside the circle) and EVERYTHING ELSE (outside it); the second mentions GEESE THAT AREN'T SWANS, GEESE THAT ARE SWANS, SWANS THAT AREN'T GEESE and EVERYTHING THAT IS NEITHER A GOOSE NOR A SWAN.

2   The first states (falsely) that there are no geese. The second states (truly) that no geese are swans.

3   The first does not state anything: the way that it is laid out (with the three circles overlapping) simply allows it to mention eight separate sets. The second makes two statements: 'No hens swim' (vertical shading) and 'All geese swim' (horizontal shading). Or we could say that it states the conjunction 'No hens swim and all geese do'.

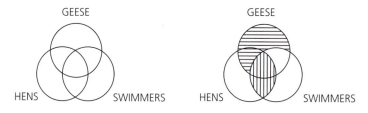

420

4   No. Like the left-hand diagram above, it simply mentions certain sets. But now the major sets are *BIRDS* THAT ARE GEESE, *BIRDS* THAT ARE HENS, *BIRDS* THAT ARE SWIMMERS, and all *BIRDS* that are none of these. Hens and geese are birds anyway, so the circles labelled 'HENS' and 'GEESE' happen to mean the same sets in each diagram. But the one labelled 'SWIMMERS' does not: in the frameless diagram it includes fish, for example. The framed one has no place for fish.

5   'All the Swiss speak French or German, but not both' is the same as 'All the Swiss speak French or German or both' (vertical shading) plus 'No one speaks both' (horizontal shading).

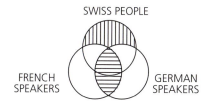

6   'All Swiss people speak French or German, or both':

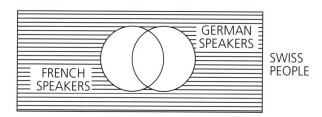

'All Swiss people speak French or German, but not both':

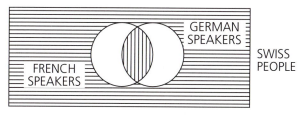

(Remember that the circles here stand for SWISS French-speakers and SWISS German-speakers. There is no place in the diagram for other kinds.)

7.

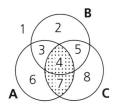

4: As that are both B and C

4+7:   As that are C

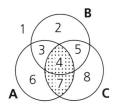

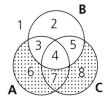

6+7+8: Everything that is A or C or both, but is not B

8   Something like this. (The dotted part is D.)

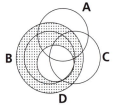

9   *ONLY A are B* is the same as *all B are A*. You know how to do that.

10   This states the same as 'All those with red hair can join the League' (horizontal shading) plus 'All those who can join the League have red hair' (vertical shading).

THOSE WITH
RED HAIR

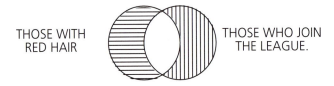

THOSE WHO JOIN
THE LEAGUE.

11 Start with the diagram above. Add a circle for the set of
    FOXES. Then shade to state that the set of FOXES
    WITHOUT RED HAIR is empty, i.e. *all foxes have red hair*. (I
    have used diagonal shading for this.)

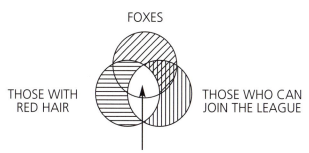

FOXES

THOSE WITH
RED HAIR

THOSE WHO CAN
JOIN THE LEAGUE

    There is now only one part of the FOXES circle that is not
    shaded, and it lies within the circle of THOSE WHO CAN
    JOIN THE LEAGUE. So all foxes can join the league.

12 None of these diagrams make any claim at all about what *does*
    exist. They only say that certain sets are empty, i.e. certain
    kinds of thing do *not* exist.

Answers to Chapter 32

1 Two: FROGS and ANIMALS; so it will need two circles.

2 **All A are B**

———————

All B are A

– though, since they are equivalent, you could say *no A is not B* instead of *all A are B*, and/or *no B is not A* instead of *all B are A*.

3 If this were valid, the part that represents B BUT NOT A would be shaded once we had drawn in our premise, to show that this set is empty. Here it is still unshaded.

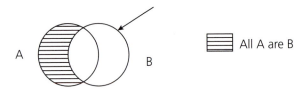

 All A are B

4 Something like:

No pig is a goat
No sheep is a goat

———————

All sheep are pigs.

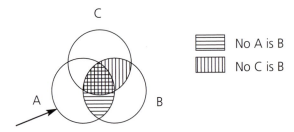 **Disgusting!**

5 Three: A, B and C (in my example these are replaced by PIGS, GOATS, and SHEEP). So it will need three circles.

6 If this were valid, the part that represents A BUT NOT C would be shaded once we had drawn in our two premises. Here part of it is still unshaded.

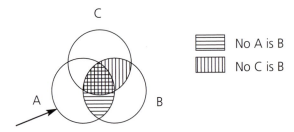

No A is B
No C is B

7 Another invalid one. The conclusion *all C is A or B* says that the set of THINGS THAT ARE C BUT NEITHER A NOR B is empty. If the argument were valid, drawing in our premises

424

would have shaded the C circle where it lies outside the A and B circles. Here it is still unshaded.

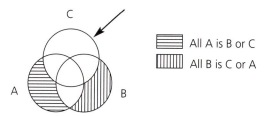

8   There are three sets here, so you will need three circles:

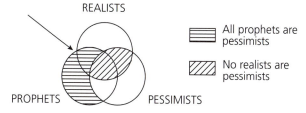

This argument is VALID. The conclusion 'No realists are prophets' says that the intersection of the PROPHETS set and the REALISTS set is empty. Look at the diagram and you will see that once we have drawn in our two premises, that part of the diagram is shaded.

9   INVALID. The conclusion says that the set of PHILOSO-PHERS WHO ARE NOT OPTIMISTS is empty, so when we have drawn in the premises the relevant part of the PHILOSO-PHERS circle should be shaded. But some of it is not.

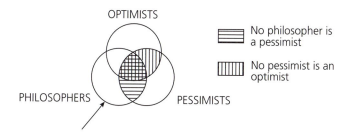

10 Conclusion:

'I can't (after all) ground a man who's crazy': in other words 'No crazy airman is someone the doctor can ground'.

Premises:

(i) All crazy airmen are airmen Doc Daneeka can ground

(ii) All airmen Doc Daneeka can ground ask to be grounded

(iii) No airman who asks to be grounded is a crazy airman.

11 The conclusion says that the intersection of the set AIRMEN THE DOCTOR CAN GROUND and CRAZY AIRMEN is empty; and once we have drawn the premises in, yes – that part of the diagram is shaded. The argument is VALID.

12 You will notice that if these premises are true, it is not just the set of CRAZY AIRMEN THE DOCTOR CAN GROUND that turns out to be empty, it is the whole set of CRAZY AIRMEN. They seem to have been argued out of existence. This highly fishy result reinforces the fishy look of the original argument, whose conclusion seems to contradict its first premise. It may be valid, but it cannot be sound.

If an argument is valid but unsound, at least one premise must be false. The obvious culprit here is the first – the alleged rule 'I have to ground someone who's crazy'. If this really were true, craziness would be a sufficient condition for being grounded – but the second part of the 'rule' takes this back. The goalposts have been moved.

 **Disgraceful!**

1   At least one *white* unicorn.
2   You need a stroke for each set:

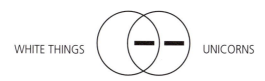

3   NO, it does not. We would need to add shading:

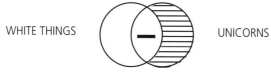

4   We want only to say that there is at least one unicorn. It/they could be white or non-white, wild or tame. To leave these open, we need a stroke that goes through all the possible sets, without limiting itself to any one of them.
5   NO. It just says that at least one unicorn does. For all we know it (or they) might be tame, not wild.
6   They just mention these sets, in a pattern that will allow us to relate them to the set of UNICORNS if we should want to.
7   Something exists that is a unicorn, and is either wild or white or both.
8   NO. (i) says 'Something is a unicorn (whether or not it's an animal) AND something is an animal (whether or not it's a unicorn)'. (ii) says 'Some animal is a unicorn AND some animal is not a unicorn'.

Since I'm both a unicorn and an animal, I could satisfy diagram (i) on my own –

but for diagram (ii), you need someone like me as well.

9 NO. (i) says 'Something is not an animal'; (ii) says 'Something is not a unicorn'.

10 NO. The first says that the set of unicorns is empty, the second says that it is occupied.

11 YES: both could be true if a unicorn existed that was not wild.

12 SHEEP 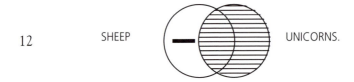 UNICORNS.

1 A figure of speech discusses A in terms of B. Often the connection is an assumed likeness: 'A rolling stone gathers no moss' is a figurative way of saying 'People who live a roving life – *who keep moving, as a rolling stone does* – do not collect worldly goods – *which attach themselves to their owner, as moss attaches itself to a stone*'. Sometimes it is some other connection, as when people use 'the Crown' to refer to the monarchy. Literal language discusses A in terms of A.

2 Something like: 'a horse-like beast with a single horn, which the speaker keeps for pleasure'.

3 A metaphor is a figure of speech that implies an analogy, like the rolling stone example above.

4 'Uncle' suggests cosy familiarity: someone a child can look to for protection. For 'Joe', see below.

5 Metaphorical: a girl is a human being, not part of a plant.

6 Up to you; but I think people usually see a Joe as informal where a Joseph is formal, relaxed where a Joseph is stiff, unpretentious where a Joseph may be pompous.

7 Mum is English demotic, Mummy is English and posher (and seen from a more childish angle). Mom and Mommy are American (less of a class difference here, but again Mommy is more from a child's angle). *Maman* is a French mother from a child's angle, Maw is a hillbilly maybe, Mamma is probably a Victorian, and the Mater is the mother of someone like Bertie Wooster.

8 Over to you (and your English literature teachers).

9 I think it depends mainly on where the names are typically used: 'Joe' at home or with friends, the full name 'Joseph' on more dignified occasions. This suggests personalities that seem better suited to one kind or the other.

10 It is cognitive because the meanings of a statement, a question and a command differ not in the atmosphere they evoke but in what they literally say. When 'You're going home now' is a statement, it *asserts* (truly or falsely) that the person addressed is going home now. When it is a question, it asserts nothing and has no truth-value: it is equivalent to 'Are you going home now?'. When it is a command, it is equivalent to 'GO home now!'. This again has no truth-value.

11 Words or gestures that we do not think of as names at all: 'this', 'that', and pointing.

12 *Either*:

My wearing these clothes today and no others is not a necessary condition for being Mary Haight – I would still be Mary Haight in different clothes; but not being a heap of mincemeat is necessary.

Or:

My being Mary Haight is not a sufficient condition for my wearing these clothes: the first does not guarantee the second. But my being Mary Haight is a sufficient condition for my being unminced: no heap of mincemeat could be Mary Haight.

1   YES: calling something 'I' describes it as *the speaker* (or writer or thinker – etc.).

2   He claimed that whenever he thought 'I think', the word 'I' must refer to something.

3   Any case where the word is being mentioned rather than used to refer to the speaker, as in '*Je t'aime* is French for *I love you*'.

4   It means that the set is not empty: at least one politician exists.

5   NO. If you think that

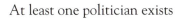

At least one politician exists

Margaret Thatcher is a politician

is valid, you're in trouble!

6   (i) 'The present King of France': NO. France is a republic.

(ii) 'The tallest man in the world': UNKNOWN. There may be several men of the same height, who are taller than anyone else: if so, no one is *the* tallest man.

(iii)'France': YES. It refers to a real country.

(iv)'The Diskworld': NO. Like 'Cinderella', this is a story-name. It merely pretends to refer (to a world described by Terry Pratchett).

(v) 'The even number between three and five': YES. It refers to four.

(vi)'The even number between four and six': NO. 'Even number' means even *whole* number, and the only whole number between four and six is odd.

7   You could do it either this way: or this:

I think the first is better. The English suggests the possibility of couples that are not American, though it says nothing about them.

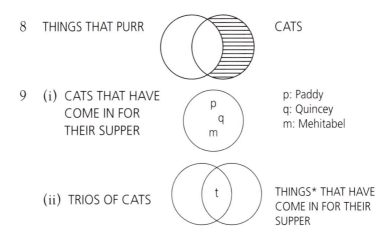

8 THINGS THAT PURR   CATS

9 (i) CATS THAT HAVE
        COME IN FOR
        THEIR SUPPER

p: Paddy
q: Quincey
m: Mehitabel

(ii) TRIOS OF CATS

THINGS* THAT HAVE
COME IN FOR THEIR
SUPPER

t: trio consisting of Paddy, Quincey and Mehitabel
* You could say TRIOS here, or GROUPS, but it is unnecessary.

10 CATS LIVING IN
    THIS HOUSE

THINGS* THAT HAVE COME
IN FOR THEIR SUPPER

* You could say CREATURES here, but it is unnecessary.

11 POP STARS   POLITICIANS

The stroke must cross the line between the two sets that Margaret Thatcher might be in: whichever she is in is occupied, but the other might not be.

12   a: Aglavaine

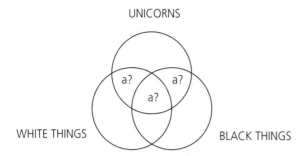

Remember that 'or' is inclusive, so there are three possibilities: all white, all black or both.

1 Without the shading for 'No dogs are cats' we would have to cover all these possibilities:

(i) No cats are dogs, cats and dogs exist and Paddy is one or the other but not both.

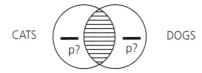

CATS   DOGS

(ii) Some cats are dogs and some are not, some dogs are not cats, Paddy is one or the other but not both.

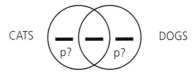

CATS   DOGS

(iii) Some cats are dogs but some are not, all dogs are cats, Paddy is one or the other but not both.

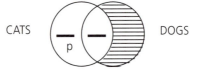

CATS   DOGS

(iv) Some dogs are cats but some are not, all cats are dogs, Paddy is one or the other but not both.

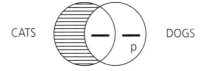

CATS   DOGS

12 Clevinger's argument is sound. The premises are true: the people shooting at Yossarian are clearly not shooting at him in particular but at everyone (from the camp) in general. And it is valid: once we draw in the premises, we can see that the set of PEOPLE SHOOTING AT YOSSARIAN is empty. Its circle has been shaded out.

PEOPLE

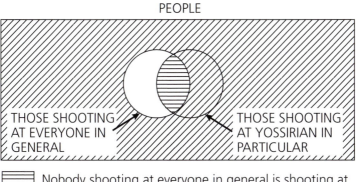

THOSE SHOOTING AT EVERYONE IN GENERAL

THOSE SHOOTING AT YOSSIRIAN IN PARTICULAR

Nobody shooting at everyone in general is shooting at Yossirian in particular

They're (all) shooting at everyone in general.

But since Clevinger and Yossarian are saying different things when they use the words 'They're shooting at Yossarian' (etc.), Clevinger is equivocating if he claims that his conclusion negates Yossarian's. Instead of two statements that contradict each other: 'They're (all) trying to kill Yossarian' and 'Nobody's trying to kill Yossarian', Yossarian's statement and Clevinger's are in fact perfectly compatible.

1   (I)   It's a plane or a bird or Superman   PREMISE
       It's not Superman   PREMISE

       It's a plane or a bird.   CONCLUSION.

   (II)   The victim died of accidental or   PREMISE
       of deliberate arsenic poisoning, or
       of gastro-enteritis due to natural causes
       She did not die of accidental or   PREMISE
       deliberate arsenic poisoning

       She died of gastro-entiritis due
       to natural causes.   CONCLUSION.

   (III)   He's telling the truth, or he's an   PREMISE
       extraordinarily good actor
       He's not telling the truth   PREMISE

       He's an extraordinarily good actor.   CONCLUSION.

2   The validity-formula is: *if (P or Q) and not P then Q*. Its table shows that it is a necessary truth: the related argument form is therefore VALID.

'Full sweep' in two stages:

ONE		P	Q	If (P or Q)	and	not P	then	Q
	(1)	T	T	T	F	F		
	(2)	T	F	T	F	F		
	(3)	F	T	T	T	T		
	(4)	F	F	F	F	T		

TWO		P	Q	If (P or Q)	and	not P	then	Q
	(1)	T	T	T	F	F	**T**	T
	(2)	T	F	T	F	F	**T**	F
	(3)	F	T	T	T	T	**T**	T
	(4)	F	F	F	F	T	**T**	F

'Fell swoop'

An argument-form is invalid if its validity-formula can be false. For this to happen, the antecedent must be true and the consequent false, i.e. Q will be false. P might be either true or false.

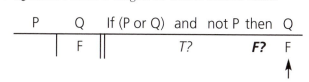

But when P is true, *not P* is false. So the antecedent (P *or* Q) *and not P* is false. This makes the formula TRUE.

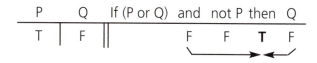

And when *P and Q* are both false, *P or Q* is false. So the antecedent (P *or* Q) *and not P* is again false, and the formula is TRUE.

P	Q	If (P or Q) and not P then Q			
F	F	F	F	**T**	F

3   R: It's a plane
    S: It's a bird
    T: It's Superman.

4   R: The victim died of accidental arsenic poisoning
    S: The victim died of deliberate arsenic poisoning
    T: The victim died of gastro-enteritis due to natural causes.

5   Form (i) substitutes T for P, and *R or S* for Q.
6   Form (ii) substitutes *not (R or S)* for the Elimination Form's second premise *not Q*.
7   It's a plane or a bird.
8   The victim died of accidental or of deliberate poisoning, or of gastro-entiritis due to natural causes.

9   **(If R then S) or (T or not R)**
Not if R then S

T or not R.

10 *If ((R or S) or T) and not T then (R or S).* It has three variables, so the table needs 8 lines.

11 I and III are valid by ELIM.

12 I   P: Randolph is asleep
       Q: Randolph is dead.

    III P: The man's naturally bad-tempered
        Q: He has been crossed in love, or his feet hurt.

1   In all cases, one formula or argument-form is a substitution
     instance for another if we *consistently* replace any wff that the
     first contains by a different wff.

     Consistency is important. For example, *(P or R) and ((P or R)
     and Q)* is a substitution instance of *P or (P and Q)*, but *(P or R)
     and (P and Q)* is not: we've substituted R for only one P, not both.

     (i)   Formula II is a substitution instance of a simpler Formula I,
           when we replace at least one wff in Formula I by a more
           complex wff. For example:

           Formula I: **P and Q**
           Formula II: **(If P then Q) and R.**

           Formula II substitutes *if P then Q* for P in Formula I, and R
           for Q. Since *if P then Q* is more complex than P (and R is
           exactly as complex as Q), Formula II is more complex than
           Formula I.

     (ii) Formula II is a substitution instance of a more complex
           Formula I when we replace at least one wff in Formula I by
           a simpler wff. For example:

           Formula I: **(If P then Q) and R**
           Formula II: **P and Q.**

           Formula II substitutes P for *if P then Q* in Formula I, and Q
           for R. Since P is simpler than *if P then Q* (and R is exactly
           as complex as Q), Formula II is simpler than Formula I.

     (iii) Argument-form II is a substitution instance of a simpler
           Argument-form I when we replace at least one wff in Form
           I by a more complex wff. For example:

           Form I: **P or Q**
                           Not Q
                           ─────────
                           P

           Form II: **(P and Q) or (R and Q)**
                           Not (R and Q)
                           ──────────────────────
                           P and Q.

     Form II substitutes *P and Q* for P in Form I, and *R and Q* for Q.
     P and Q is more complex than P, and *R and Q* is more complex
     than Q; so Form I is simpler than Form II.

(iv) Argument-form II is a substitution instance of a more complex Argument-form I when we replace one or more wffs in Form I by a simpler wff. For example:

Form I: **(P and Q) or (R and Q)**

Not (R and Q)

P and Q

Form II: **P or Q**

Not Q

P.

Form II substitutes P for *P and Q* in Form I, and Q for *R and Q*. P is simpler than *P and Q*, and Q is simpler than *R and Q*; so Form I is more complex than Form II.

2   **If P then Q**

P

Q.

3   *Argument I*

P: That malicious little creep sets foot in the house

Q: I leave.

4   *Argument III*

P: The Snake will accept

Q: The Snake will die in the attempt, or he will live but fail, or he will succeed.

5   The most detailed one is:

If P then (Q or (R or S))	P: The Snake will accept
P	Q: The Snake will die in the attempt
----	R: The Snake will live but fail
Q or (R or S).	S: The Snake will succeed.

(You could bracket the first premise and the conclusion in several ways.) But less detailed ones would also do, for example

If P then (Q or R)	P: The Snake will accept
P	Q: The Snake will die in the attempt
----	R: The Snake will live but fail, or he will
Q or R.	succeed.

6   The form in question is **If P then Q**

                            P

                         —————

                          Q.

In the first version above, Q *or* $(R$ *or* $S)$ replaces Q. In the second, Q *or* R replaces Q. (P is the same.)

7   The first premise affirms *if P then Q*: a conditional whose antecedent is P. The second affirms P.

8   I 'Fell swoop'.

    Try to construct a line where the validity-formula is false. The antecedent must then be true and the consequent false, i.e. Q will be false. P might then be either false or true.

    (a)

P	Q	If (if P then Q) and P then Q
T	F	F *F?* F

    (b)

P	Q	If (if P then Q) and P then Q
F	F	T *F?* F

But if P is true, *if P then Q* is false. So the antecedent *(if P then Q) and P* is false, and the whole formula is not false but TRUE.

    (a)

P	Q	If (if P then Q) and P then Q
T	F	F F **T** F

And if P is false, *(if P then Q) and P* is again false. And again, the whole formula is TRUE.

    (b)

P	Q	If (if P then Q) and P then Q
F	F	F F F **T** F

II 'Full sweep'.
By now you can cope with the whole thing at once, not by stages.

	P	Q	If (if P then Q)	and	P	then	Q
(1)	T	T	T	T	T	**T**	T
(2)	T	F	F	F	T	**T**	F
(3)	F	T	T	F	F	**T**	T
(4)	F	F	T	F	F	**T**	F

9 (i) YES. P is *S or R* and Q is T.
   (ii) NO. This is not a substitution instance of MPP. In the first premise, S and T are the wrong way round: it should be *if T then S*.
   (iii) YES. P is R and Q is R. (Unusual perhaps, but legitimate.)

10 It is a substitution instance of MPP. For P, we substitute Q; and for Q we substitute P.

11 Yes, but we will need to use it more than once. The rule works on just two premises at a time.
   (i) From 'If Fang is a dog, he's a mammal' and 'Fang is a dog' we may infer 'He's a mammal'.
   (ii) From 'If he's a mammal, he's a vertebrate' and 'He is a mammal' we may infer 'He's a vertebrate'.
   (iii) From 'If he's a vertebrate, he's an animal' and 'He's a vertebrate' we may infer 'He is an animal'.

12 1. If P then Q   PREMISE
    2. If Q then R   PREMISE
    3. If R then S   PREMISE
    4. P   PREMISE
    5. Q   1, 4 MPP
    6. R   2, 5 MPP
    _____
    7. S   3, 6 MPP.

P: Fang is a dog   R: Fang is a vertebrate
Q: Fang is a mammal   S: Fang is an animal.

**CONGRATULATIONS! YOU NOW KNOW
HOW TO WRITE A PROOF.**

1   The first premise is a conditional statement, whose consequent is *Amanda bit Billy* (ignore differences in surface grammar like 'would have'). The second premise denies this consequent.

2   I   If he's telling the truth, I'm a Dutchman   (spoken)
        I'm no Dutchman   (unspoken)
        ───────────────────────────────
        He's not telling the truth.   (unspoken)

    II   If I agreed to ride in that car of yours I'd be tired of life
         I'm not tired of life
         ───
         I won't agree to ride in that car of yours.

    III If he had caught the 3:10 train he'd be here
             by now   (spoken)
         He's not here now   (unspoken)
         ───
         He did not catch the 3:10 train   (spoken)

3   (i) YES, used twice. Here is a proof:
        1. If S then R   PREMISE
        2. Not T   PREMISE
        3. If R then T   PREMISE
        4. Not R   2,3 MTT
        ───────────────────────────────
        5. Not S   1,4 MTT.
        In step 4 we substitute R for P and T for Q; in step 5 we substitute S for P and R for Q.
    (ii) NO: this form is not a substitution instance of MTT. R and S in the first premise are in the wrong order: it should be *if S then R*.
    (iii) NO. It is valid by ELIM.

4   I NO. Its only form in statement logic is   P
                                                         Q
                                                        ──
                                                         R.

    It is a valid argument, but statement logic will not show this.

i   II   YES, it is valid by MTT.

III   NO: this one's not even valid. Its most detailed form is

If P then not Q

Not Q

P

not a substitution instance of MTT. The second premise does not deny the consequent of the first one, it restates it.

5   In II, P is 'You are a fish' and Q is 'You have feathers'.

6   The validity-formula is

If (if P then Q) and not Q then not P.

I   'Fell swoop'.

Try to construct a line where the validity-formula is false. The antecedent must then be true and the consequent false, i.e. *not P* will be false; so P will be true. And since the antecedent is a conjunction, both its conjuncts must be true. One of these is *Not Q*, so Q will be false.

P	Q	If (if P then Q) and not Q then not P
T	F	T? F? F

But if P is true, *if P then Q* is false. So the antecedent (*if P then Q*) *not Q* false, and the whole formula is not false but TRUE.

P	Q	If (if P then Q) and not Q then not P
T	F	F F T **T** F

II   'Full Sweep'.

	P	Q	If (if P then Q) and not Q then not P
(1)	T	T	T F F **T** F
(2)	T	F	F F T **T** F
(3)	F	T	T F F **T** T
(4)	F	F	T T T **T** T

7   NO. It is not a substitution instance of MTT. The consequent of the first premise is *not R*: in MTT this is what replaces Q. But then the second premise should be *not not R*.

8   They are equivalent.

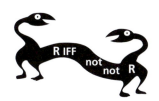

9
	P	P	iff	not	not	P
(1)	T	**T**	T	F
(2)	F	**T**	F	T

(Remember that a biconditional statement is TRUE when the formulae joined by 'iff' have the same truth-value, and FALSE when they do not.)

10 (i) is valid by DN and MTT.
    (ii) would be valid by ELIM if properly bracketed, but without brackets its first premise is not a wff.
    (iii) is valid by MPP. For P in MPP we substitute *not P*, and for Q we substitute *not Q*.

11 1.   If R then not Q   PREMISE
    2.   Q   PREMISE
    3.   Not not Q   2 DN
    _____
    4.   Not R   1, 3 MTT.

12 Strictly, we cannot write a proof of (ii) because its first premise is not a wff. But we can if we bracket it.

    PROOF of (ii)
    1.   (P or Q) or R   PREMISE
    2.   Not R   PREMISE
    _____
    3.   P or Q   1, 2 ELIM.

449

PROOF of (iii)

1	If not P then not Q	PREMISE
2	Not P	PREMISE

| 3 | Not Q | 1, 2 MPP. |

1   Validity-formula: *If P and Q then (P and Q)*.
     'Fell swoop'
     For this formula to be false, the antecedent must be true and
     the consequent false. In this case it's clearly impossible; but you
     can show it by table if you want to. The antecedent can be true
     in just one case: when both P and Q are true. But then the
     consequent *P and Q* is true, making the whole conditional
     TRUE.

P	Q	If P and Q then	(P and Q)
T	T	T	**T** T

     'Full sweep'
     The full table for &I's validity-formula is:

	P	Q	If P and Q then	(P and Q)
(1)	T	T	T	**T** T
(2)	T	F	F	**T** F
(3)	F	T	F	**T** F
(4)	F	F	F	**T** F

2   The argument-form   **Q and P**   is a substitution instance of
     &E. Substitute   **Q**   Q is for P, and P for Q. And
     it doesn't matter in what order conjuncts occur: 'and' just
     means 'both are true' – so when we're GIVEN *P and Q*, we're
     also GIVEN *Q and P*.

3   Validity-formula: *If P and Q then P*.
     'Fell swoop'
     Try to construct a line where the antecedent is true and the
     consequent false. As before, the antecedent – *P and Q* – will be
     true in just one case: when both P and Q are true.

P	Q	If P and Q then	P
T	T	T	**T** T

     But then the consequent P is true, making the whole condition
     TRUE.

'Full Sweep'.

	P	Q	If P and Q then P
(1)	T	T	T **T** T
(2)	T	F	F **T** F
(3)	F	T	F **T** F
(4)	F	F	F **T** F

4–12

1. If your cat bites my cat, I'll put a spell on you — PREMISE
2. If I put a spell on you, your roses will die or your hens will stop laying — PREMISE
3. If your roses die, you won't win a prize at the flower show — PREMISE
4. If you cross my palm with silver, you'll win a prize at the flower show — PREMISE
5. My cat chases yours and your cat bites my cat — PREMISE
6. You cross my palm with silver — PREMISE
7. Your cat bites my cat — 5 &E
8. I'll put a spell on you — 1,7 MPP
9. Your roses will die or your hens will stop laying — 2, 8 MPP
10. You'll win a prize — 4, 6 MPP
11. It's false that you won't win a prize — 10 DN
12. Your roses won't die — 3, 11 MTT
13. Your hens will stop laying — 9, 12 ELIM

---

14. Your roses won't die but* your hens will stop laying. — 12, 13 &I.

* Remember that, truth-functionally, 'but' is equivalent to 'and' (see Chapter 18).

452

1   He came through the hole in the roof.
2   ELIM.
3   He did not come through the door, the window or the chimney.
4   He was concealed in the room.
5   If he did not come through the door, the window or the chimney, and was not concealed in the room, then he came through the hole in the roof.
6   The letters D, R and H are short for particular statements. When a letter is a variable in an argument-form, it's a hole that we can replace by *any* statement.
7   **H.**
8   **Not D.**
9   **Not R.**
10 **If not D and not R then H.**
    (You could also write it *if not (D or R) then H*, but the first way is easier for our proof.)

11–12

1.	Not D	PREMISE
2.	Not R	PREMISE
3.	If not D and not R then H	PREMISE
4.	Not D and not R	1, 2 &I
5.	H	3, 4 MPP.

1   Arguments to which CH applies have the form

    If P then Q
    If Q then R

    If P then R

and therefore the validity-formula *if (if P then Q and if Q then R) then if P then R.*

'Fell swoop'

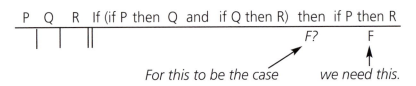

When *if P then R* is false, P is true and R is false. Q may be either true or false.

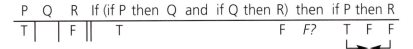

But if Q is TRUE, *if Q then R* is false. So the antecedent *if P then Q and if Q then R* is FALSE;

P	Q	R	If (if P then Q and if Q then R) then if P then R
T	T	F	F T F F *F?* T F F

and if Q is FALSE, *if P then Q* is false, so again the antecedent *if P then Q and if Q then R* is FALSE.

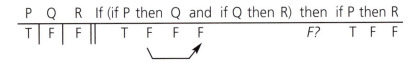

And when its antecedent is false, the validity-formula is not false but TRUE:

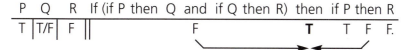

P   Q   R   If (if P then Q and if Q then R) then if P then R
T |T/F| F || F   **T**   T F F.

So there is no line in its table where it is false: it's a necessary truth. The related argument-form is valid, and therefore CH is a valid rule.

2   FANG PROOF 2 (using CH twice and MPP once)
    1. If Fang is a dog then he is a mammal   PREMISE
    2. If Fang is a mammal then he is a vertebrate   PREMISE
    3. If Fang is a vertebrate then he is an animal   PREMISE
    4. Fang is a dog   PREMISE
    5. If Fang is a dog then he is a vertebrate   1,2 CH
    6. If Fang is a dog then he is an animal   3,5 CH

    7. Fang is an animal   4,6 MPP.

3. (i) is INVALID.
    (ii) is VALID, but not by CH or CH plus another rule. It is valid by MTT alone.
    (iii) is VALID by CH plus MPP. Q replaces CH's P, and S or T replaces CH's Q.

4   1. If Q then (S or T)   PREMISE
    2. If (S or T) then R   PREMISE
    3. Q   PREMISE
    4. If Q then R   1,2 CH

    5. R   3,4 MPP.

5   The validity-formula is *if (if P then R and if Q then R) then if (P or Q) then R*. With three variables a full table would be very long, so let's use the 'fell swoop' method.

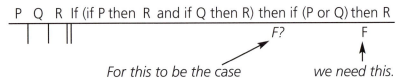

For this to be the case　　　　we need this.

But *if (P or Q) then R* will be false only when *P or Q* is true and R is false.

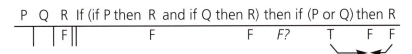

We also need a true antecedent; but in that case *if P then R* and *if Q then R* must both be true.

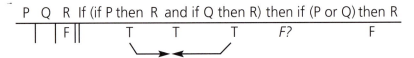

When R is false, this means that P and Q must both be false as well.

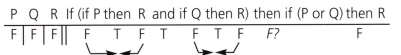

But if so, *P or Q* is false, which makes the consequent not false after all, but TRUE.

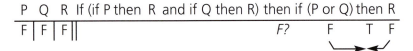

And if the consequent is true, so is the whole validity-formula. The related argument is therefore VALID and DIL is a valid rule.

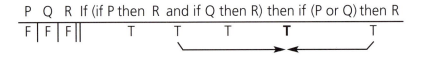

6   P: I don't sit the exam   Q: I do sit the exam
     R: I fail the course.

7   (Whatever happens) I get a penny from Grandpa.

8   When I go to see Grandpa:

1. (Either) I cry or I don't cry	PREMISE
2. If I cry I need cheering up	PREMISE
3. If I need cheering up I get a penny from Grandpa	PREMISE
4. If I cry I get a penny from Grandpa	2, 3 CH
5. If I don't cry I'm good	PREMISE
6. If I'm good I get a penny from Grandpa	PREMISE
7. If I don't cry I get a penny from Grandpa	5, 6 CH
8. If I cry or I don't cry I get a penny from Grandpa	4, 7 DIL

---

     9. (Whatever happens) I get a penny from Grandpa   1,8 MPP.

9

1. Fang is a dog	PREMISE
2. If Fang is a dog, he is a mammal	PREMISE
3. Fang is a mammal	1,2 MPP
4. If he is a mammal, he is a vertebrate	PREMISE
5. If he is a vertebrate, he is an animal	PREMISE
6. If he is a mammal, he is an animal	4,5 CH

---

     7.   Fang is an animal   3,6 MPP.

10   I will need a separate letter to abbreviate each of the three, plus two more for the other possibilities:

         D: He came through the door
         W: He came through the window
         C: He came down the chimney
         R: He was concealed in the room
         H: He came through the hole in the roof.

11   P: No concealment is possible.
     Then my new premise is *if P then not R*.

12   HOLMES PROOF 2

1. R or ((D or (W or C)) or H)*	PREMISE
2. If P then not R	PREMISE
3. P	PREMISE
4. Not R	3,4 MPP
5. (D or (W or C)) or H	1, 4 ELIM
6. Not (D or (W or C))	PREMISE

---

     7.   H   5,6 ELIM.

     * You could also bracket it *R or (((D or W) or C) or H)*. Other ways make it a bit harder.

457

1   In this argument-form P is substituted for CONTRA's Q, and vice versa.

2   Since CONTRA is an equivalence rule, its validity-formula uses 'iff', not 'if-then'. Its table is quite a simple one:

	P	Q	If P then Q	iff	if not Q then not P
(1)	T	T	T **T** F		F F
(2)	T	F	F **T** T		T F
(3)	F	T	T **T** F		F T
(4)	F	F	T **T** T		F T

3   (i) is valid by CONTRA plus MPP: see proof 1 below. In (i), CONTRA's P is replaced by *P or Q*, and CONTRA's Q is replaced by P. (ii) and (iii) are invalid.

4   (i) is also valid by MTT alone: see proof 2 below.

PROOF 1
1. If (P or Q) then P   PREMISE
2. Not P   PREMISE
3. If not P then not (P or Q)   1, CONTRA
_____
4. Not (P or Q)   2,3 MPP.

PROOF 2
1. If (P or Q) then P   PREMISE
2. Not P   PREMISE
_____
3. Not (P or Q)   1,2 MTT.

5   *Not P and not Q.*
    P: They CAN climb trees
    Q: They CAN jump this high.

6   (i) negates (a). When P and Q are the same as in the answer to 5, the form of (i) is *P or Q*. Remember that this means 'P or Q or both': if any of these is true, (a) is false; and if (a) is false, at least one of these is true.
    (ii) does not negate (a). It states only one of the three possible ways in which (a) could be false.

(iii) negates (a). It is therefore equivalent to (i).

7 Remember that '...or vice versa' means that *not P and not Q* and *not (P or Q)* are equivalent; so instead of *if-then*, our validity-formula uses *iff*. We therefore need a 'full sweep', as we did for DN and CONTRA.

	P	Q	(Not P	and	not Q)	iff	not	(P or Q)
(1)	T	T	F	F	F	**T**	F	T
(2)	T	F	F	F	T	**T**	F	T
(3)	F	T	T	F	F	**T**	F	T
(4)	F	F	T	T	T	**T**	T	F

8 These two formulae have different truth-values for lines 2 (P true, Q false) and 3 (P false, Q true). So – obviously – they are not equivalent.

	P	Q	Not P	and	not Q
(1)	T	T	F	F	F
(2)	T	F	F	F	T
(3)	F	T	T	F	F
(4)	F	F	T	T	T

	P	Q	Not	(P and	Q)
(1)	T	T	F	T	
(2)	T	F	T	F	
(3)	F	T	T	F	
(4)	F	F	T	F	

9 (For example)
  P: 2 is even
  Q: 2 is odd.

'2 is not both odd and even' is TRUE: no number is both odd and even; but '2 is not odd and 2 is not even' is FALSE: 2 is even.

10 These again have different truth-values for lines 2 (P true, Q false) and 3 (P false, Q true). So they are not equivalent.

	P	Q	Not P or not Q		
(1)	T	T	F	F	F
(2)	T	F	F	T	T
(3)	F	T	T	T	F
(4)	F	F	T	T	T

	P	Q	Not (P and Q)	
(1)	T	T	F	T
(2)	T	F	F	T
(3)	F	T	F	T
(4)	F	F	T	T

11 (Again) P: 2 is even
            Q: 2 is odd.

'Two is not odd or 2 is not even' is TRUE, since 2 is not odd; but 'It's false that 2 is odd or even' is FALSE: 2 is even.

12 *Not (P or Q)* or – since they are equivalent – *not P and not Q*. Yes, we could use NNOR on either of these forms, to conclude the other.

1   NO: they are incompatible. No two could be true at once. So if a given set of premises proves any one of them, the other two must be false.

2   The logical form of a conjunction is *P and Q*. So we might prove any of these conclusions by &I, if we had the appropriate P and Q. And since substitution in rules is allowed, we might also prove any of them by a rule whose conclusion is a single variable – for which we substituted our conjunction. These rules are:

    ELIM   (conclusion Q)
    MPP   (conclusion Q)
    DN   (when we use it to conclude P from *not not P*,
                rather than vice versa)
    &E   (conclusion P).

    For example, *P and Q* is substituted for ELIM's Q in the following proof (and R is substituted for ELIM's P):

    | 1. R or (P and Q) | PREMISE |
    | 2. Not R | PREMISE |

    | 3. P and Q | 1, 2 ELIM. |

    (We can't use any rules except those above: the others yield conclusions of the wrong logical form.)

3   NO, for all three.

4   (a) We could get this if we had 'Lily is not an agent'. ELIM used on Premise 1 ('Either Hank is an agent, or Lily is') would give us 'Hank is an agent'; we could then combine this with 'Lily is not an agent' using & I. Or we could get it by ELIM from Premise 4 ('The CIA don't know it') if we had 'Either the CIA know it, or Hank is an agent and Lily is not'.

    (b) We could get this in a similar way from Premise 1 (using first ELIM and then & I) if we had 'Hank is not an agent'. Or again we could get it by ELIM from Premise 4 ('The CIA don't know it') if we had 'Either the CIA know it, or Lily is an agent and Hank is not'.

    (c) We could get this by ELIM from Premise 4 ('The CIA don't know it') if we had 'Either the CIA know it, or both Hank and Lily are agents'.

461

5   We haven't any of the statements given above that would let us use ELIM on Premise 4. But we could try MTT on Premises 3 and 4. This gives us the next step:

1. Either Hank is secret agent, or Lily is.   PREMISE
2. If Lily is a secret agent, Hank knows it.   PREMISE
3. If either Dimitri knows it or Hank knows it, the CIA know it.   PREMISE
4. The CIA don't know it.   PREMISE
5. It is false that Dimitri or Hank knows it.   3, 4 MTT.

6   Step 5 has the form *not (P or Q)*.

This should make you think of NNOR. Used on step 5, NNOR would allow us to conclude that 'Dimitri doesn't know it and Hank doesn't know it'. Is that any use?

It is a conjunction, which should make you think of &E. &E will give us either conjunct on its own. Look at our premises, and you will see that we can use 'Hank doesn't know it' with Premise 2 and MTT to get step 9: exactly what we need to finish the proof.

7   'Hank doesn't know it' plus Premise 2, with MTT, will give you 'Lily is not a secret agent'. Look back at your answer to question 4: you can now prove (a).

8   1. Either Hank is secret agent, or Lily is.   PREMISE
    2. If Lily is a secret agent, Hank knows it.   PREMISE
    3. If either Dimitri knows it or Hank knows it, the CIA know it.   PREMISE
    4. The CIA don't know it.   PREMISE
    5. It is false that Dimitri or Hank knows it.   3, 4 MTT
    6. Dimitri doesn't know it and Hank doesn't know it.   5, NNOR
    7. Hank doesn't know it.   6, &E
    8. Lily is not a secret agent.   2, 7 MTT
    9. Hank is a secret agent.   1, 8 ELIM
    _____
    10. Hank is a secret agent and Lily is not.   8, 9 &I.

9   Premises: 1. H or L
                           2. If L then K
                           3. If (D or K) then C
                           4. Not C.
      Conclusion: H and not L.

10 Premise 3 has (*inter alia*) the form *if P then Q*. This – plus the word 'transformed' – might make you think of CONTRA. If we use CONTRA on Premise 3 we get 'If the CIA don't know it, then it's false that Dimitri or Hank knows it'.

11 'If the CIA don't know it, then it's false that Dimitri or Hank knows it', plus Premise 4 and MPP, yields 'It's false that Dimitri or Hank knows it'. This is the same as step 5 above: we can now go on as before.

12 1. H or L   PREMISE

     2. If L then K   PREMISE

     3. If (D or K) then C   PREMISE

     4. Not C   PREMISE

     5. If not C then not (D or K)   3, CONTRA

     6. Not (D or K)   4, 5 MPP

     7. Not D and not K   6, NNOR

     8. Not K   7, &E

     9. Not L   2, 8 MTT

     10. H   1, 9 ELIM

     ———————————————————————————

     11 H and not L   9, 10 &I.

1 *Not P or not Q.*   P: The spreckle is twigging
                     Q: The crackshot is delivering enough
                        power.

2 *P and Q.*   (P and Q as above.)

3 Either you haven't got chickenpox, or you haven't got measles, or you've got neither.

4 'She's an angel – and she loves me!' is false iff one of these is true:

   (i) she's an angel, but she doesn't love me
   (ii) she loves me, but she's no angel
   (iii) she's no angel, and she doesn't love me.

5 STAGE ONE

	P	Q	(Not P	or	not Q)	iff	not	(P and Q)
(1)	T	T	F	F	F		F	T
(2)	T	F	F	T	T		T	F
(3)	F	T	T	T	F		T	F
(4)	F	F	T	T	T		T	F

STAGE TWO

	P	Q	(Not P	or	not Q)	iff	not	(P and Q)
(1)	T	T	F	F	F	**T**	F	T
(2)	T	F	F	T	T	**T**	T	F
(3)	F	T	T	T	F	**T**	T	F
(4)	F	F	T	T	T	**T**	T	F.

6 (i) is valid by NAND plus DN and ELIM;
   (iii) is valid by NAND plus MTT, and also by NAND plus CONTRA and MPP.
   (ii) is valid but does not use NAND: it uses NNOR plus &E.

464

7 Any of these would do:

(i)	1.	Not (Q and R)	PREMISE
	2.	R	PREMISE
	3.	Not Q or not R	1 NAND
	4.	Not not R	2 DN

	5.	Not Q	3, 4 ELIM.

(iii a)	1. If Q then (R and S)	PREMISE
	2. Not R or not S	PREMISE
	3. Not (R and S)	2 NAND

	4. Not Q	1, 3 MTT.

(iii b)	1. If Q then (R and S)	PREMISE
	2. Not R or not S	PREMISE
	3. Not (R and S)	2 NAND
	4. If not (R and S) then not Q	1 CONTRA

	5. Not Q	1, 4 MPP.

8–12

1.	Ginger can join the Red-headed League if and only if he has red hair and is of Irish descent	PREMISE
2.	Ginger can join the Red-headed League if he has red hair and is of Irish descent; and if he has red hair and is of Irish descent, Ginger can join the Red-headed League	1 IFF
3.	If he has red hair and is of Irish descent, Ginger can join the Red-headed League	2 &E
4.	Ginger can't join the Red-headed League	PREMISE
5.	It's false that he has red hair and is of Irish descent	3, 4 MTT
6.	Either he hasn't red hair, or he is not of Irish descent	5 NAND
7.	Ginger has red hair	PREMISE
8.	It's false that Ginger hasn't red hair	7 DN

9.	Ginger is not of Irish descent	6, 8 ELIM.

1   From the premises   **If (T or S) then not Q**
                            If not Q then R
                            If Q then R
and rules 1 and 2 (ELIM and MPP) you can prove nothing.

2   You could use rule 4 (DN) to prove various things, for example:

1. If (T or S) then not Q	PREMISE

2. Not not if (T or S) then not Q	1 DN

or 1. If Q then R   PREMISE

2. Not not if Q then R	1 DN

– and go on using DN indefinitely if you liked, proving conclusions with more and more negatives:

1. If Q then R   PREMISE
2. Not not if Q then R   1 DN
3. Not not not not if Q then R   2 DN…*etc.*

Or, since DN is an equivalence rule, you could use it to go back to where you started:

1. If Q then R   PREMISE
2. Not not if Q then R   1 DN
3. Not not not not if Q then R   2 DN
4. Not not if Q then R   3 DN

5. If Q then R	1 DN.

MTT is useless with these premises. To use it you would need *not not Q* or *not R*, and there is no way you can get them.

3   You could prove *if (T or S) then R*, using rule 5 (CH):

1. If (T or S) then not Q   PREMISE
2. If not Q then R   PREMISE

3. If (T or S) then R	1, 2 CH

Rule 6 (&E) is useless here: it works only on conjunctions.

4   From the premises   **If (T or S) then not Q**
                               If not Q then R
                               If Q then R
with rule 7 (&I) you could prove the conjunction of any two
premises: for example

    1. If not Q then R   PREMISE
    2. If Q then R   PREMISE

    3. (If not Q then R) and if Q then R   1, 2 &I

and conjunctions of conjunctions, ad infinitum: for example

    1. If not Q then R   PREMISE
    2. If Q then R   PREMISE
    3. (If not Q then R) and if Q then R   1, 2 &I

    4. ((If not Q then R) and if Q then R)
        and if Q then R   2, 3 &I.

You could also use DIL to prove if (Q or not Q) then R:

    1. If not Q then R   PREMISE
    2. If Q then R   PREMISE

    3. If (Q or not Q) then R   1, 2 DIL.

5   Of rules 9 and 10 (CONTRA and NNOR), only CONTRA is
    any use with these premises, because they are conditionals. For
    NNOR you need either the form *not (P or Q)* or the form *not P
    and not Q*.

    You can always use CONTRA to change the form of a
    conditional. For example from the second formula above, you
    could conclude *if not R then not not Q*. (Remember that it must
    be *not not Q* rather than just Q: an exact substitution instance
    of CONTRA.) In fact (as with DN), you can go on forever,
    getting conclusions with more and more negatives:

    1. If not Q then R   PREMISE
    2. If not R then not not Q   1, CONTRA
    3. If not not not Q then not not R   2, CONTRA...etc.

    – or since CONTRA is an equivalence rule, you could go back
    again to where you started, and so on forever:

2.	If not R then not not Q	1, CONTRA
3.	If not not not Q then not not R	2, CONTRA
4.	If not R then not not Q	3, CONTRA
5.	If not Q then R	4, CONTRA...

if you have nothing better to do with your time.

6   Rules 11 and 12 (NAND and IFF) are useless here. NAND works only on premises whose form is *not (P and Q)* or *not P or not Q*; IFF works only on premises with the form *P iff Q* or *(if P then Q) and if Q then P*.

7   You could take the premises and steps is various orders, but in each case you'll need CH and DIL. For example:

1.	If (T or S) then not Q	PREMISE
2.	If not Q then R	PREMISE
3.	If (T or S) then R	1, 2 CH
4.	If Q then R	PREMISE

5.	If ((T or S) or Q) then R	3, 4 DIL.

Your proof strategy should be:
   (i)   What's my conclusion?
         If ((T or S) or Q) then R.
   (ii) What is its overall form?
         It's an if-then statement, whose antecedent is the disjunction *(T or S) or Q*.
   (iii) Does this form recall any rule? (Check the list of rules.)
         Yes. DIL could give a conclusion of this form.
   (iv) What would I need to get that conclusion with DIL?
         I would need two premises, in which *T or S* represents DIL's P, and Q and R represent DIL's Q and R. In short, I need *if (T or S) then R* and *if Q then R*.
   (v)   Have I got them?
         I've got *if Q then R.*
   (vi) Could I get *if (T or S) then R*? Does its form, plus the forms of my premises, recall any rule?
         Yes: CH. *T or S* would represent CH's P, *not Q* would represent CH's Q, R would represent CH's R. Then I could conclude *if (T or S) then R* from my first two premises...EUREKA!

8   You can't prove *not Q* from the premises

> **If (T or S) then not Q**
> **If not Q then R**
> **If Q then R.**

If you had *T or S*, you could get it from this and the first premise by MPP; if you had *not R* you could get it from that and the third premise either by MTT (in one step) or by CONTRA and MPP (in two). But you haven't.

9   Any of them:

(i) *T or S* because we can prove *if (T or S) then R* (look at step 3 in the answer to 7);

(ii) *(T or S) or Q* because we can prove *if ((T or S) or Q) then R* (look at step 5 in the answer to 7);

(iii) *Not Q* because we've got the premise *if not Q then R*;

(iv) *Q* because we've got the premise *if Q then R*.

In each case, the rule you need is MPP.

10 Question 4 shows that you can use DIL to prove *if (Q or not Q) then R*. Any statement with the form *Q or not Q* is necessarily true. (If in doubt, do its truth-table.) So you could assume it as a premise, and then use MPP:

1.	If not Q then R	PREMISE
2.	If Q then R	PREMISE
3.	If (Q or not Q) then R	1, 2 DIL
4.	Q or not Q	PREMISE (new)
5.	R	3, 4 MPP.

11

1.	(If P then (not R or not Q)) and P	PREMISE
2.	If P then (not R or not Q)	1, &E
3.	P	1, &E
4.	Not R or not Q	2, 3 MPP.

Your proof strategy should be:

(i) What's my conclusion?
    Not R or not Q.

(ii) Does it match anything in my premise?
    Yes: it's the consequent of *if P then (not R or not Q)*, which is a conjunct of my premise.

(iii) If I could get *if P then (not R or not Q)* from my premise, would it help?

Yes, if I also had P. Then I could use MPP to get my conclusion.

(iv) Can I get these from my premise?

Yes. The premise *(if P then (not R or not Q)) and P* is the conjunction of these formulae, so I can get both from it, using &E (twice)…EUREKA!

12 *Not R or not Q* should make you think of NAND: it is a substitution instance of NAND's *not P or not Q*.

NAND says we may conclude *not P or not Q* if we are given *not (P and Q)*. So the premise you need is the appropriate substitution instance of *not (P and Q)*: that is *not (R and Q)*. Then the proof is

1.	Not (R and Q)	PREMISE

2.	Not R or not Q	1 NAND.

 WORK FROM BOTH
ENDS
and
START BACKWARDS.

1   The argument-formN for this rule is **P**

   ────────

   P or Q.

The validity-formula is *if P then (P or Q)*.

TRUTH-TABLE

	P	Q	If P	then	(P or Q)
(1)	T	T	T	**T**	T
(2)	T	F	T	**T**	T
(3)	F	T	F	**T**	T
(4)	F	F	F	**T**	F.

2   (iii). It is the simplest, and the original argument-form is a substitution instance of it.

3   The validity-formula is *if P and Q then if P then Q*.

TRUTH-TABLE

	P	Q	If P and Q	then	if P then Q
(1)	T	T	T	**T**	T
(2)	T	F	F	**T**	F
(3)	F	T	F	**T**	T
(4)	F	F	F	**T**	T

   The table shows that this formula is necessarily true: it never has a true antecedent and a false consequent. So the related rule will never allow a false conclusion from true premises.

4   **GIVEN P or Q, we may conclude P** is not a possible rule. It would allow a true premise and false conclusion. For example

   2 is odd or 2 is even   (TRUE)

   ────────────

   2 is odd.   (FALSE)

5   The argument-form for this rule is   **P**

   ──

   P.

The validity-formula is *if P then P*.

TRUTH-TABLE

	P	Q	If P	then	P
(1)	T	T	T	**T**	T
(2)	T	F	F	**T**	F.

6   A valid argument can't have true premises and a false conclusion. So if an argument we know to be valid has a false conclusion, we know that it has at least one false premise.

7   TRUTH-TABLE

	R	R and	not R
(1)	T	**F**	F
(2)	F	**F**	T

8   'I agree in some respects, but not in others' has these forms in statement logic:

(i) R   R: I agree in some respects, but not in others

(ii) Q and R   Q: I agree in some respects
                   R: I disagree in others

(iii) Q and not R Q: I agree in some respects
                   R: I agree in other respects.

9   You could do this in two ways.

A	1.	Everything has a cause	PREMISE
	2.	Causes can't go back forever	PREMISE
	3.	If causes can't go back forever, there was a First Cause	PREMISE
	4.	If there was a First Cause, not everything has a cause	PREMISE
	5.	If causes can't go back forever, not everything has a cause	3, 4 CH
	6.	Not everything has a cause	2, 5 MPP

| | 7. | Everything has a cause and not everything has a cause | 1, 6 &I. |

B	1.	Everything has a cause	PREMISE
	2.	Causes can't go back forever	PREMISE
	3.	If causes can't go back forever, there was a First Cause	PREMISE
	4.	If there was a First Cause, not everything has a cause	PREMISE
	5.	There was a First Cause	2, 3 MPP
	6.	Not everything has a cause	4, 5 MPP

| | 7. | Everything has a cause and not everything has a cause | 1, 6 &I. |

10	1.	*Everything has a cause*	PREMISE*
	2.	Causes can't go back forever	PREMISE
	3.	If causes can't go back forever, there was a First Cause	PREMISE
	4.	If there was a First Cause, not everything has a cause	PREMISE
	5.	There was a First Cause	2, 3 MPP
	6.	It's false that not everything has a cause	1 DN
	7.	There was no First Cause	4, 6 MTT
	8.	There was a First Cause and there was no First Cause	1, 7 &I.

| | 9. | IT IS NOT THE CASE THAT everything has a cause | 1, 8 RAA. |

* Hypothesis.

11 Yes, given the right premise/s. Make Q the negation of what you want to prove. If you can derive *not* Q by RAA, DN will give you what you want.

Suppose you are given premises 1, 3 and 4 above, and want to prove that causes *can* go back forever. Premise 2 negates this. I have already given you a proof by RAA that 2 is false, on page 301. You could use that, plus one more step:

| 8. | It's not the case that causes can't go back forever | 2, 7 RAA |

| 9. | Causes can go back forever | 8 DN. |

* Hypothesis.

(You will have noticed by now that we can derive more than one contradiction from 1, 2, 3 and 4 taken together. Any of these will do.)

12 RAA requires that we *derive* a contradiction, so we can't just say:

1. *I am a poached egg and I am not a poached egg*   PREMISE*

---

2. IT IS NOT THE CASE THAT I am a poached
   egg and I am not a poached egg   1 RAA.
* Hypothesis.

But we can do it in just one more step, using SELF:

1. *I am a poached egg and I am not a poached egg*   PREMISE*
2. I am a poached egg and I am not a poached egg   1 SELF

---

3. IT IS NOT THE CASE THAT I am a poached
   egg and I am not a poached egg   1, 2 RAA.
* Hypothesis.

In this gem of a proof, no premises are given; 'I am a poached egg and I am not a poached egg' replaces Q, and 'I am a poached egg' replaces R.

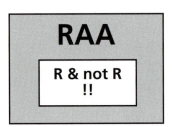

1   However we may formulate our premises, what RAA says we may conclude from them is *Not Q*. So if RAA is a valid rule, *not Q* is the formula that must not be false, when our premises are true.

2   These are the lines where P is false.

3   We can ignore lines 1 and 2: here *if P and Q then (R and not R)* is false, because *P and Q* is true. So when P, Q and R have the truth-values given for these lines, *R and not R* is not validly derived.

	P	Q	R	If P and Q then	(R and not R)	then not	Q
(1)	T	T	T	T	**F**	F	
(2)	T	T	F	T	**F**	F	
(3)	T	F	T				
(4)	T	F	F				
(5)	F	T	T				
(6)	F	T	F				
(7)	F	F	T				
(8)	F	F	F				

4   In both the lines that remain, the validity-formula is true. This is because in these lines P, Q and R have truth-values which make the formula's consequent *not Q* true. But the antecedent *if P and Q then (R and not R)* is true in these lines as well, which can only be the case when *P and Q* validly entails *R and not R*. When P, Q and R have the truth-values given them in lines (3) and (4), we therefore have the conditions that RAA specifies. And the validity-formula's truth shows that these are also conditions where we may conclude *not Q*.

	P	Q	R	If P and Q then	(R and not R)	then not	Q
(1)	T	T	T				
(2)	T	T	F				
(3)	T	F	T	F	T	F	**T** T
(4)	T	F	F	F	T	F	**T** T
(5)	F	T	T				
(6)	F	T	F				
(7)	F	F	T				
(8)	F	F	F				

5 (i) is valid by RAA and two other rules. RAA's P is the premise *not Q*, RAA's Q is *Q and P*.

(ii) is invalid.

(iii) is valid by RAA. RAA's P is P, RAA's Q is *not (P or Q)*.

6 PROOF of (i)

1.	*Q and P*	PREMISE*
2.	Not Q	PREMISE
3.	Q	1 &E
4.	Q and not Q	2,3 &I
5.	Not (Q and P)	1, 4 RAA.

PROOF of (iii):

1.	*Not (P or Q)*	PREMISE*
2.	P	PREMISE
3.	Not P and not Q	1 NNOR
4.	Not P	3 &E
5.	P and not P	2,4 &I
6.	Not not (P or Q)	1,5 RAA
7.	P or Q	7 DN.

* Hypothesis.

7 P: Gussie is a male newt
   Q: Gussie can propose to Madeline

8 P: Gussie is a male newt   P as it happens is the same
   Q: Madeline loves Gussie   Q is not.

9 P: Gussie is a male newt
   Q: Madeline is a female newt
   R: Madeline loves Gussie.

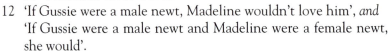

10 P: Madeline is a female newt
    Q: Gussie loves Madeline.

11 P: Madeline is a female newt
    Q: Gussie is a male newt
    R: Madeline loves Gussie.

12 'If Gussie were a male newt, Madeline wouldn't love him', *and* 'If Gussie were a male newt and Madeline were a female newt, she would'.

'If Madeline were a female newt, Gussie wouldn't love her' *and* 'If Madeline were a female newt and Gussie were a male newt, he would'.

1   Gussie is a male newt and Madeline is a female newt.
2–5

1. If Gussie loves Madeline and can propose
    to her, he will   PREMISE (i)
2. If Madeline loves Gussie and Gussie
    proposes, Madeline will accept   PREMISE (ii)
3. If Gussie were a male newt, he could
    propose to Madeline   PREMISE (iii)
4. If Gussie were a male newt and Madeline
    were a female newt, Madeline would love
    Gussie   PREMISE (iv)
5. If Gussie were a male newt and Madeline
    were a female newt, Gussie would love
    Madeline   PREMISE (v)
6. *Gussie is a male newt and Madeline is a
    female newt**   *PREMISE (vi)**
7. Gussie loves Madeline   5, 6 MPP
8. Madeline loves Gussie   4, 6 MPP
9. Gussie is a male newt   6 &E
10. Gussie can propose to Madeline   3, 9 MPP
11. Gussie loves Madeline and can propose to her   7, 10 &I
12. Gussie will propose to Madeline   1, 11 MPP
13. Madeline loves Gussie and Gussie will propose   8, 12 &I

---

14. Madeline will accept   2, 13 MPP.
* Hypothesis.

6   It does not follow that Madeline will not accept Gussie.
    'If Gussie is a male newt and Madeline is a female newt,
    Madeline will accept' does not say that their being newts is a
    necessary condition for Madeline's accepting. It merely says
    that it is sufficient. Other sufficient conditions could bring
    about the same result; in fact later in the story this happens.

7   We use RAA in conditions that show us our hypothesis must
    be rejected as false. With CP our hypothesis could be either
    true or false. The point being made is a conditional one, about
    what would be the case IF (given P) it were true.

8   We can ignore any line where *if P and Q then R* is false: line (2), for example. Since we can also ignore (5)–(8), this leaves lines 1, 3 and 4. In all of these our formula is TRUE.

	P	Q	R	If (if P and Q then R) then if Q then R			
(1)	T	T	T	T	T	**T**	T
(2)	T	T	F				
(3)	T	T	T	F	T	**T**	T
(4)	T	F	F	F	T	**T**	T

This means that whenever *if P and Q then R* and *P* are both true, so is *if Q then R*. So we are justified in concluding *if Q then R* whenever CP's conditions hold. CP is a valid rule.

9   No. If we use CP in the middle of an argument, later steps can lead to another form of conclusion.

10 In (i), CP's P is the conjunction of premises *P or Q* and *if P then S*. CP's Q is *not S*.

1.	P or Q	PREMISE
2.	If P then S	PREMISE
3.	*Not S*	*PREMISE**
4.	Not P	2,3 MTT
5.	Q	1,4 ELIM

6.	If not S then Q	3,5 CP.

* Hypothesis.

11 In (ii), CP's P is the conjunction of premises *P and Q* and *if P then S* and CP's Q is *R*. (ii) illustrates the fact that CP's Q can be totally unrelated to the premises in P.

1.	P and Q	PREMISE
2.	If P then S	PREMISE
3.	P	1,2 &E
4.	S	2,3 MPP
5.	*R*	*PREMISE**

6.	If R then S	3,5 CP.

* Hypothesis.

12 In (iii), CP's P is the conjunction of premises *P or Q* and *if P then R*. CP's Q is *if Q then R*.

1.	P or Q	PREMISE
2.	If P then R	PREMISE
3.	*If Q then R*	*PREMISE**
4.	If (P or Q) then R	2, 3 DIL
5.	R	1, 4 MPP

6.	If (if Q then R) then R.	3, 5 CP.

* Hypothesis.

Answers to Chapter 50

Here are the three final rules, for reference:

13 **SELF-ENTAILMENT (SELF): GIVEN P, we may conclude P.**

14 **REDUCTIO AD ABSURDUM (RAA): GIVEN** a set of premises whose conjunction is P: if adding a further premise Q allows us to derive R *and not* R, we may conclude *not* Q.

15 **CONDITIONAL PREMISE (CP): GIVEN** a set of premises whose conjunction is P: if adding a further premise Q allows us to derive R, we may conclude *if Q then R.*

1 From SELF and
> If (T or S) then not Q
> If not Q then R
> If Q then R.

you can prove nothing new, if you have no other rules. All that SELF can do is derive a statement (as conclusion) from itself (as premise). For example:

1. If (T or S) then not Q	PREMISE

2. If (T or S) then not Q	1, SELF.

SELF writes into our system something we already knew: that a circular argument is valid. Now and then it is important to point this out: see my discussion of induction in Chapter 14.

2 From RAA and these three premises you can prove nothing. You would need &I to put together a statement of the form *R and not R*, without which RAA can't work. Even with &I, you cannot do much until you have other rules, though it allows you to prove formally something else that we already knew: when a premise is true, its negation is false. For example

1. If Q then R	PREMISE
2. *Not if Q then R*	PREMISE*
3. (If Q then R) and not if Q then R	1, 2 &I

4. NOT not if Q then R	1, 3 RAA.

* Hypothesis

3   From   **If (T or S) then not Q**
            If not Q then R
            If Q then R

and CP, you can prove nothing. CP works by adding a new premise (hypothetically) and using it to derive a conclusion. For that you need other rules.

4   NO: if Q is a self-contradiction you can prove that it is false using RAA and SELF, without &I. The Poached Egg argument at the end of Chapter 47 is a case in point.

5   With CP and SELF you can show that whenever a statement is true, *any* other statement materially entails it. This is one of those side-effects of the truth-functional 'if-then' that people find odd; but I hope you are used to it by now. It makes a straightforward point: once something *is* true, it is true regardless of whatever else may be so.

For example in a world where Gussie loves Madeline, then if fish have feathers Gussie loves Madeline AND if they have not, Gussie loves Madeline. Using CP we can prove both.

(A) 1. Gussie loves Madeline   PREMISE
     2. *Fish have feathers*   *PREMISE**

     3. If fish have feathers then Gussie loves
         Madeline   1, 2 CP.
     * Hypothesis.

(B) 1. Gussie loves Madeline   PREMISE
     2. *Fish don't have feathers*   *PREMISE**

     3. If fish don't have feathers then Gussie
         loves Madeline   1, 2 CP.
     * Hypothesis.

6   When a premise is hypothetical, we only treat it as true 'for the sake of argument'. This allows us to show its real status by the end of the proof. When we assume it for RAA, we show that it is in fact false. When we assume it for CP it may be true or false, but we make no claim either way: what we show is that it is the antecedent of a true 'if-then' statement.

7   Assume 'Not (your conclusion)'. If you can then prove 'NOT not (your conclusion)', DN will give you what you want.

Here we want to prove R. Look at the two premises with R in them: *if not Q then R* and *if Q then R*. If you assume *not R* you can use MTT on both, and get the two halves of a self-contradiction. Then you can prove R by RAA:

1.	If not Q then R	PREMISE
2.	If Q then R	PREMISE
3.	*Not R*	*PREMISE**
4.	Not not Q	1, 3 MTT
5.	Not Q	2, 3 MTT
6.	Not Q and not not Q	4,5 &I
7.	Not not R	3,6 RAA

8.	R	7 DN.

* Hypothesis.

Whenever your premises do not show an obvious way to your conclusion, RAA is worth trying.

8   In the Poached Egg argument we used RAA to show that the self-contradiction 'I am a poached egg and I am not a poached egg' is false. Since *Q or not Q* is a necessary truth, its negation is also a self-contradiction. Assume it hypothetically, and RAA will prove that it is false. Then use DN to show that *Q or not Q* is true.

1.	*Not (Q or not Q)**	*PREMISE**
2.	Not Q and not not Q	1 NNOR
3.	Not not (Q or not Q)	1,2 RAA

4.	Q or not Q	3 DN.

* Hypothesis.

9   Offend the Fatal Four and you die!
    If B then D.

To speak of roses to Giulio is to offend the Four, as is any reference at all to violets.
    If (G or V) then B.

Looking too long at Wang's moustache is to offend the Four, if you wear a moustache yourself.
> **If (W and M) then B.**

Wear an emerald in Lucy's presence, and you offend the Four.
> **If L then B.**

Mention wasps to Anastasia and you offend the Four, unless you smile as you speak.
> **If (A and not S) then B.**

10 Smiling as you speak, you mention wasps and violets to Anastasia.
> **(A and S) and V.**

11–12

1.	*Not D*	*PREMISE**
2.	If B then D	PREMISE
3.	Not B	1, 2 MTT
4.	If (G or V) then B	PREMISE
5.	Not (G or V)	3, 4 MTT
6.	Not G and not V	5 NNOR
7.	Not V	6 &E
8.	(A and S) and V	PREMISE
9.	V	8 &E
10.	V and not V	7, 9 &I
11.	Not not D	1, 10 RAA

12.	D	11 DN.

* Hypothesis.

1–8 PROOF 1

1.	(U and R) or ((U and not R) or not U)	PREMISE
2.	If (U and not R) then not P	PREMISE
3.	If not U then not P	PREMISE
4.	If ((U and not R) or not U) then not P	2, 3 DIL
5.	P*	PREMISE*
6.	Not not P	5 DN
7.	Not ((U and not R) or not U)	4, 6 MTT
8.	U and R	1, 7 ELIM
9.	U	8 &E
10.	If P then U	5, 9 CP
11.	If W and (if P then U) then S	PREMISE
12.	W	PREMISE
13.	W and (if P then U)	10, 12 &I

14.	S	11, 13 MPP.

* Hypothesis.

9–10 PROOF 2

1.	(U and R) or ((U and not R) or not U)	PREMISE
2.	If U and not R then not P	PREMISE
3.	If not U then not P	PREMISE
4.	If ((U and not R) or not U) then not P	2, 3 DIL
5.	P*	PREMISE*
6.	Not not P	5 DN
7.	Not ((U and not R) or not U)	4, 6 MTT
8.	U and R	1, 7 ELIM
9.	If P then (U and R)	5, 8 CP
10.	If U and R then P	PREMISE
11.	(If P then (U and R)) and if U and R then P	9, 10 &I

12.	P iff (U and R)	11 IFF.

* Hypothesis.

11–12 The conclusion of Proof 1 is that I should use induction; but none of the premises on which this depends either say or entail that induction is infallible. All they show is that it's my best bet, and even best bets can lose.

The conclusion of Proof 2 is that I will make reliable predictions if and only if I use induction and it's reliable; but this says only that *I make reliable predictions* and *I use induction and it's reliable* always have the same truth-value. This is to say that induction is not just my best bet, it's my only hope. But even an only hope can fail: 'I make reliable predictions' and 'I use induction and it's reliable' could both be false.

1 '(Whatever happens) the Foundation is not conquered.'
2 'Either the general is not strong, or the general is strong and the emperor is not, or the general is strong and the emperor is strong.' This covers all the possibilities. Barr does not state it, but he clearly assumes it, since he works out what each disjunct in turn seems to entail.
3 'A strong general during the time of a weak emperor would never have endangered us either' - in other words 'If the general is strong and the emperor is not, the Foundation is not conquered.'
4 'If the Emperor is strong, the general is not strong.'

5 SUBSIDIARY ARGUMENT I

1.	If the general is strong and the emperor is not, the general attacks the emperor	PREMISE
2.	If the general attacks the emperor, he does not attack the Foundation	PREMISE
3.	If the general does not attack the Foundation, it is not conquered	PREMISE
4.	If the general attacks the emperor, the Foundation is not conquered	2, 3 CH

5.	If the general is strong and the emperor is not, the Foundation is not conquered	1, 4 CH.

6 PREMISE 1:
'A strong general during the time of a weak emperor…would have turned his arms toward a more fruitful target (events have shown that three-fourths of the emperors of the last two centuries were rebel generals).'

PREMISE 2:
'A strong general during the time of a weak emperor would never have endangered us [because] he would have turned his arms toward a more fruitful target.'

7   SUBSIDIARY ARGUMENT II

1	If the emperor is strong, he permits no strong subjects	PREMISE
2	If the emperor permits no strong subjects, the general is not strong	PREMISE

3	If the Emperor is strong, the general is not strong	1, 2 CH

8   'But, what keeps the Emperor strong? It's obvious. He's strong, because he permits no strong subjects.'

9   'A weak general could never have endangered us, obviously': in other words, 'If the General is not strong, the Foundation is not conquered.'

10–18

1.	Either the general is not strong, or the general is strong and the emperor is not, or the general is strong and the emperor is strong	PREMISE
2.	If the general is not strong, the Foundation is not conquered	PREMISE
3.	If the general is strong and the emperor is not, the Foundation is not conquered	PREMISE
4.	*The general is strong and the emperor is strong*	*PREMISE**
5.	If the emperor is strong, the general is not strong	PREMISE
6.	The emperor is strong	4, &E
7.	The general is not strong	5, 6 MPP
8.	The general is strong	4, &E
9.	The general is strong and the general is not strong	7, 8 &I
10.	It is false that the general is strong and the emperor is strong	4, 9 RAA
11.	Either the general is not strong, or the general is strong and the emperor is not	1, 10 ELIM
12.	If either the general is not strong, or the general is strong and the emperor is not, the Foundation is not conquered	2, 3 DIL

13.	The Foundation is not conquered	11, 12 MPP.

* Hypothesis.

19–20

1.	(Not G or (G and not E)) or G and E	PREMISE
2.	If not G then not C	PREMISE
3.	If G and not E then not C	PREMISE
4.	G *and* E	*PREMISE**
5.	If E then not G	PREMISE
6.	E	4, &E
7.	Not G	5, 6 MPP
8.	G	4, &E
9.	G and not G	7, 8 &I
10.	Not (G and E)	4, 9 RAA
11.	Not G or (G and not E)	1, 10 ELIM
12.	If not G or (G and not E) then not C	2, 3 DIL

_____

13. Not C   1, 12 MPP.

* Hypothesis.

21–24

SUBSIDIARY ARGUMENT I

1.	If G and not E then A	PREMISE
2.	If A then not F	PREMISE
3.	If not F then not C	PREMISE
4.	If A then not C	2, 3 CH

_____

5. If G and not E then not C   1, 4 CH.

SUBSIDIARY ARGUMENT II

1.	If E then not S	PREMISE
2.	If not S then not G	PREMISE

_____

3. If E then not G   1, 2 CH.

Subject index

In the subject index, references are usually to the main text, not the answers. The main text will lead you on to the answers, where relevant. Where I refer to the answers section, it is because the entry is something you might be looking for on its own, like a particular definition or truth-table.

('*Passim*' means 'throughout the book' and 'ff' means 'and on the following pages'.)

affirming the antecedent, see 'rules...MPP'
'all' 11; in Aristotelian logic, 197
'ALL A IS/ARE B' 194, 197 ff; Aristotelian sense, *defined* 197; in logic of sets, *defined* 197
ambiguity, see under 'formula', 'statement' etc.
analogy and equivocation, 93 ff; and metaphor, 221 ff, *defined* 361; argument by ix, 89 ff, 115; invalid form, 89 ff, 99, *defined* 89; valid form, 90 ff, 99, *defined* 90; bad, 92; inappropriate, 92; shaky, 92
analytic statement, 48 ff, 53 ff, *defined* 48
'AND' in statement logic, 131 ff, 371 ff, 377; truth-table for P and Q, 139
'and' introduction, see 'rules...'
'and/or' see 'OR...inclusive'
antecedent (of a conditional), *defined* 153
argument, *passim*, esp. 3 ff, *defined* 3; analysed step by step, 263 ff; demonstrative, 103-4; inductive, see 'induction'; interpreting an argument 73, see also 'clarity', 'implicit', 'logical form and surface

form', 'putting words into someone's mouth'; requirements for, 352
argument-form, *passim*, esp. 59 ff; more than one per argument, 63 ff; in statement logic, 115 ff; invalid, see 'invalid argument'; of a valid argument, 75 ff, 354 ff; requirements for, 352; substitution instance of, 243 ff
arguments, representative: Agent, 283 ff; Alice's Identity, 234 ff; Clevinger's Equivocation, 236 ff; Creep, 61; Devil, 22 ff; Fang, 64, 161 ff, 249 ff; First Cause, 300 ff; Forgeries, 71, 94; Foundation, 325 ff; Grandpa (dilemma), 269; Granny, 3 ff, 75; Gussie's Problem, 305 ff; Holmes, 263 ff; Lewis Carroll's puzzle, 194 ff; Miss Nightingale's, 67 ff, 93, 238; Opium, 27 ff; Pub, 25 ff; Real men and Rabbits, 60; Rape, 26, 265; Sheep, 62 ff; Spider, 6 ff; Tapestry, 89 ff; Uncle, 35 ff; Yossarian (Catch-22), 214 ff
axiom, 332

begging the question, see 'fallacies'

Name index